The Planets
and their Psychological Meaning

Capabilities and Tools of the Personality

Detailed Descriptions of
the Ten Horoscope Planets

Bruno & Louise Huber

HopeWell
Knutsford, England

Originally published in German entitled
'Planeten als Funktionsorgane'
by Bruno & Louise Huber
Copyright © 2002 API-Verlag, Adliswil/ Zürich
(Switzerland)

First published in English in 2006 by HopeWell

HopeWell,
PO Box 118, Knutsford
Cheshire WA16 8TG, U.K.

English translation
copyright © 2006 HopeWell and Louise Huber.

All rights reserved. No part of this publication may be reproduced, sorted in a retrieval system, or transmitted in any form or by any means, electronic or otherwise, without the prior permission of the publisher.

Translated by Heather Ross
English version edited by Barry Hopewell

Jacket: adapted from original by Michael Huber
Graphics: adapted from originals by Michael Huber
Horoscopes: Huber-Method
(drawn up with MegaStar software)

ISBN 978-0-9547680-2-7

Planetary Symbols

Sun	☉		♂	Mars
Moon	☽		♃	Jupiter
Saturn	♄		♅	Uranus
Mercury	☿		♆	Neptune
Venus	♀		♇	Pluto
ascending Moon Node	☊			

Sign Symbols

Aries	♈		♎	Libra
Taurus	♉		♏	Scorpio
Gemini	♊		♐	Sagittarius
Cancer	♋		♑	Capricorn
Leo	♌		♒	Aquarius
Virgo	♍		♓	Pisces

Acknowledgements

Special thanks to David Kerr and Joyce Hopewell for checking the translation of this book for accuracy and the terminology for consistency with current English usage.

The following acknowledgements appear in the original German edition.

First of all we would like to express our gratitude and highest appreciation for Bruno Huber, who very intuitively described the qualities of the ten planets, making sophisticated horoscope interpretation possible. Recordings of the many lectures he gave in his career formed the basis for a large part of this book. This allowed us to complete it, although he is no longer with us.

Our thanks also go to all those who have made transcripts of the recordings over the years and made them available to us. In particular, we would like to thank all the active API students and colleagues who have collaborated on this book by proofreading, producing drawings, making corrections, preparing manuscripts and additional references and providing encouraging suggestions. We have also included a deep psychological description of planetary configurations by Wolfhard König, who also deserves our thanks. The profound psychological observations contained in his article complete the picture of the influence of the planets. We are convinced that everyone who has waited such a long time for this book will not have waited in vain.

We are now delighted to have finished the last volume in this series on Astrological Psychology with your help and repeat our thanks for your collaboration on this book:

Daniel Cuny	Rita Keller
Taomir Ebersold	Johanna Kohler
Lotti Ehrat	Wolfhard König
Monika Gubler	Heinz Russman
Elke F. Gut	Edith Sager
Anita Haas	Rita Schafroth
Michael-A Huber	Ruth Schmidhauser
Martin Kannenberg	Beatrice Solér
Annegret Kaufmann	Barbara Zollinger

Contents

Foreword	1
1. The Functionality of the Planets	**3**
Introduction	4
Astronomical Connections	4
Astronomical Planetary Data	**5**
The Planets as Functional Organs	7
The Main Significance of the Planets	8
The Five Layers of the Horoscope	8
Interpretation Process	8
Planetary Symbols	**10**
Planetary Table	**14**
Division into Three Levels and Three Columns	14
Planets in the Columns (Vertical)	16
Planets in the Three Levels (Horizontal)	17
Libido Planets	18
Intelligence Planets	21
Middle Level: Ego Planets	25
Top Level: Spiritual Planets	26
Summary of the Planets	28
2. The Seven Classical Planets	**29**
Introduction	30
Three Ego Planets: Sun, Moon, Saturn	**31**
The Sun: Autonomous Self-Awareness	32
The Moon: The Feeling Self	37
Saturn: The Physical Self	41
Four Tool Planets: Mercury, Venus, Mars, Jupiter	**46**
Mercury: The Winged Messenger	46
Venus: The Feminine	52
Mars: The Masculine	59
Jupiter: The Eye	65
Attribution of the Planets	**71**
A) To the Three Crosses	71
B) To the Four Temperaments	75
C) To the Seven Rays	76
3. The Three Spiritual Planets	**77**
Uranus, Neptune, Pluto:	**78**
Transpersonal Essential Forces	

The Zeitgeist: Collective and Individual Effects	78
Collective Models	79
Expansion of Consciousness	79
Esoteric Function of the New Planets	80
Transformation Model	80
Chart "Amphora"	**81**
Transformation through the Spiritual Planets	82
Esoteric Psychology	82
The Three Stages	83
Uranus: The World Improver	83
Neptune: Looking for Love	85
Pluto: The Superman (Master)	88
Transformation of the Personality:	**91**
Personal and Spiritual Psychosynthesis	
Strong and Healthy Ego	91
Interpretation Guide	91
House Position of the Ego planets	92
Integration of the Personality	93
Psychosynthesis and Love	93
Wholeness	94
Developmental Tendencies	94
Transformation of the Ego planets	96
Simultaneity	96
The Spiritual Path	96
Saturn Levels	97
Moon Levels	99
Sun Levels	101
Ego Fears and How to Overcome Them	104
Initiation and Transformation	**106**
Esoteric Astrology	
Initiation in Antiquity	106
Initiation Today	106
Initiation Crises	107
Initiation Levels	107
Saturn-Uranus Transformation: 1st Initiation	108
Moon-Neptune Transformation: 2nd Initiation	111
Sun-Pluto Transformation: 3rd Initiation	115
4. Rules for Interpreting the Planets	**119**
Introduction	**120**
The Planetary Level	
Energy from the Centre of Being	120
Tools for Self-Actualisation	121
Disposition and Behaviour	122

The Aspect Pattern	122
The Ego Planets	123
The Moon Nodes	123
Interpretation in the Signs of the Zodiac	123
Planetary Rulers in the Signs of the Zodiac	**124**
Sun in Leo	125
Moon in Cancer	125
Mars in Aries and Scorpio	125
Venus in Taurus and Libra	125
Mercury in Gemini and Virgo	125
Jupiter in Sagittarius and Pisces	126
Saturn in Capricorn and Aquarius	126
Interpretation Rules	**126**
15 points	127
Special Planetary Positions	128
According to the Planetary Table	128
Aspects in the Columns	128
Unaspected Planets	129
Tension Rulers	129
15 Point List (Einstein)	130
House Positions	131
Sign/ House Distinction	132
Four main Criteria	132
Combinations	134
Example Horoscope	136
Attribution of the Planets to the Aspects	137
Planets in Aspect Figures	138
Aspect Colours on Planets	**139**
Single-Coloured Aspects	139
Missing Colours	140
House Horoscope	140
Conjunctions	140
Three-Coloured Aspects	141
Two-Coloured Aspects	**142**
a) blue-red, b) red-green, c) blue-green	
Sun, Moon, Saturn, Mercury, Venus	142 - 146
Mars, Jupiter, Uranus, Neptune, Pluto	147 - 151
Planetary Connections	**152**
Interpretation in Keywords	152
Sun Aspects, Moon Aspects, Saturn Aspects	152 - 153
Mercury Aspects, Venus Aspects, Mars Aspects, Jupiter Aspects	153
Spiritual Aspects	153
Planetary Interpretation on Three Levels	**154**

The Three Levels: 1 – Physical, 2 – Feeling, 3 – Mental	154
The Ten Planets at the Three Levels	155
Ptolemaic Planetary Sequence	157
Year Rulers, Days of the Week	157
The Four Quadrants	**158**

5. The Planets in the Houses — 159

Sun, Moon, Saturn in the Horoscope Hemispheres — 160

The Threefold Personality	160
Sun in the Upper Hemisphere	160
Sun in the Lower Hemisphere	161
Sun on the I-Side	161
Sun on the You-Side	162
Moon on the You-Side	162
Moon on the I-Side	162
Moon in the Upper Hemisphere	163
Moon in the Lower Hemisphere	163
Saturn in the Lower Hemisphere	163
Saturn on the I-Side	164
Saturn on the You-Side	164
Saturn in the Upper Hemisphere	165

Sun and Saturn in the Twelve Houses — 165

Introduction	165
The Signs of the Zodiac	166
Three Zones in one House: Cardinal, Fixed, Mutable	167
1st House: Sun, Saturn	168
2nd House: Sun, Saturn	173
3rd House: Sun, Saturn	176
4th House: Sun, Saturn	180
5th House: Sun, Saturn	183
6th House: Sun, Saturn	188
7th House: Sun, Saturn	192
8th House: Sun, Saturn	198
9th House: Sun, Saturn	204
10th House: Sun, Saturn	210
11th House: Sun, Saturn	217
12th House: Sun, Saturn	225

6. Planets in the Zodiac Signs using the example of the Moon — 233

The Man in the Moon – or the Moon in Man, Bruno Huber — 234

Anima and Animus	234
Role Models	234
The New Interpretation	236
The Feelings	237

Mother	237
Saturn	237
Paradigm Shift	238
The Moon as our Feeling Nature, Louise Huber	**239**
Reflection	239
Dependencies	240
Learning Processes	240
The Here and Now	240
Subjective I-Experience	241
Theories and Methods	241
Transformations of the Moon Ego	242
The Refined Moon	242
The Child within Us	243
The Moon in the Zodiac Signs	**244**
Combinations and Analogies	244
The Three Crosses	245
Development Processes	245
Table of Planetary Rulers (Exoteric and Esoteric)	246
The Moon in the Cardinal Signs	**247**
Aries	248
Cancer	250
Libra	252
Capricorn	254
The Moon in the Fixed Signs	**257**
Taurus	259
Leo	261
Scorpio	264
Aquarius	266
The Moon in the Mutable Signs	**269**
Gemini	272
Virgo	275
Sagittarius	278
Pisces	281
7. Special Planetary Positions	**285**
Planets and Ascendants	**286**
The Influence of the Birth Process on the Ego	286
Sun, Moon, Saturn, Mercury, Venus	286 - 289
Mars, Jupiter, Uranus, Neptune, Pluto	290 - 293
The Family Model	**294**
Sun: Father, Saturn: Mother, Moon: Child	294
The Parents as Archetypal Role Models	295
Aspects between the Family Planets	296

Phases of Ego Development	299
Exposed Planetary Positions	**302**
The Psychodynamics of Fear in the Horoscope - Wolfhard König	
What is Fear?	302
Planetary Configurations and the Development of Fear	302
1st Case - The Normal Position	304
2nd Case - The Weak Position	304
3rd Case - The Strong Position	305
1. Unaspected Planets	306
2. Pulling Position	306
3. Congestion Position	307
Example Horoscope	308
The Three Charts	**310**
Data for Example Horoscopes	**311**
Bibliography	**312**
Contacts and Resources	**314**

Abbreviations Used

AC	= Ascendant	MNH	= Moon Node Horoscope
IC	= Imum Coeli	HC	= House Cusp
DC	= Descendant	LP	= Low Point
MC	= Medium Coeli	BP	= Balance Point
AP	= Age Point	GM	= Golden Mean

Aspect Colours			
	Trine and Sextile	= Blue	△ ✶
	Square and Opposition	= Red	□ ☍
	Semi-Sextile and Quincunx	= Green	⚺ ⚻
	Conjunction	= Orange	☌

Element colours		
	Fire	= Red
	Earth	= Green
	Air	= Yellow
	Water	= Blue

Numbers in (round brackets)
Refer to books in the Bibliography on page 312. For example (2).

Text in [square brackets]
Amplifying notes inserted by the Editor.

Foreword

Dear Readers,

We have for over 30 years been teaching a dynamic astrological approach based on the holistic concept of psychosynthesis developed by Dr. Roberto Assagioli (Florence). Since 1973 we have offered an established astrological professional training course leading to a diploma, which has been completed by more than 1,500 students. Bruno Huber created this course, and it was his many years of research work that brought psychosynthesis into astrology. This created a new approach to astrology, which forms the basis for this book about the planets.

Since Bruno left us on 3rd November 1999, our son Michael and I and a qualified teaching staff have continued to run the Institute in his spirit. Astrological Psychology also continues to exist through our books. It provides many people with a valuable tool for gaining self-knowledge and has been used for many years as a diagnostic tool in psychological consultation. We have set out the whole concept of Astrological Psychology (Huber Method) in eight volumes. This book is probably the last in this series, finally making the whole collected works of the Huber Method available to students, experts and lay people alike.

This volume, dealing with the functionality of the ten planets, is particularly important for the interpretation of the horoscope. The planets represent fundamental archetypal qualities that are present in everyone and enable us to live a conscious life. They are the cornerstone in the building of the horoscope, and influence each of its five levels. The position of the ten planets in a zodiac sign, in a house and with certain aspects, allows accurate psychological observations to be made about people, and also informs us on how to live a successful life.

In this book we have tried to give as thorough a definition as possible of the meaning of each planet as it relates to basic human needs. We begin by describing the seven classical planets, followed by the three spiritual ones. The latter function primarily as collective models, transformation processes and paths to initiation for evolved people. These days, many students seek a spiritual orientation in astrology, which is why we have also given the transformed level as a development goal in the description of the different levels of the planets.

As you can see, this is not a recipe book that you can dip into to find, for example, the meaning of an opposition between Saturn and Sun. It is a study book aimed at the development of the student's interpretative abilities. We show how meaning can be derived from the positions of the planets, explaining first the principles and then the effects. Students can learn to work out the interpretation for themselves from these principles.

The study of astrology as an instrument for the development and understanding of the self is based not on new discoveries, but on deep cosmic interconnections. We therefore proceed from the assumption that astrology in general is a form of psychology. It deals with the psyche and, via the ten planets, offers an excellent representation of all human functions, needs, energies and drives that are based on actual human experience as well as observations and records throughout the centuries.

We therefore hope that this book will enable you to understand, cultivate and experience your own planetary powers more successfully.

Adliswil, April 2002   Louise Huber

1. The Functionality of the Planets

Introduction
• Astronomical Connections •
• The Planets as Functional Organs •
• The Main Significance of the Planets •
• The Five Layers of the Horoscope •
• Interpretation Process •

Planetary Symbols
• Sun • Moon • Saturn •
• Mercury • Venus • Mars • Jupiter •
• Uranus • Neptune • Pluto •

Planetary Table
• Division into Three Levels and Three Columns •
• Three Columns (Vertical) •
• Feminine/Masculine • Neutral Planets •
• Planets in the Columns (Vertical) •
• Left Column • Middle Column • Right Column •
• Planets on the Three Levels (Horizontal) •
• Bottom Level: Tool Planets •
• Libido Planets • Intelligence Planets •
• Middle Level: Ego Planets •
• Top Level: Spiritual Planets •
• Summary of the Planets •

Introduction

Astronomical Connections

In order to understand the planets, we need to have a little basic astronomical knowledge. Most people know that the sun rises in the east and sets in the west, and that the moon can be full or new. We also know that the seasons depend on the movement of the sun. In the summer, it moves northwards from the Equator, and in the process rises further and further north-east and sets further and further northwest. It reaches its most northerly point on 21st June, the summer solstice, which is the longest day and the shortest night. From there the sun moves southwards again; we experience this as the shortening of the days and the lengthening of the nights in summer and winter.

Just as the sun influences the seasons and the length of the days on earth and the moon affects the tides of the seas, the other planets (each in its own way) also have a certain influence on everything on earth, not only in a physical way but also on a mental and spiritual level. This fact means that we should know something about the movement of the planets, so that we can interpret them astrologically.

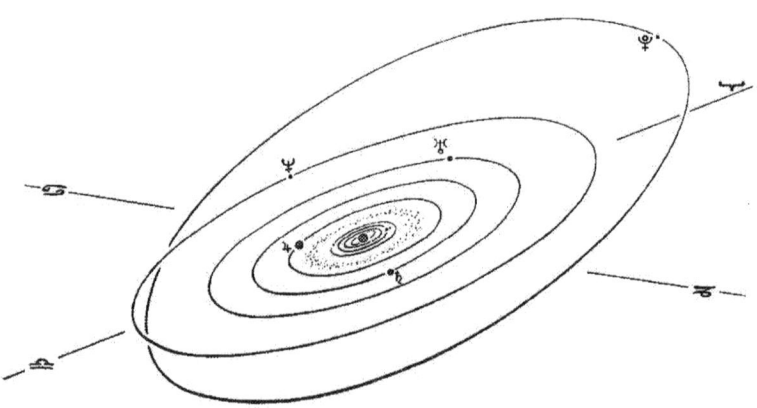

Planetary system

In the planetary system diagram we can see the planets arranged in different circles around the Sun. Nearest to the Sun are Mercury, Venus, Earth and Mars, then the Asteroid Belt (indicated by dots) and then the orbits of Jupiter, Saturn, Uranus, Neptune and Pluto.

Planets	Orbit time	Distance from Sun			Diameter		Orbit	Moons
	(years)	Earth=1	x1000km	light mins	in km	Earth = 1	inclination	
Sun	0	0	0	0	1,392,000	109	0	–
Mercury	0.240	0.38	57,910	3.51	4877	0.38	7°00'11"	–
Venus	0.615	0.72	107,910	5.98	12103	0.94	3°23'37"	–
Earth	1	1	149,530	8.30	12756	1	0	1
Moon	27.32 days		To earth = 384	0.02	3476	0.27	5°08'43"	–
Mars	1,880	1.52	227,700	12.64	6793	0.53	1°51'01"	2
Jupiter	11.861	5.20	777,900	42.84	142803	11.2	1°18'31"	16
Saturn	29.457	9.55	1427,000	79.21	120002	9.4	2°29'33"	17
Uranus	84.016	19.2	2868,900	159.24	50800	4.0	0°46'21"	15
Neptune	164.774	30.1	4496,900	249.61	48600	3.8	1°46'45"	2
Pluto	247.700	39.5	5869,660	327.00	2390	0.2	17°08'44"	1
Asteroids	2-3	2-3	320-470000		about 1-800		–	

Astronomical Planetary Data

The planets therefore orbit the Sun in a particular order, the duration of the orbit depending on their distance from the Sun. We differentiate between the slow-moving planets that take years, like Jupiter, Saturn, Uranus, Neptune and Pluto, and fast-moving planets like the Moon, Mercury, Venus and Mars. The old astrological rule applies here: the faster a planet moves, the smaller its influence, the longer it stays in a certain point, the stronger its effect. We should remember this distinction. For quick reference, we have given the rounded up orbit times of the planets in the table below. You can find more accurate information on the exact astronomical data in the table on page 5 or in the *Astro Glossarium*, page 82 (1).

Movement of the Planets (rounded up)

Sun	365 days	Jupiter	12 years
Moon	28 days	Saturn	30 years
Mercury	88 days	Uranus	84 years
Venus	225 days	Neptune	165 years
Mars	687 days	Pluto	247 years

As the planets are in perpetual motion, their influence on the Earth is always coming from a different angle. These constantly changing positions of the planets in the zodiac are listed in the *Ephemerides* (36). There we can find the exact angular position of each planet for a given birthday. The position in the individual horoscope depends on time and place of birth, and must be specially calculated. Nowadays this is done by computer using specialist software programs (4). It is also possible to calculate your own horoscope yourself (15).

The Planets as Functional Organs

The planets represent special functional organs within us, with which we act and react and can perceive and influence the environment. Tuned in to cosmic energies, planets are forces that affect each one of us. So we must not think that it is the planets out there in space that send us these special abilities, but rather energies and powers existing within ourselves and controlled by the influences of the planets. It is the micro-macro-cosmic process, illustrated by the hermetic saying "As above, so below, as within, so without".

From a psychological point of view, the planets are our tools, our resources, which enable us to deal with life's many and varied tasks. They are essential archetypal physical forces embedded within us. Planets have an intrinsic, deep-seated reaction pattern that is formed, modified and consolidated in the course of human development. From this point of view, the planets are qualities or properties that enable us to act in certain ways. This is reflected in a specific behaviour and attitude unique to this planet. So when interpreting planets we can infer reactions that correspond to these archetypal properties.

The planets are therefore basic functions present in all of us. They cannot be conclusively defined or expressed completely by one word, for they are always combined and linked in different ways. One of the ten basic human functions can hardly be meaningfully used by itself without considering certain other elements in the horoscope.

The ten planets are arranged differently in every horoscope. They are in a different place for each person, i.e. in a particular zodiac sign, area of the horoscope and house. They also have different aspects and are connected to other planets, which strengthen or weaken their influence. If a planet is badly placed, it is difficult to ensure the corresponding life function. We can therefore make statements based

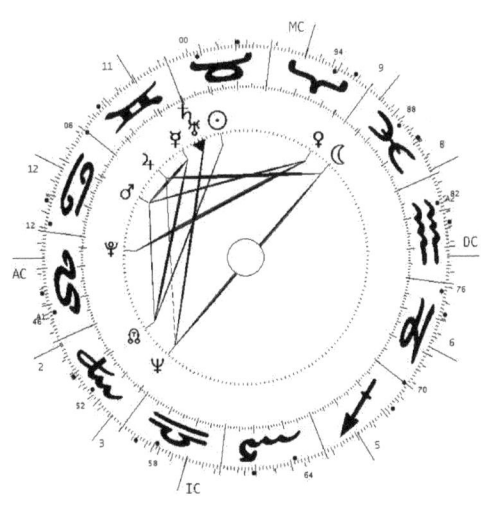

Example Horoscope
10.05.1942, 11.30 Zürich/Switzerland

on the positions of the planets. In the interpretation of a horoscope we must always assume the planets to be the instruments of the personality.

The Main Significance of the Planets

The planets have a central role in the horoscope, which is obvious from the chart. They are arranged around the middle ring and we can see how they connect the outside and the inside. We distinguish between the three personality planets, Sun, Moon and Saturn as the structure of our personal power on the three levels: mental, emotional and physical. We also see the three spiritual planets Uranus, Neptune and Pluto, which constitute a higher, transpersonal level of our I-experience. We are familiar with the four planets Mercury, Venus, Mars and Jupiter whose main function is to satisfy creatural needs. In addition, the ascending Moon Node features in aspect patterns, and represents the first step in the development of the personality (18).

The Five Layers of the Horoscope

We divide the horoscope into five distinct layers or levels, as shown in the illustration opposite. On the third layer from the bottom, right in the middle, you can see the ring of the planets. The layer above that is the aspect pattern, which represents the structure of human consciousness. Right at the top is the centre of being as the overarching energy. The layer below the ring of planets is formed by the twelve zodiac signs, which give the planets a particular quality. The twelve houses make up the very bottom layer. They show how a planet influences the environment. Wherever planets lie in the house system or the zodiac system, we react consciously to the environment. We lack the means to be active in the houses and signs in which we have no planets. However, this does not mean that we cannot get anything done in these areas of life. Even if there are no planets present, the house is made viable by the character of the sign.

Interpretation Process

Because the planets influence all the layers of the horoscope, the connection between these layers must also be interpreted. We briefly describe this interpretation process once again. Firstly we establish how the planet appears in the aspect pattern and which other planets it is linked to. Here it is important to see which aspect figures it features in (21). We then find out which zodiac sign it lies in and describe the specific quality that it expresses there (20). Finally we look in the house

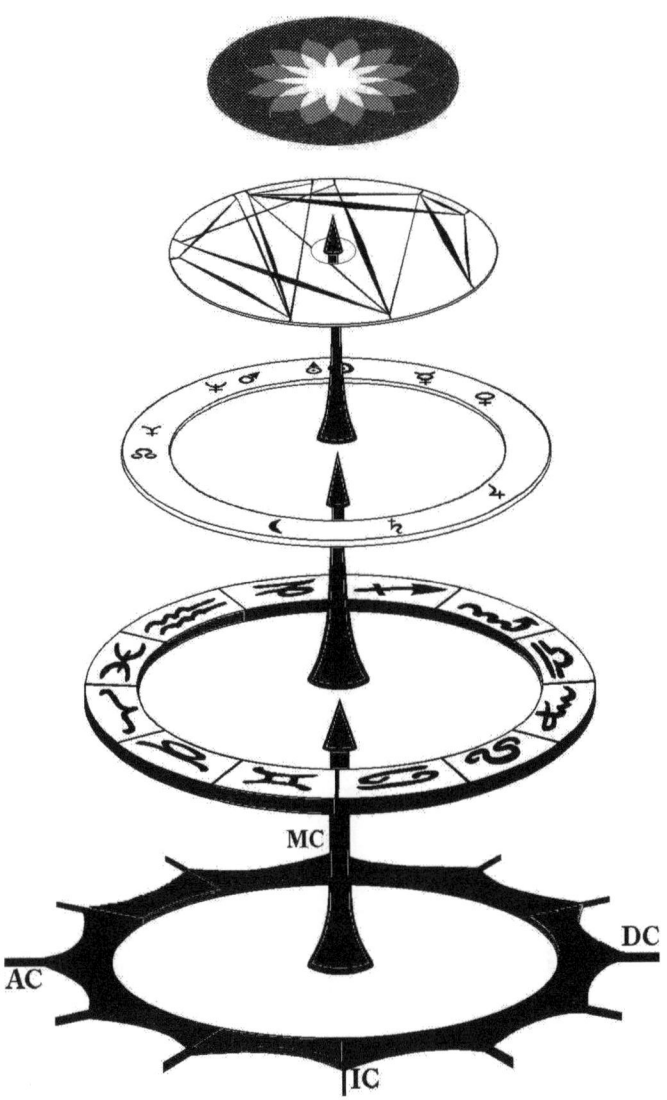

The Five Layers in the Horoscope

that shows how it interacts with the environment (16). The art of interpretation consists in combining all these levels in the right way so as to establish the effectiveness of the planet's qualities.

This book deals with all these elements systematically. However, our first task is to familiarise ourselves with the actions and qualities of each planet and study their diverse effects. We start with the importance of the symbols that are used to denote them in this book.

Planetary Symbols

Symbols play a very important role in astrology, and horoscope interpretation would be impossible without them. They are meaningful because they represent things graphically. Symbols allow a great deal to be expressed allegorically, immediately evoke impressions and insight, and allow the comprehensive interpretation of a planet's significance and influence. Symbols express intrinsic properties that can only be comprehended in image form, the interpretation of which arouses the intuition and persists indefinitely. The language of astrological symbols must be learnt to be able to understand what we mean when we talk about "Sun" or "Saturn". Symbols represent forces and energies that can immediately be incorporated into a reading by the initiated. The language of symbols is universal and understood by most people. It has had the same meaning for thousands of years and is used everywhere, in mysticism, religion, magic, runes, tarot and astrology. A brief summary of the most important symbols follows, including those for the planets.

The Five Basic Symbols

Cross	Circle	Dot	Semicircle	Line/Arrow
✚	○	●	◖	↗
Form Structure Manifestation	Space Content Collection	I Definition Concentration	Sensitivity Receptivity Perception	Direction Movement Activity

The cross is a well-known symbol for matter. The circle represents an enclosed sphere; with a central dot it means the I or the human self. The semicircle or crescent is attributed to the principle of receptivity and sensitivity. A line or arrow means movement toward a goal.

Sun ☉

The Sun is represented by a dot inside a circle. It is an enclosed, self-sufficient figure concentrated on its centre. The symbol of the circle has always represented unity, the self-contained person. The dot in the centre symbolises the I, individuality, self-awareness and the formative, creative principle. The sun is the star all the other planets orbit around, the centre of our solar system, and it represents the source of all life. It provides man's will to live, vitality and energy. It shows the striving for autonomy, awareness, but also for personal recognition, prestige and esteem.

Moon ☽

The Moon is represented by a crescent. The semicircle symbolises susceptibility, receptivity and impressionability. The moon is our contact self, our emotional nature, our psychological make-up, the changing, mutable principle. Unlike the shining sun, the moon can only reflect and collect. It is concerned with our feelings and emotions and therefore symbolises our subjective reactions and our needs for love, security and understanding. The Moon is therefore also the symbol for moods and changes of opinion. This changeability is reflected in the ebb and flow of the tides of the seas, a well-known lunar rhythm in nature.

Saturn ♄

The symbol shows a cross at the top and two semicircles at the bottom. As mentioned above, the cross is the symbol for matter, structure and form. The cross at the top means that for Saturn, matter rules everything, including the sensitive side (the two semicircles) at the bottom. Saturn therefore has a hard and a soft side; the latter is often forgotten. It represents the principles of both form and sensitivity. For the spirit and the soul, form always means austerity, limitation and restraint. The soul, the sensitive element, would, however, drift into a maelstrom of events if it were not tied down in some way. This is why Saturn is also the protector and the lawgiver. The soul and form can work together to produce optimum stability and security.

Mercury ☿

There is a semicircle at the top, a circle in the centre and a cross at the bottom. It is therefore open at the top, lets everything flow down through it and return to matter. Mercury is the mediating principle, the winged messenger that takes messages back and forth between gods and men. The symbol shows this clearly: the semicircle, the receptive principle; then the circle, the personality, but without a dot in the middle, therefore neutral and permeable; and below the cross – the symbol of matter, which symbolises the passing on of what was received and allows concrete interpretations.

Venus ♀

Here we have a circle with a cross beneath it. Matter, the cross through the circle, is thus made integrated and bearable. Venus strives for roundedness, harmony and beauty, and tries to achieve them by perfecting and cultivating. The circle at the top indicates perfection, so Venus is always trying to reach and maintain the highest state of harmony and beauty. It tries to compensate for what is lacking in all things, thus creating a harmonious, rounded whole, a coherent synthesis. Underneath is the earthly cross, which means that Venus is also attached to the terrestrial, enjoying what life has to offer. Venus is also the symbol for female sexuality. Her highly-developed selectivity means that she only chooses what suits her and what corresponds to her nature, and rejects everything else.

Mars ♂

This symbol is a circle with an arrow protruding from the top right. The arrow shows that something is being ejected. We all know that Mars is the masculine principle, it symbolises the motor impulse, without which nothing would be done and nothing would move. It provides the courage, bravery and readiness to act that is required to attain goals. Mars is dynamic energy and removes obstacles or limiting influences. It stands for wishes and longing, drive, activity, passions and the energy to get things done. It brings dynamism to the horoscope and also symbolises the rashness and bravado of youth. Mars usually employs its energies to satisfy personal wishes and goals. It can also be motivated by ideals, or by distress to rectify unpleasant situations.

Jupiter ♃

The symbol for Jupiter shows a left-facing semicircle, connected to the material cross. The dish resembles an inwards-facing parabolic reflector that picks up all impressions. Jupiter represents sensory perception that connects us to our environment. It symbolises observation, perception, watching. At the same time the senses are directed to form and matter symbolised by the cross. Sensory perception and the conscious management of the sensory organs allow matter to be understood and used. Expansion and determined development lead Jupiter to complete mastery of form. This has correctly earned Jupiter the name of the "lucky planet". The conscious person does not just master matter and form, he is also in the right place at the right time and reacts immediately to opportunities for expansion, success and progress.

Uranus ⛢ or ♅

The symbol ♅ shows a circle with a dot in the centre and an arrow pointing upwards, thus representing a combination of the symbols for the Sun and Mars. The arrow points straight upwards. In Uranus, the centre is known as the starting point of the path of expansion, the direction of which is established by the vertical arrow. It indicates a deliberately creative individuality that knows what to aim for in order to change the world. It expresses the individual act, the principles of change, metamorphosis and awakening. Uranus provides a purposeful will to realise knowledge, as seen in the technical and scientific discovery process. It always points to the new, to the revolutionary. It is usually in a strong position in the horoscopes of inventors, scientists and also astrologers.

[The symbol ⛢ is commonly used in the English-speaking world. Here the circle of spirit is transformed through the cross of matter conditioned by semicircles of soul. - Ed]

Neptune ♆

This symbol has a large dish that reaches out like a receiver above the earthly sphere. The vertical line of the cross extends into the dish to pick up higher frequencies and to be receptive to more subtle matter from other dimensions. This is the planet of universal human kindness, the seer and the mystic; it enables identification in the spiritual sense with divine love. It therefore stands for inspiration, idealism, altruism, self-sacrifice and the desire to help. It can also lead to the spheres of dreams, manias, addictions and rare states of consciousness that can have a confusing and deluding effect on real life.

Pluto ♇ or ⯓

The symbol ⯓ consists of two semicircles connected by the vertical line of a cross. It symbolises the desire for transformation and is considered to be the primeval impulse for evolution. Armed with the highest will power, it keeps evolution going, both destroying and transforming matter. It is the pattern-changing principle, which brings about great metamorphoses, both on an individual and worldwide level. It intensifies all elements, houses, aspects and planets to which it is linked in the horoscope.

[The symbol ♇ is commonly used in the English-speaking world. Here the circle of spirit dominates the cross of matter through the medium of the semicircle of soul. - Ed]

Planetary Table

The planetary table on the facing page serves as the basis for everything to do with the planets in the Huber Method. Bruno Huber worked on it for many years until he was satisfied with it. We are now able to say that it contains all we need to know about the effect of the planets. Please note that the Sun and Moon have been singled out from the seven classical planets since time immemorial. They are the only two that we can see clearly with our own eyes. The Sun rules the day, it lights up the skies; the Moon is mainly visible at night – two shining bodies in the sky that light the day and night. The other planets appear in the skies as shining dots of various sizes and can only be seen in detail with a telescope, for example we know that Venus has phases, like the Moon. The changing sizes of the Moon can be seen with the naked eye. It gets smaller and smaller until it almost disappears, then grows to the full moon once more.

Division into Three Levels and Three Columns

In the planetary table the planets are arranged in three rows or levels one on top of the other, and in three columns next to each other. Each level is described on the far left. The life-sustaining functions can be found on the animal level in the unconscious realm. The personality or ego planets are situated in the middle row, in the field of everyday awareness with the different roles of the ego. At the top is the spiritual level, with three spiritual planets in the superconscious realm.

Three Columns (Vertical)

The three vertical columns are arranged in order of gender: feminine, neutral and masculine. The planets in each column share similar qualities and motivations. Venus, Saturn, Uranus in the left column are feminine; Mercury, Jupiter, Moon, Neptune in the middle are neutral and Mars, Sun, Pluto in the right column are masculine.

Feminine/Masculine

By **feminine** we mean a passive, receptive attitude, such as we find with Venus, Saturn and Uranus. It is harder to imagine the feminine element in the case of Uranus, as its dynamism disturbs the status quo to find new opportunities for development. However, its motivation is feminine, as it strives for a security that is greater and more promising than what went before. All three spiritual planets are actually also hermaphroditic, i.e. they have both feminine and masculine sides. Therefore Uranus is associated with the principle of life improvement.

Planetary Table

DEVELOPING AREA ASPIRATIONS SPIRITUAL GROWTH		CREATIVE INTELLIGENCE MOTHER ♅ IMAGO Occultist Methodology Ideal of the perfect world Organising	ALL – LOVE (Christ) CHILD ♆ IMAGO Mystic Mediation Ideal of unconditional love Serving	SPIRITUAL WILL FATHER ♇ IMAGO Magician Metamorphosis Ideal of the perfect human being Creating
PERSONALITY (EGO)	Supraconscious realm Spiritual level	**BODY** Self-Confidence **Immunity** ♄ **Security** housekeeping closing MOTHER heteronomous	**FEELING** You-awareness **Sensitivity** ☽ **Sympathy** learning opening CHILD ambivalent	**MENTALITY** Self-awareness **Vitality** ☉ **Mental capacity** growing radiating FATHER autonomous
ROLES OF THE EGO Interests and Motivation	Daily awareness Personal level	**Enjoying** **AESTHETIC** **Assimilation** ♀ **Selection** Woman Fruitfulness	**Learning** **DEDUCTIVE** ☿ **SENSORY** **Formulation** **Evaluation** **Information** **Perception** Human Receptivity	**Achieving** **MOTOR ACTIVITY** **Achievement** **Activity** ♂ Man Potency
Drive-Instinct = Achievements LIFE-SUSTAINING FUNCTIONS	Unconscious realm Animal level	Feminine Matter Holy Spirit Shiva	Neutral Awareness Son Vishnu	Male Spirit
Father
Brahma
© API				

In principle, all feminine planets let things come to them, choose what is suitable for them and appropriate it. The feminine is adaptable and supple; it avoids unpleasantness and conflicts, to name just a few of its qualities.

Masculine is the opposite. Masculine energy is directed outwards to goals and objects, and is found with Mars, Sun and Pluto. They form and change the status quo and sometimes disturb it too. The masculine wants to create something new, clears obstacles out of the way and is ready to fight. To express it another way: the masculine force is directed towards the environment to produce effects; the feminine reacts to external influences. The movement from inwards to outwards is masculine; the movement from outwards to inwards is feminine. The left is the feminine side of the body; the right is masculine. Men and women are capable of both attitudes, both masculine and feminine, even though one is more familiar than the other.

In the astrological approach to the planets, we identify the opposition between masculine and feminine separately from biological gender, a very helpful distinction in the interpretation of the planets. It addresses the ancient astrological principle of polarity. There are masculine and feminine signs in the zodiac too: Aries is a masculine sign, Taurus feminine, Gemini masculine and so on...

Neutral Planets

Planets that are neither masculine nor feminine are neutral and have quite different properties. The neutral planets Mercury, Jupiter, Moon and Neptune are concerned with understanding connections. They are sentient, open to contact, sensitive, perceptive, observant and imaginative. Their sphere is the interconnectedness of all things.

Planets in the Columns (Vertical)

Left Column   ♀ ♄ ♅

The left column in the planetary chart symbolises the feminine side. At the bottom in the unconscious realm we find Venus, with Saturn above in the conscious realm and Uranus in the superconscious realm. These three planets have thoroughly feminine qualities. On the animal level, Venus corresponds to the eternal feminine. Saturn is feminine as the physical self on the personality level; with its ability to set boundaries it protects and maintains the status quo. Uranus is feminine on the spiritual level. It symbolises the higher Mother Imago, an ordering power that ensures security and brings about life improvement by innovation.

Middle Column ☿ ♃ ☽ ♆

The middle column features Mercury/Jupiter at the bottom, Moon above them and Neptune at the top. They are the neutral, sensitive planets, naturally connected because they belong to the same principles of communication and love. They are all sentient and react spontaneously in relationships and on social occasions. The crescent symbol is common to all of them; it occurs in the Moon, at the top for Mercury, on the left for Jupiter and at the top for Neptune. It symbolises sensitivity and receptivity, characteristic properties of these four planets.

When the crescent faces to the left, it signifies getting to the bottom of things. If it faces to the right, it represents openness to contact. If it faces upwards, as in the case of Neptune, it denotes impressionability and the characteristics of a receiving station. Mercury is the messenger who brings messages from the gods down to mankind, symbolised by the cross.

Right Column ♂ ☉ ♇

This column symbolises the masculine side of human nature, e.g. activity, willpower, self-assertion. In the case of Mars, the masculine aspect corresponds to the libido, motor energy, fighting power and achievement. In the case of Sun, it is self-generated will power that pursues its goals regardless of the opinions of other people. In the case of Pluto, we find the higher model of the Father, whose will is powerful and who constantly and irrevocably changes the world in his image.

Planets in the Three Levels (Horizontal)

The planets are divided into three horizontal levels in the table on page 15. On the bottom level are the instinctive human functions, on the middle level are the three personality or ego planets Saturn, Moon and Sun, while the three spiritual planets are on the top level, having a transpersonal function as ideal models.

Bottom Level:

Tool Planets   ♀ ♃ ☿ ♂

The Planets Venus, Jupiter, Mercury and Mars appear on the bottom level. These planets mainly serve basic functions, geared towards drives and instincts, representing the automatic processes that ensure survival. They still function if we are unconscious. They also take care of the survival of life and species in the animal kingdom.

These planets are not concerned with personality-forming energies in the sense that they contain a sense of self, or that they mean the ego in a direct sense. They are abilities or tools available to the ego with which it can express itself – but they are not the ego. Our ego powers are found in the three main planets: Sun, Moon and Saturn. Mars is pure power; it is also the masculine libido that is controlled by the ego. Its power, fighting energy, courage and potency must be manipulated and managed. Let us illustrate this using the example of the car.

The car has an engine. This engine is like Mars. If we turn on the engine and let the car run, it will do so until the petrol runs out. The car does not move, it is stationery and just pollutes the air and achieves nothing. If it is put into gear and allowed to move, it will crash into the nearest wall, maybe go off the nearest cliff. In other words: to achieve anything meaningful with Mars, someone must be present to guide and steer it, to give it direction. The ego planets in the middle row do this. This is true for all four planets in this group, not just for Mars. They must be used and guided correctly, which can only be done by a self that has goals and takes control.

Libido Planets

Venus and Mars   ♀ ♂

On the first level we find Venus in the feminine column on the left, and Mars in the masculine column on the right. They are the prototypes of femininity and masculinity, where the factor of gender comes into effect. It would be true to say that Venus is the feminine libido and Mars the masculine – but there is more to it than that. Every man and woman has Mars and Venus in their horoscope, i.e. everyone has a masculine and a feminine side. It has been scientifically proven that the human body does not produce only the gender-specific hormones, but also those of the opposite sex, i.e. oestrogen in men and testosterone in women, although in smaller quantities.

Both planets have other functions too. They are responsible for the balance of energy and matter in the body, mind and even the brain. Venus deals with the balance of matter, and Mars with the balance of energy. It is quite hard to illustrate how these processes work in humans, so we will use an example from the animal kingdom.

Venus/Mars Function in the Wild

A lion lies basking in the sun or better still in the shade. He ate well the previous day, feels good and does not feel like running around looking for food. At this point he is in a late Venus stage. He is passive, enjoys the warmth and light, does nothing at all and does not need to. But at some point his stomach will start to rumble, thus ending the Venus stage. Venus reports that supplies are running low. The feeling of hunger means that food must be found, so the lion starts to move. As he gets up, adrenaline, which is known to be a masculine hormone, is released. It allows sugar to be transformed into energy inside the muscle tissue, thereby generating power. The second burst of adrenaline follows when the lion gets wind of some animal. He follows his nose, a specifically masculine organ (often experienced astrologers can tell something about the position of Mars in a horoscope from a person's nose). The sense of smell and the ability to smell are both expressed by Mars. It is necessary to get wind of an animal in order to catch and eat it. Animals can do this well because their sense of smell is not as limited as that of humans. After the lion scents his prey, the third adrenaline burst occurs, he starts to run and tries to catch it. That is a significant expenditure of energy. After the ensuing hunt, the lion sits down in front of the dead animal. The influence of Mars is now fading away and he needs the remaining energy to devour his prey. After the meal, the lion is calm again, and as such in a comfortable Venus state. He enjoyed his feast and now his body can digest it.

Venus: The Sense of Taste

Venus provides the sense of taste: the ability to select what does us good and what suits us from what is available. It is also involved in choosing furniture, clothes or works of art. In art we talk about powers of aesthetic discrimination. As far as food is concerned, Venus chooses the right thing that will not harm the body. Venus tastes the quality of the food. We also add seasoning when cooking. Seasoning means checking that things are as they should be. When food reaches the stomach, the chemical process of assimilation begins. In the stomach and the intestine, food is broken down into its constituent parts and transformed into substances that can be stored in tissues or eliminated. Stores of various substances are laid down – mainly sugar as energy for movement, which the body uses later as required. Other nutrients are eliminated so that the body can continue the regeneration process, and part of the energy from the food is used immediately. Deliberately eating certain food with a high energy value, like meat broth, stimulating drinks or glucose rapidly restores energy. They are substances that are ready for immediate use.

Antagonism

The biological balance of energy and matter is in a constant state of flux between Mars and Venus. Each function leads inevitably to the other after a while – a true antagonism. They are two forces that work in opposing directions, but together they accomplish something that neither could do alone. That is the real characteristic of polar forces. One uses energy, the other stores it for later use. It is a life-supporting process that continues indefinitely. These two forces are interdependent, and many partnerships could work better if they adapted to the man and wife model of the couple. The person who understands these two forces as natural polarities finds it easier to accept that the two are meant for each other.

Male and Female functions

Mars and Venus also represent sexuality. A woman will identify herself more with the Venus in her horoscope and less with the Mars, and vice versa for a man. However, as both planets are present for both sexes, the woman also has masculine functions and vice versa. This can be understood as follows: all processes that use energy are masculine; all pleasure and enjoyment functions are feminine. If a woman stands at the oven and cooks, she is using Mars energy, she is doing something. Household chores involve a large amount of masculine energy. When a man appreciates beautiful things, art, furniture or clothes, he is expressing his feminine side. Even the selection process is a feminine Venus function, as the beautiful is distinguished from the ugly. Beauty is meant in another sense here, purely in the area of fashion.

A man identifies himself by the position of Mars in his chart, but he experiences the feminine with the women he meets who represent Venus in his chart. Venus in a man's chart works like the lodestar for femininity, seeking it out. His Venus helps him to know which type of woman will suit him. This usually happens unconsciously. When the right woman comes along, his Venus "signal" is set off. How he deals with that is another matter. Women have a kind of Mars "signal", which goes off when the right man comes along. The planet of the opposite gender is a kind of searching tool, in sexual terms. In a woman's horoscope, the Mars position shows what kind of man she is looking for. This is a projection of her own masculinity, which she carries within herself and is not really able to express. This is why she looks for a man who possesses these qualities.

On our planetary table on page 15 Mars and Venus are quite separate, which illustrates their polarity. There is a great affinity that corresponds to this large gap. In the interpretation of the horoscopes of couples, the distance between Mars and Venus shows the strength of the affinity. You can read more about this in *Astrological Psychosynthesis* part 3 'Love and Relationships in the Horoscope' (14).

Intelligence Planets

Jupiter and Mercury ♃ ☿

These two planets are placed closed together on the planetary table. The small distance between them means that they are not very different. They are actually much more alike than one would think, although there is a certain polarisation. The two functions are not fundamentally different though, as we have seen in the case of Mars and Venus; it is rather a question of a different approach to perception and learning ability.

People's learning ability is ruled primarily by the planets Jupiter and Mercury. There is more to it than that, of course, but it is these two bodies that enable us to learn. They allow us to perceive, to observe and to differentiate. We learn to avoid the unpleasant or the defective so that we do not have to experience it again. Human learning ability is so developed that we can get to the root of things, draw the right conclusions and then make decisions based on very little experience.

Jupiter is our sensorium that enables us to observe and to learn. We have five senses with which we can observe the world and draw conclusions from what we perceive. Only then do we start to think and interpret what we perceive. Thought must be fed by information, which is obtained from Mercury.

Jupiter ♃

Jupiter rules sensory perception. The Jupiter function enables us to learn without outside help, as long as we keep our wits about us and gather our experiences. Back in childhood we learn the difference between cold and hot, thick and thin, wood and metal. Children do this by holding things and putting them in their mouths, in other words, by exploring them with their senses. From this perception we learn to assess substance, realities, situations and even people correctly. Good judgement is the result of a well-functioning Jupiter. Good observation and careful evaluation lead to the correct assessment. We can distinguish wood from metal and know precisely that wood is useful for some things and metal for others. Metal does not burn when put into the fire, and the fire must be extremely hot even for it to melt, but it does not actually burn as wood does. These are real experiences that enable us to evaluate objects correctly and there is nothing subjective about them, unlike, for example "I like fire or I don't like fire". They are evaluations to distinguish what can be used for which purpose and what is right. That is how we learn for ourselves.

Mercury ☿

With Mercury, there is a second way of learning, that is, from other people. Mercury acquires information from all quarters so as to be well informed. It is constantly collecting knowledge, whether it needs it or not. Mercury does not discriminate according to value or quality as Jupiter does. Nowadays there are countless books on the market that are full of trivia. In schools, teachers tell us many things, and we learn from this knowledge transfer. This is quicker than learning by experience.

If every new-born baby had to learn by the Jupiter method, i.e. by his own sensory perception and observation abilities, it would take them a very long time to become "viable" people. These days, children are sent to school early so that they can learn things. At home they are given books and are also taught  daily about various practical aspects of life. This is really all second-hand information. It is not self-acquired but borrowed and drummed into them. If one reads a book, one can either accept or reject the contents if one does not have the necessary experience. One is not at all sure, which is why under the influence of Mercury one reads more books on the same subject but by different authors. If they all say the same things, then they are probably correct. Differences immediately cause insecurity, though.

Mercury provides the ability to put thoughts into words and words into sentences. That is a fantastic human talent, without which we could not understand each other. In the course of evolution, the human larynx has developed to make speech possible. Noises can become words and words are put together so that they make sense. This is how the power of speech developed, which has enabled man to convey his thoughts and ideas to others. Speech is a way of conveying ideas and thoughts.

Mercury makes human learning potential highly developed. The speed of learning has increased as speech has become more complex. If you look at the information networks that surround us today, you must admit that this data flow is almost too much to take in. But all Mercurial activity is dedicated to bringing us information that we cannot obtain by ourselves. One example is the internet, which more and more people want to be connected to so that they can communicate with the whole world.

Jupiter/Mercury Antagonism   ♃ ☿

The most highly developed form of learning ability is that based on the antagonism of Jupiter and Mercury. If we doubt a book's accuracy, we have no alternative but to find out for ourselves. Consulting the works of other authors does not reassure us of the truth, for they can be wrong too. Even as readers of this chapter, you have no way of checking what you are reading. Only by making your own observations and gathering your own experiences can you be at all sure if something is true or not. Words are really only air. With words one can do anything; in our world they are powerful tools, which can easily deceive.

Only by checking, i.e. by thinking, observing and experimenting with our own senses can we be sure if information we have received is correct or not. A little observation does lead to certain conclusions, but it is possible that they are not really valid. More observation is then required to see if that brings more consistency.

As mentioned above, the Jupiter way of learning is always via the senses and the Mercury way could be described as intellectual. A strong mercurial tendency is characteristic of our society. In schools, children are stopped from Jupiter learning and forced more and more towards Mercury, which makes it hard for them to experience as many things as they should. They are often bad students although they are not stupid, they just work differently – they learn visually. Experience shows that it is easier for them to memorise by seeing a picture while hearing a sound. Simple learning processes are more successful when done together than when done separately.

Astrological Psychology is also Jupiter/Mercury influenced. The two intelligence planets work antagonistically in that the whole aspect pattern can be perceived sensually with the eyes and described with Mercury. Observations that are made with Jupiter cannot be expressed with the senses. Mercury is required to express and explain. It can draw logical conclusions because it possesses the terminology to express the logic of things.

The assimilation range of Jupiter is a great deal larger than that of Mercury. It has been measured how many bits per second (a bit is a unit) is used for a single unit of information in Information Technology. A red spot is a single unit of information that Jupiter can assimilate. The quantity is an order of magnitude higher than for Mercury. Jupiter always brings whole images, while Mercury brings words one after the other. Even when we read we must read words one after the other; information reaches us in discrete packets that are sequenced together with others. That is why mercurial thinking is purely linear, while Jupiter thinking is two- or even three-dimensional.

Our society would indeed be well-advised to respect Jupiter more. There are movements and undercurrents that attempt this, but they do not get very far. Mercury learning is still favoured in schools, with the other just done for fun as a sideline. Many have not yet understood how important it is to also encourage children to look within. It is not enough to just introduce this in music, because it remains a special department.

The self-test to determine your own type consists of working out whether you think primarily in words or in images. If the answer is in words, then you are mercurial; if in images, then you are more influenced by Jupiter. The ideal is to be able to do both. In the verbal process it is easy to set performance targets in which a certain amount of information must be assimilated, organised and reproduced in a certain time. This cannot be done with Jupiter.

Expressed in simple terms, there are visual and verbal types. The visual type corresponds to Jupiter and the verbal type to Mercury. All those who function with language and words and all the professions that use them are mercurial. However, a strong Jupiter is shown in the explorer, the nature-lover, the skier or the person who gets to grips with realities. They must demonstrate a pronounced sensuality. You can read more about this in *Astrological Psychosynthesis* part 1 'Intelligence in the Horoscope' (23).

Middle Level:

Ego [or Personality] Planets ☉ ☽ ♄

The Planets Saturn, Moon and Sun on the second, middle level of the planetary table on page 15 are concerned with the awareness of the personality or the 'little ego'. This level is connected to the daily awareness by which a person knows he is unique. Here he lives as an independent being and can function as a personality that looks for and goes his own way. It is often experienced as loneliness, something that animals do not feel, as they are instinctively connected with members of their own species and the whole natural world.

These three planets form the personality awareness, or the identity of the person, and this can only be done by these three planets and their functions. We can of course draw on other planets to help to do this, and base our self-awareness on our achievements or even on our beauty or ability to enjoy. They have no substance; they are distractions, as if one first has to look in the mirror in order to know oneself. This requires objects, subjects, articles, situations, while with the three main planets one can have direct experience of oneself as an identity.

It is important to see that we have three levels of personhood. We are beings who are bodies that also feel and think. We possess the ability to change levels several times a day. Sometimes we are more intellectual, sometimes more emotional, sometimes more physical. This is a tangible fact. The mind is classified as masculine and physicality as feminine, without making any value judgements.

We therefore assume three different types of individual awareness that together form the personality awareness. Two of them are "lights", plus Saturn. It is interesting to note here that, in traditional astrology, Sun and Moon are considered to be the planets of personality awareness. The Sun has always symbolised self-awareness. The term awareness also appears on the planetary table, which means that a person is aware of himself by means of the Sun. For Saturn, the word "mother" is also still used, which irritates many classical astrologers. Saturn rules physicality and matter. It guarantees protection and security from possible danger, just as the mother does.

Saturn therefore represents the mother, Sun represents the father and Moon the child. This attribution is the result of years of research work, which showed overwhelmingly that the position of Saturn in individual horoscopes gives precise information about the mother-child relationship. The Moon does not show the mother herself, but traces of the mother that remain in the child's psyche.

Saturn represents physical self-awareness. If you are physically healthy, you feel good, which leads to a feeling of well-being and self confidence. If you are physically unwell, you become apprehensive and enjoy life less. If you are physically injured, Saturn perceives that as danger and pain. As the physical self, it immediately counteracts with measures to restore order. In the three-fold personality structure it is the head of security responsible for the survival and health of the body. Always managing to feel well and healthy boosts our self-confidence and increases our vitality.

The **Moon** is our emotional nature, which is almost always contrasted with our intellectual nature (Sun). Many problems arise if the polarity between feeling and thinking cause conflicts in the environment. Our emotional nature and its needs connect us closely to our environment, and we are easily moved and jostled by its movements. With the Moon we learn predominantly by contact and less by self-observation.

The **Sun** represents the main principle of human self-awareness. It is the entity that can consider itself, refer to itself and say "I am". The Sun shines with its own energy out in space; it does not need anyone to shine on it. It is autonomous and imposes its own will to achieve its goals. This is illustrated by the symbol for Sun ☉, the circle with a dot at the centre: a closed, self-contained figure concentrated on its centre.

Top Level:

Spiritual Planets   ♅ ♆ ♇

The orbits of **Uranus, Neptune and Pluto** lie outside that of Saturn. These so-called new planets cannot be seen with the naked eye. They symbolise three general principles that function mainly on the spiritual level and are insignificant in terms of our physical make-up. It could even be said that we could live without them. They affect most people as collective currents that are followed unconsciously. To individualise them we need to know them so that they can be cultivated in our personal lives. We will go into this in more detail in a later chapter.

In the columns of the planetary table on page 15, we find Uranus on the feminine side, Neptune in the neutral column and Pluto on the masculine side. However on this transpersonal level there is no clear division into masculine and feminine and these planets should be considered more as androgynous, i.e. they can be either gender.

In Chapter 3, we go into detail on the deeper significance of the three spiritual planets for human spiritual development. The transformation of the three-fold personality to the transpersonal level is a particularly fascinating area that interests many people today.

Summary of the Planets

Symbol/Name		Motivation	Energy	Function
☉	Sun	Cardinal	Masculine	Thinking self Self-awareness
☽	Moon	Mutable	Neutral	Feeling self Sympathy-antipathy
♄	Saturn	Fixed	Feminine	Physical self Immunity, limits
☿	Mercury	Mutable	Neutral	Logic Language, communication
♀	Venus	Fixed	Feminine	Aesthetic Selective harmony
♂	Mars	Cardinal	Masculine	Motor function Strength to achieve
♃	Jupiter	Mutable	Neutral	Sensory function Perception Awareness of value
♅	Uranus	Fixed	Feminine	Perfect world Creative thinking
♆	Neptune	Mutable	Neutral	Ideal love Unconditional love Idealistic
♇	Pluto	Cardinal	Masculine	Perfect being Metamorphosis Essence, will, absoluteness
☊	Moon nodes	Correction point	Neutral	First step Signpost for further development

2. The Seven Classical Planets

Introduction

Three Ego Planets
Sun, Moon, Saturn
• The Sun, Autonomous Self-awareness •
• The Moon, the Feeling Self • Saturn, the Physical Self •

Four Tool Planets
Mercury, Venus, Mars, Jupiter
• Mercury, the Winged Messenger •
• Venus, the Feminine • Mars, the Masculine •
• Jupiter, the Eye •

Attribution of the Planets
A) To the Three Crosses
B) To the Four Temperaments
C) To the Seven Rays

Introduction

The Seven Classical Planets

The seven classical planets are those that can be seen with the naked eye, without a telescope. In astrology they have always been interpreted as basic human abilities. While the Moon is, of course, not really a planet but the satellite of our Earth, for the purposes of astrology it is interpreted as a planet. The Sun is the central star of our solar system and is orbited by the planets, including the Earth. The three new planets were only discovered later, as explained in Chapter 3.

The seven classical planets are initially broken down into three ego planets and four tool planets. The three ego planets Sun, Moon and Saturn are vitally important in the Huber Method, because through them everyone can experience and actualise their self potential. The four tool planets Mercury, Venus, Mars and Jupiter are responsible for all natural survival functions. There are therefore seven basic qualities that everyone possesses.

In order to understand how these seven planets work in the horoscope, we should familiarise ourselves with the astrological knowledge accumulated over centuries as well as with new psychological insights. A one-sided interpretation such as the Sun in Leo or Mars in Sagittarius will very rarely be found in this book. We always proceed from a holistic pattern, in which the effects of the planets in the horoscope depend on the zodiac sign, the house in which it lies, and the aspects that it forms with other planets. First of all we shall describe the psychological qualities, the archetypes and a few mythological connections of the seven planets in some detail.

Because many modern students of astrology are seeking an orientation for their spiritual development, we have also included the transformed stage as a development goal in the descriptions of the planets on different levels.

Three Ego Planets

Sun, Moon, Saturn

As already described in chapter 2, the Sun is our thinking self in the composition of the three-fold personality. It is autonomous and can take decisions independently. The Moon is the feeling self, with which we seek contact and love and in which everything to do with our feelings is reflected. Saturn is the physical self, or more simply, physical awareness. Its basic motivation is security. You can read more on this in the section on "The Personality and its Integration" in *Astrological Psychosynthesis* (19).

For further study, it is important to differentiate between the three levels of life experience, which anchor our personality as three facets of the ego. These are areas of experience of the self and can be perceived relatively easily with our normal human awareness. It is obvious that it is impossible to do any physical work or perform any actions without a physical body. The body is an essential tool that we need to live and to realise goals. Everyone has feelings and wishes they would like to fulfil, and many people go to great lengths to satisfy them. The mind accounts for a large part of our lives, it is constantly active creating new ideas so that we can understand life. Every day we learn new things that have to be processed by the mind. Nobody can deny these three facts. They are simple and obvious because they are organic realities. We distinguish between:

1) The autonomous-thinking self: Sun

2) The emotional-feeling self: Moon

3) The physical self: Saturn

The Sun ☉

Autonomous Self-Awareness

> **Affinities**
>
> Masculine Planet (right column)
> Mars and Pluto
> Ruler of Leo
> Day of the week: Sunday
> Metal: Gold
> Aspect: Conjunction
> Cardinal Cross
> Fire Signs: Aries, Leo, Sagittarius
> Fire Houses: 1, 5, 9
> Mental Thinking Self
> Self-awareness, I-sense
> Competitiveness
> Good position in horoscope: top
> Will and Power
> Father

Of all the planets, the Sun has always been considered as the most important way of expressing the personality. It symbolises self-awareness, so is the most effective I-entity of the human personality. The Sun is able to form a secure, stable self-awareness independent of any recognition from the environment. It is the powerful formative, creative principle and symbolises the source of all life, including the will to live, vitality and human spiritual energy. In the horoscope, it represents individuality, self-awareness and the thinking and discriminating self. The self-awareness of a person is therefore dependent on Sun's sign position, house position and aspects.

Know thyself

The Sun ego enables us to reflect upon ourselves, to know ourselves and deliberately change things. As the thinking self on the mental level, we are standing on an observation post that gives us an overview of our lives. We see our strengths and weaknesses and can decide freely what we want to do. If we entertain thoughts of development, we set out with determination to work on ourselves, avoid making the same old mistakes and change unwanted habits. Everyone can develop their will and use creative thinking to form a new and better personality that corresponds more and more closely to their inner nature.

Goethe the Thinker
After the painting by Tischbein, 1776

Mentality

On the thinking level, the position of the Sun indicates a person's mentality. If it lies in a cardinal sign (Aries, Cancer, Libra, Capricorn), we think in terms of hierarchical power, are career-minded, strive toward goals and judge others by their position of power. In a fixed sign (Taurus, Leo, Scorpio, Aquarius), the thinking processes are economical; we are sparing with our thoughts and only speak if we have something to say. In a mutable sign (Gemini, Virgo, Sagittarius, Pisces) we adapt to circumstances and often change our minds, but usually judge according to humanitarian standards.

The Sun is creative on the mental level according to the motto: "We are what we think". If we think badly of ourselves, that we are worthless and will never be able to achieve our goals, we make it happen. However, if we think positively and believe in the creative potential of Sun's energy within us, our whole lives are positively affected. With the thinking Sun ego we can recognise when negative feelings rise from the subconscious and depress us, and go on to use willpower to resolve and eliminate them. We can also transform them with the power of creative thinking and replace them with positive feelings. By so doing we experience the power of our own thought, deepen our sense of self, strengthen our inner values and radiate increasing self-confidence.

I think, therefore I am

Descartes famously said: "I think, therefore I am." One could also say: "I do, therefore I am." When we do something ourselves that produces a result, we can see that we have done something worthwhile that gives pleasure to ourselves and to others. By what we are and what we have done, we affirm and value ourselves. We do not need acknowledgement from our environment. As self-awareness grows and we believe in ourselves, we actualise ourselves in our own right.

Depending on sign, with Sun consciousness we stick to our own thoughts, convictions and opinions. We say without fear of criticism, that is my opinion, my experience, no-one can take it away from me. The thinking self therefore has the most direct and visible function of consciousness and that is why the "I think" is the most impressive sign of an aware and intelligent person.

From the very start, the Sun's self-awareness is to a certain extent differentiated. We can deliberately confront the other "I"s that we meet, objectify our thinking, and differentiate our powers of discrimination and judgement. In this way we can relate clearly and lucidly to the world and react with ever-greater self-confidence, as a real I-entity taking full responsibility for its actions. We have the right to be what we are. We are just right as we are and can say "yes" to ourselves. This is the point at which the integration of the personality is very significant. How many people have had their self-confidence knocked in their youth? They were not trusted with anything and not given opportunities to learn. They were made to feel that they couldn't come up to scratch, that no one needed them and their particular abilities weren't required. An environment offering no support for development reduces self-confidence and creates future ego problems.

Ego **Problems**

Ego problems like these can be seen in the horoscope. We can establish how strong and autonomous a person's self-awareness is and how it can be made effective in their life as a support and a relational pole. We can also see to what extent the environment is favourable or not for building self-confidence. That is largely dependent on Sun's sign and house position and aspects. If the Sun is not prominent, it is not sufficiently or successfully expressed in life. As the most important aspect of the ego, its short- or long-term functional problems can obviously affect vitality.

It is a fact that people cannot assert themselves in life if they have little self-confidence. They do not achieve their goals and are unhappy. If they do feel satisfied with less success, they easily become resigned. However, one must learn how to live, even with a so-called "weak Sun position". To learn with which of the three ego planets we can most easily do this, though, is an art that takes time to learn, either by means of what has formed us in life or what we can see in our horoscope.

Self-Awareness

What is self-awareness? The term is composed of two parts: self and awareness. True self-awareness is a prime indication of a person's awareness of their inner strength and creative power. It allows him to realise the purpose of his life and to set life goals that suit him, as well as a developed and well-planned life programme.

For this, it is necessary to know oneself and to check constantly whether one is living according to one's intrinsic nature or according to the opinions of others. Intelligence, mental perception and a certain amount of integrity are necessary along with this evolved self-awareness. This requires constant work. The autonomous Sun ego enables us to observe and analyse ourselves and to decide to expand our minds, free them from negative thoughts and fill them with new vital strength, so that positive Sun energy grows within us thus reducing anxiety, worries and depression.

Willpower

One of the most important functions of the evolved and autonomous Sun in the horoscope is the individual will that can choose and decide freely. Sun's position gives significant indications as to the strength of willpower and the ability to assert the self. Will is developed by having a clear goal to aim for and directing all one's strengths towards it. Concentrating on one goal extends our knowledge, sharpens our minds and ability to think. We develop new abilities in a specific and planned way and build our own future. Sun corresponds to the cardinal principle, and stimulates a person's active, motivating energies that guide him in a certain direction according to the type of cross, causing him to pursue some things and not others. These motivating energies do not just come from the Sun, but also from the aspect pattern and all three ego planets.

Sign and House Position

When interpreting the Sun, as with all planets, we distinguish between its position in a sign (situation), in a house (behaviour) and its aspect (motivation). Only this combination can provide a correct assessment of the overall quality. The vital Sun principle in the houses indicates a person's interests that express character and reveal conscious motivation. We deal with this in Chapter 5. His inner goals are actualised in the sign. In cardinal signs, his will-drive is directed towards reaching personal goals, in fixed signs he searches for security in everything and in mutable signs he tries to improve human relationships.

The Sun as a Father Image

The position of Sun in the horoscope provides useful psychological information about our father. It shows how we live the masculine-paternal principle and can realise it within ourselves. The

Sun corresponds to the patriarchal system that ruled much of society in the past. The archetypal function of the father is to be a model for an independent, strong-willed personality who can stand on his own two feet and is strong enough to confront all obstacles and to actualise himself. The position of Sun usually tells us something about our real father. If he was a strong personality, he set us a good example, by which we could orientate and develop self-awareness. If he was a weak figure, then we too lack self-confidence, are afraid to assert ourselves and frequently suffer from low self-esteem.

Sun Position and Female Emancipation

In patriarchal times, the solar level was only available to men. The woman was restricted to the lunar level to play out her serving role. These days, many women have transferred their awareness from the lunar level to the solar level. Countless women have been gripped by the urge to emancipate themselves and work more and more on the solar level. They want equality with men and jobs that bring them satisfaction and recognition; like men they strive for self-actualisation.

Individuation Process

This process involves the expansion of Sun awareness as an autonomously functioning whole that aims to liberate and become the self. Only the Sun is able to combine all parts of the personality into a functional whole and to mobilise energies towards a goal. That is the integration of the personality, in which we become increasingly aware of our personal strength and self-reliance. We learn that we can act without having to wait for commands or orders from others. On the contrary, a self-aware person avoids following others, wants to lead and set the tone himself and decide what has to be done.

Transformation

Willpower and intelligence are strong enough, according to sign and house position, to devote oneself to spiritual goals and renounce personal power. In the transformed Sun, a person tries for higher goals and is prepared to liberate himself from all the limitations of the "little personality". This usually only happens when he knows exactly what he does and does not want. To the extent that motivations change and individual awareness evolves, the sense of responsibility also grows. Such a person is then not only there for himself, but also for others. He can do things for society and complete them conscientiously without abuse of power. He can be relied on and trusted with projects that he can manage and realise. A person with a transformed Sun exudes strength, wisdom and integrity and is a role model for many people.

The Moon ☾

The Feeling Self

> **Affinities**
>
> Neutral, sensitive planet (centre column)
> Jupiter, Mercury, Neptune
> Ruler of Cancer
> Day of the week: Monday
> Metal: Silver
> Aspect: Conjunction
> Mutable Cross
> Water signs: Cancer, Scorpio, Pisces
> Water houses: 4th, 8th, 12th
> Feeling Self, You-sense
> Reproductive Instinct
> Good position in the horoscope: You-side
> Humanity, sympathy and antipathy
> Love and Contact
> Child

In the case of the Moon, the motivation is for others. It needs the environment to be able to live as an I. With the feeling self we need approval from the You. The Moon is not able to give approval to itself as the Sun is; it requires constant encouragement from others. This makes it dependent on those around it at any one time. This second level of the personality is comparable to water. The feeling self is reflected in it, as is everything to do with a person's feelings.

Reflection

The Moon is a heavenly body unable to emit light itself but has a great ability to reflect light. It reflects almost 100% of the light it receives from the Sun. The symbol of the Moon is a crescent facing either to the left or the right, depending on whether it was waxing or waning at the time of birth – it is shown as such on our horoscopes. A waxing Moon faces inwards and can get right to the bottom of things; a waning Moon faces outwards, is sensitive to the environment and can express its own wishes.

The reproductive or sex drive is attributed to the Moon as a contact planet. It drives us to connect with a You, a lover. We need loving contact, relationships, love, harmony, and beauty around us, for only then do we feel joyful and happy; if nobody pays attention to us and ignores us, our feeling self feels pain – we suffer.

New Moon

The Moon uses any means available to communicate its need for contact with the environment, as it feels neglected without this. There is nothing there at all at the time of the New Moon because the light shines on it from the wrong side. For five days every month, the Moon is not visible at all, there is a kind of feelings vacuum. The feelings are untouched, nothing is experienced, as if it is non-existent. When we have our personal new Moon, we usually complain of loneliness, lovelessness or boredom. Loneliness is hard for the Moon to bear, because it is then unable to perceive anything by itself.

Full Moon

When the Moon is full, it is completely illuminated by the Sun and its perceptions are heightened. The emotional nature is particularly stimulated and many people do strange things. They become active and try to fulfil their wishes. During the full Moon, the ego feels approval, as if someone is saying: "I love you". The feeling self thus receives fulfilling approval. Many people think that the full Moon approval must always be present, forgetting that the Moon is governed by cycles over which we have no control. It is as well to understand these natural laws of ebb and flow as soon as possible to avoid disappointment. There is a difference between blaming one's partner when the full Moon is over and knowing that it is caused by the Moon's cycle. We must know that a new Moon is always followed by a full Moon, and that the vicissitudes of our feelings are determined by cosmic laws.

The Feeling Level

The feeling level is a world of contradictions: feelings of joy and love, of sympathy and antipathy, ebb and flow, symbolised by the phases of the Moon. This is just like our feeling self, depending on sign and house position: unstable, changeable, moody and dependent on the environment. We want to be loved and approved of and admired by others. We are afraid of being alone and having to live without love. When left alone, we often react to some experiences negatively, standoffishly, coldheartedly or too subjectively, i.e. egocentrically. In doing so, we often hurt other people; it is our fault if they go away.

Probing Device

The Moon enables the perception of initial opportunities for contact on psychic levels. It is a kind of encounter, an inner feeling, an identification. When we meet someone, we immediately feel a kind of attraction or rejection, sympathy or antipathy. Other people radiate something that attracts or repels us. The Moon seeks out all sympathetic waves like a radar screen and tries to avoid less sympathetic people. Seen in this way, it is a probing device, a warning signal. Everyone has had the experience of picking up good vibes from some people and bad vibes from others. That is a purely Moon function. A highly sensitive Moon ego enables us to immediately recognise friend or foe and make quick, spontaneous decisions whether to open ourselves up or shut down and defend ourselves. If the Moon allows us to sense a potentially sympathetic person, initially we think: "I would like to know that person better". But whether we go to them and initiate an encounter usually depends on other factors. The Moon reports opportunities for contact, we then usually make decisions with the Sun or Saturn.

The Need for Contact

For the Moon, contact means self-affirmation. The feeling self experiences itself through contact and the love between two people. There are people who are not, or perhaps no longer, in the position to make positive contact or to love other people. What do they do? They gossip and moan about the neighbours. That is negative contact affirmation. Squabbling and criticising are also forms of contact, albeit not very productive or beneficial. But if one is not capable of doing otherwise, it is frequently a necessary compensation. On the feeling level there is a wide variety of compensatory behaviour; now and again everyone needs a treat or a substitute to be able to deal with disappointments or feelings of being unloved.

The Child Within

The position of the Moon in the horoscope also tells us which experiences as a child have marked our contact behaviour. Psychological findings show that the reasons for many behavioural problems in young people are to be found in unresolved early childhood experiences. The child naturally  expects that the world will correspond to her innermost ideas; she lives on the feeling level and is almost always identified with the Moon ego. All experiences, good and bad, are fixed in the feeling self and are the causes of later interpersonal behaviour patterns. If the parents as key figures do not disappoint their children, the feeling self can grow unscathed. A healthy overall attitude to life can develop and the child can cope with difficult tasks and adversity later in adult life.

However, if a child's initial sense of trust, belief and security are betrayed, she will withdraw into herself and construct a defence against outside contact for her own protection. Later on, this must be recognised as such and then dismantled, which is a difficult process. Conversely, the parents can also project ideals onto the child that she cannot fulfil because they do not correspond to her natural abilities. This usually occurs when the Moon is in the upper area of the horoscope, i.e. in the 9th or 10th house. We reach a point where we must liberate ourself even from projections like these in order to find ourself, which is where astrology can be very helpful.

An individual horoscope is a neutral instrument and does not respond to wishful thinking. It is objective and shows a person's true nature. There are often deceptions in the very assessment of the feeling level, and wrong beliefs due to the reflection of external judgements and deeply ingrained personal wishes.

Transformation Work

From the Moon's position in the horoscope we can work out how we react to life's ups and downs and to the contradictions inherent in this level. Do we swing from one extreme to the other, from activity to passivity, from love to hate, from attraction to repulsion or do we keep calm? Do we lose ourselves completely in other people because we are emotionally dependent and do not want to grow up? How do we cope when love goes wrong? Do we still believe in love despite bad experiences and remain open to contact and love, or do we become closed and embittered and seek revenge. Do we learn from experience and try to avoid these swings and achieve stability and balance? Which consequences do we draw from these pairs of opposites and how do we overcome the subjectivity of the feeling self?

We deal with all these questions when we look at the position of the Moon in the horoscope. The Moon in the twelve signs of the zodiac is described in detail in Chapter 6, together with descriptions of the material and transformed levels.

Saturn ♄
The Physical Self

> **Affinities**
> Feminine Planet (left column)
> Venus and Uranus
> Ruler of Capricorn and Aquarius
> Day of the week: Saturday
> Metal: Lead
> Aspects: Opposition, Quincunx
> Fixed Cross
> Earth signs: Taurus, Virgo, Capricorn
> Earth houses: 2nd, 6th, 10th
> Physical Self, Self-preservation drive
> Good horoscope position: bottom
> Responsibility and discipline
> Self-confidence and security
> Sense of touch, the skin
> Mother

The state of self-awareness is different for Saturn, symbol of the physical dimension that reveals much about the relationship to one's own body and therefore also to mother. It is a psychological fact that our I-experience in the body is to a large extent dependent on the relationship of symbiosis with mother in the first two years of life. If this symbiotic phase was problem-free, then physical existence is tolerable, even enjoyable. The absence of this phase is often indicated by a lack of vitality or bad health. We learn this by asking ourselves: "Do I feel well?" or "How dangerous is life for me at the moment?" We can feel the answer on our skin. If we feel well, we can let ourselves be touched; if we feel unwell, we avoid physical contact. Pain can also be felt on the skin. It is our natural boundary with the environment and is controlled by Saturn.

Boundary

Saturn perceives by means of boundaries, from both a physical and mental point of view. The more successful the boundaries, the more secure it feels, resulting in self-assurance and physical well being. Saturn symbolises the human drive for self preservation. We must also make sure that we preserve what doesn't hurt us, intrude upon us or make us ill. We also ensure that we eat well and healthily. These abilities are usually learnt from mother. From a very young age, she tells us what to do and what not to do. Mother's many instructions, prohibitions and reprimands aid security and survival. We store them in memory and use them as a basic code of behaviour for use on the material level of existence. So with Saturn we perceive all survival-related functions and act accordingly in a careful, responsible and realistic manner. The better we preserve ourselves, the more self-assured and strong we are.

If we fall ill or get injured, our self-assurance crumbles. We become anxious, suffer and do something to get rid of the pain. Here Saturn usually behaves defensively and builds defence mechanisms that can even be aggressive, depending on character and temperament. Saturn's position in the horoscope can indicate how we react in dangerous situations. It's basically a defensive mechanism, not offensive – Saturn cannot go out and fight. It can behave like a wall made of brick or glass though. Closing up and locking down are Saturn's specialities. From a biological point of view, Saturn represents the immune system, which ensures the survival of the body.

Recognisable Identity

Saturn's identity awareness is physical. Our physical appearance reveals what and who we are. The way we hold ourselves shows the world where our boundaries are, so that others automatically keep their distance. When we show that we can protect ourselves from the environment, people take us seriously. Setting boundaries is the prerogative of Saturn; in a biological sense it provides immunity. If we do this successfully, we have a recognisable identity in the eyes of others. We all do this in our own way, according to Saturn's horoscope position. Identity must be shown to the world. Self-awareness needn't be visible to the environment; it doesn't need attention to be drawn to it. Identity definitely requires a setting in which it can prove itself. One way to do this is to be bursting with health; another is to have a bulging bank account. If one has one of these and has a "cushion", some security, one is externally strong and invulnerable. Bank accounts impress others and give a sense of security. So Saturn enables us to do our own public relations. We can flaunt our possessions, train our bodies and show our muscles, or pose wearing expensive clothes. These are all examples of typical Saturn showing off.

Thoughts of Security

What's mine is mine, Saturn tells himself; he doesn't give it away easily. He's talking about substance, reserves. Reserves mean security, typical of Saturn. The possession of reserves ensures survival in times of need. Many animals also lay down reserves. The squirrel collects hazelnuts in autumn. Every hoarding instinct is Saturnine. Looking after oneself, gaining security, being able to ensure personal survival are all ways in which Saturn builds self-confidence. This also helps identification with the environment.

If someone is unable to survive, they go down in other people's estimations. Whether it is their fault or not, they are shunned, considered a failure, a loser – a harsh judgement. Someone who shows that he can make it, that he has resources, possessions and space around him, makes an impression. He is a strong figure who commands respect. Such people can be trusted with duties and responsibilities.

Saturn's position in the horoscope also indicates whether or not we are healthy, strong and secure, can take care of ourselves, and whether we are able to set boundaries naturally and therefore possess defensive strength (immunity). It also shows whether we look for weak, ill, anxious and insecure protection and security in other people. Saturn also tells whether or not we are capable of bearing responsibility and to what extent we take physical reality seriously. It confers a sense of reality and its importance. Saturn leaves no margin for error and eventually leads us to a clear awareness of reality.

The Memory

From another point of view, Saturn is also memory that stores every experience and warns us of danger. Experience teaches us to avoid repeating the same mistakes. Saturn also symbolises the wealth of experience: that which we have lived and suffered. It is the ability to remember, memory, and also conscience and in many cases the "nay-sayer". On one hand it is our anxiety that helps us to avoid danger, and on the other hand the primal belief and knowledge that Mother Nature watches out for her children and provides them with what they need to survive.

Saturn, the great Mother

In connection with the Earth and matter, Saturn has been known as the great Mother since time immemorial. We know from our own experience how feelings of wellbeing and protection provided by mother can make us feel good about our selves. Saturn's maternal nature demands that everything is in order and all dangers and sources of disruption are eliminated. As a protective power, Saturn wants to be completely sure that everything runs smoothly. That is the minimal demand for the basic need for security. A mother constantly watches over her child so that it comes to no harm. She is always on call and sees to the vital necessities. For the child she is the life-preserving entity who provides everything, feeds, protects and guides. As the maternal function, Saturn brings up the child to be a responsible adult who is able to look after himself and control matter. Saturn's position in the horoscope reveals the influence of mother, and also the existential possibilities in the family. If there was material deprivation or instability, or the child grew up without a mother, these insecure conditions can cause many people to be unable to cope with material life.

Inactivity - Inertia

Inactivity is a weakness that can easily occur if one has an excess of pleasant things. If security and survival are guaranteed, the body wants to feel better and better, so becomes more and more lazy and comfortable. A sign of such an oversaturation of Saturn in the horoscope is if all aspects are blue. This increases the need for comfort and therefore to have a nice, comfortable, cosy and constantly improving life. The armchair and sofa become plumper and softer as energies become saturated. Our civilisation is greatly influenced by Saturn's need for comfort. Everyone strives for material security, wealth and perfect health. There are typical Saturn processes like stagnation, crystallisation and the ageing process. Saturn's energies can easily go into reverse, so we must be on our guard here and constantly work on our flexibility and perceptiveness and broaden our minds with the aid of the other planets.

Saturn the Keeper of the Threshold

In many writings, Saturn is also referred to as the "Keeper of the Threshold". As the most distant planet that can be seen with the naked eye, it is the frontier guard of the visible and therefore deserves this name. Before we can experience the spiritual planets Uranus, Neptune and Pluto, which are too far away for our eyes to see, we must cross the path of Saturn's orbit. It guards the stages of the transcendental, which we can only enter safely with a stable grasp of reality.

As "Keeper of the Threshold", Saturn represents the total amount of mental and spiritual factors that limit spiritual development. These must be acknowledged and transformed before we can make our way towards the spiritual planets. This does not happen by repressing unwanted emotions or by compensation methods, but by understanding that life means constant movement and change and that we must become permeable to the subtler radiations of our soul. Saturn offers the protective security and assurance that we need to be able to work on ourselves and prepare to venture safely into the spiritual dimensions. As ruler of matter and form, Saturn protects our souls and the spirit of the earth on which we may safely live out our physical existence. Nowadays, Saturn has an important maturing function to fulfil, in which we have to learn to deal responsibly with the earth's resources.

The Evildoer

In the last 2000 years, the so-called Age of Pisces, Saturn was known as the "great Evildoer". This period demonised the physical and the body was considered to be sinful. We still feel the effects of this today, which explains why so many people have problems with their bodies. This attitude towards Saturn has caused the body to be neglected and has complicated physical existence. In olden times, the lives of many people were not pleasant; how many times did plagues and other diseases strike mankind, which was powerless to protect itself? It was no wonder that Saturn was demonised and also acted as the Evildoer in astrology. This can still be seen today in the old astrology books. This error of judgement is still felt by many people, although the care of the body is now fashionable.

The Integration of Saturn

According to Robert Assagioli, founder of Pychosynthesis (6), we can only integrate what we love. It is therefore obvious that we have to change our attitude towards Saturn. For the purposes of integration, it is necessary to free Saturn from the "demonisation theory". We can and should accept it as the precious bodily self, without which physical existence would be impossible. In the horoscope, Saturn not only represents the mother that gives us life, but also provides us with a quite different attitude towards our bodies by means of modern hygiene and medicine. The glorification of the body as the necessary swing of the pendulum to the opposite extreme is catching on everywhere; we can see this on pictures in magazines or in the way that modern man cherishes his body as an important instrument for his wellbeing. We only have to think of the number of books on correct nutrition, skin care, health and physical therapies. Our entire physical existence has improved compared to the old days. We can be glad that technological achievements have made our lives easier and safer. Survival is no longer a problem for most people. It is frequently up to ourselves to stay physically healthy. This also enables us to become more and more fond of Saturn and to free him of his old curse.

☿

Four Tool Planets
Mercury, Venus, Mars, Jupiter

Mercury ☿
The Winged Messenger

> **Affinities**
> Neutral Planet (middle column)
> Jupiter, Moon, Neptune
> Ruler of Gemini and Virgo
> Day of the Week: Wednesday
> Metal: Quicksilver
> Aspects: Semi-sextile, Aspect Figure "Eye"
> Mutable Cross
> Air Temperament
> Communication, Information
> Speech and Sense of Hearing
> Combination Theory

Mercury is equated in mythology with the Greek god Hermes and the Egyptian god Thoth, both of whom act as mediators in the world of the gods. We imagine the winged messenger to be a winged being that can move freely in the sky and travel everywhere. In mythology, Mercury was described as "carrying messages at the speed of light between men and the gods". His task was to convey the will of the gods to men and also to carry the wishes and worries of men back to the gods as quickly as possible. He was a true go-between. He was very good at his job of mediating between above and below, between creator and created and all areas in between. It made him very happy to deal with everything as fast as possible. The image of the fleet-footed messenger has always suited Mercury; every new burst of speed was a pleasure for him. He was mainly concerned with obtaining the most effect with as little energy expenditure as possible, with saving time and being present in several places at the same time.

Mercury Today

The planetary principle of Mercury is also that of an intermediary. It is involved in all forms of human relationship. It stimulates us to connect, to make contact, to exchange thoughts, it creates a communication platform and reciprocal connections. Mercury works ceaselessly to connect everything together and to maintain the network. It is always there when information has to be exchanged and passed on. The flow of information must not be interrupted, indeed, new ways of transporting all messages even faster must be found. So Mercury is the planet of the present. It rules means of communication like the telephone, radio, newspapers, internet and also the roads, cars, railways, planes, satellites and space stations – in fact, everything that serves to exchange and transport information, goods and people.

Speaking and Listening

The ability to speak and listen is required to communicate. Speech allows people to make contact, even with other cultures and language groups. The exchange of thoughts enables us to get to know each other and to know if we are talking to a kindred spirit or not. Speech connects; it conveys both thoughts and feelings that may also be expressed in words. If we observe ourselves talking, we are aware if our words accurately express what we think and feel. We notice if we hurt others with our words or make them happy by saying nice things. The awareness with which we use words also tells us something about ourselves. Conversely, thoughts are also stimulated by talking. Necessary insights often come only after an exchange of thoughts.

We cannot give the right answers unless we listen carefully. Listening is also connected with Mercury. Speaking and listening belong together, for true understanding can only be reached when they are combined. If we analyse this more closely, speaking and listening are unbelievably complicated processes that astound us and make us ask "Just who invented them?" If we think of the throat, which performs the complex task of speech, then of the structure of the vocal chords, the soft palate that separates the oesophagus from the trachea, the breath with which we send forth spoken words and give them the correct sound. Finally, the larynx that is in constant motion and gives nuance to the sound we produce. Without these vocal organs we would not be able to speak to each other, we could not

The Winged Messenger
Giovanni da Bologna, ca. 1550

understand each other and we would be dumb. The speech organs are therefore a valuable tool for interpersonal contact and enable the exchange of thoughts. So Mercury has an extremely important place in our lives.

Combinatory Intelligence

Mercury gives us not only the gift of speech, but also intelligence. Among the mythological gods, he was considered to be outstandingly clever, smart and even sly. He wants to use language to wield influence and announces his message with great skill and cleverness so that he moves others and convinces them to listen.

Mercury symbolises combinatory intelligence; he invents terms for objects, impressions and experiences. He is able to bring things together. This requires language, self-expression and skill with words and writing. The position of Mercury in the horoscope tells us to what extent a person can express their thoughts clearly, how they put them into words and sentences and express them so that they can be understood by others. With strong Mercury positions, all these qualities are present; with weaker ones they are more limited. Hence difficulties with speech and expression, errors in reasoning and misunderstanding in the case of tense Mercury aspects. In traditional astrology, a Mercury-Moon or Mercury-Neptune aspect (square and opposition) is called a "Delusion Aspect", because emotions and fantasy influence the thoughts, making it difficult to be objective.

The Trader

The above descriptions show a basic quality of flexibility of thought and action, of mental agility but also in manual dexterity. Mercury is also involved in the practical side of daily life, in our movements and actions. Mercurial people are born traders, who certainly know how to advertise and sell their wares. No sooner have they bought something nice than they immediately want to pass it on. Ancient literature even called Mercury the "planet of merchants and thieves".

Today, mercantile abilities are very sought-after and highly valued in business, particularly in advertising. When we watch advertisements, the images, language and sound arouse our need to want the product that is being advertised. This quality is also present in intellectual areas like speaking, translating, calculating, in newspapers and in books, where the most varied aspects of life are described and put into words to be shared with others and disseminated. In all these and a thousand other similar forms of expression, we see the basic principle of Mercury at work passing on information or associating things. Writing is one of the most important of these abilities. For example, a writer usually has Mercury well-positioned in his horoscope; he can convey his thoughts to others via the written word. He can describe both what he thinks and imagines, and also objective reality. It is up to him whether he makes something up or reports facts.

The Provider of Knowledge

Mercury is also jointly responsible for learning, for education. He gives us curiosity and the desire to experience new things. The joy of exchanging information, of discussion, debating and negotiating is typically Mercury. He is always looking for opportunities for talking and for expression. He enjoys arguing and debating for hours, as politicians often do. Whether a conclusion is reached or not is another question; often it is not, as Mercury is not at all creative. He collects all the necessary information and passes it on as accurately as possible. Help from other planets like Uranus, Jupiter and Sun is required in order to find workable solutions for existing problems. Together they complement each other and act intelligently, finding new ways, looking into the future and creating functional plans.

Modern Education

Mercury plays a significant part in our schools and education system, where the main priority is learning by heart and the accurate reproduction of subject matter. Someone who has a good Mercury can quickly memorise the required information and reproduce it just as quickly. He is able to formulate this information so that it can be understood. With these abilities one can do well at school today. However, in the future, the intellectual ability of Mercury alone will not be enough to understand an ever more complex world. The collaboration of Jupiter is required to relate the information to reality via the senses. This is the only way to organise a holistic and meaningful education system.

Quicksilver

As befits the mutable principle, Mercury is linked to the metal mercury (quicksilver). Mercurial people frequently say and do unbelievable things and are hard to pin down. Just like quicksilver they move around all over the place and always find a way out. Mercury weighs up all the possibilities in a flash and sets off quickly if he sees an opportunity somewhere. He does not hold onto anything, just lets everything flow through him. His symbol shows this too: the dish at the top catches everything that falls, lets it fall into the circle and then passes it on to the real world. Mercury does not relax until he has found a form of expression and come up against a counterforce. Only this can stop, form or turn around his flux. He often thinks in circles. In the case of a square with Uranus, for example, we talk about increased nervousness as well as sleep disturbances, especially if there are only red and green aspects and no blue ones. Then he can hardly stop thinking.

The Frivolous

Social gossip, ubiquitous tittle-tattle, sensation-seeking tabloid journalism are all aspects of the mercurial. Mercury has no philosophical or ethical standards. He does not distinguish between high or low values, for him the value of everything is the same. This leads to the debasement of all values and the frivolous irresponsibility of idle gossip. The words say nothing to us, they are superficial and empty. If Mercury follows a certain aim and wants to achieve something specific, he can always find the right words to win people over and bend them to his will. Many cannot resist his reasoning; he gets what he wants and uses connections for his own ends. If he is exposed, he doesn't take it seriously. He relativises his weaknesses, making a thousand excuses and confusing justifications. He does not care if this leads to conflict. He skilfully uses flattering words to lull others into a sense of security. If he deliberately manipulates, it can naturally lead to malicious affectation, simulation and deception in order to achieve a certain goal. He is not hindered by any moral or ethical considerations.

The Control of Mercury

The shadow sides of Mercury make it clear that he should not obtain too much power and influence. He must be controlled and sometimes stopped altogether. In astrology, this can be done by Saturn, Pluto or Sun, also Jupiter – as the god Zeus – is qualified to steady him. Rounded intelligence can emerge from the combination with Jupiter as the organ of perception and observation. Mercury by itself, like Hermes, is incapable of knowing right from wrong. He got up to all kinds of mischief in Olympus: he pinched his father Zeus's sceptre, stole Mars's sword and even the girdle of Venus was not safe from his nimble fingers. It is quite clear that Mercury thoroughly deserves his nickname "the unreliable".

The Transformed Mercury

An evolved person who works consciously on himself will constantly monitor and discipline himself in the case of potential

"Mercury damage", and curb the tendency to gossip as well as the irresponsible circulation of information. In the transformation work, it depends which planet Mercury is linked to, in which sign and house it lies and which aspects it forms. This can only be seen from the individual horoscope, when we then know to what extent inner work is necessary.

The transformed Mercury finds its highest expression combined with Jupiter, Venus and the spiritual planets in melodious and stylish speaking, singing and writing. These abilities can also be learnt. It is a joy to listen to someone speak faultlessly. A transformed Mercury orients itself towards the truth, checks information for its real truth content and avoids making errors of judgement. Combined with Saturn, the spoken word is carefully and scientifically considered and used. Alongside the spiritual planets, Mercury is used in the realisation of higher ideals, also in spiritual education work and for the complete description of eternal wisdom.

So this Mercury truly is the winged messenger, who only passes on that which serves humanity and evolution. These days, when channelling (spiritual transmission of information from ethereal levels) is almost the order of the day, we can well imagine that "channelled knowledge" will become the most important source of information for the spiritually inclined. More and more people will then be able to log on to the "spiritual internet" with the help of developed senses (Jupiter/Mercury combined with the three spiritual planets Neptune, Uranus, Pluto) and receive information directly that benefits their development in the deepest sense.

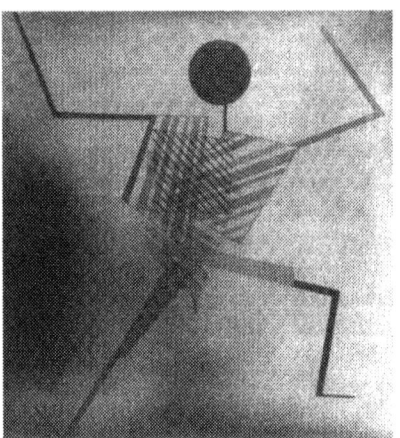

The Jumper, a representation of Mercury
By Paul Klee, 1930

♀
Venus ♀

The Feminine

> ## Affinities
>
> Soft, Feminine Planet (left column)
> Saturn and Uranus
> Ruler of Taurus and Libra
> Day of the Week: Friday
> Metal: Copper
> Aspects: Sextile and Small Talent Triangle
> Fixed Cross
> Water Temperament
> Sense of Taste
> Feminine Libido
> Harmony and Beauty
> Security

As the feminine principle, our Venus enjoys beauty and grace, emphasises the pleasant side of life and aims for wholeness and perfection. She brings relaxation, balance and harmony wherever she goes. For this she uses development; rises onto a level on which life appears enjoyable and greets us lovingly. She is happy if everyone else is happy and does much to increase the comfort of others. She wants to live in harmony with people and all creation and to live life to the fullest. Back in Greek mythology, where she was called Aphrodite, she was the favourite daughter of Zeus, who pandered to her every whim. As the goddess of love and beauty, she was welcome everywhere. In art she is represented as graceful, physically perfect and wreathed in flowers. Good taste and a natural sense of style stop her from clashing with people or things that do not agree with her own nature.

Sense of Taste

On the physical level, Venus is the sense of taste. Our tongues tell us if something tastes sweet, sour, bitter or salty. Our mouths water when we smell good food. Mars and Venus work together here, for Mars controls the nose. Something that smells unpleasant arouses feelings of repugnance, of disgust. Like a sensory organ Venus reacts immediately to good and bad odours. She always looks for that which is beautiful and does good, whether it is food, clothes, in the home, etc. As a feminine planet, her territory is the primal instinct for survival and

"The Birth of Venus" Sandro Botticelli
1486, Florence, Uffici

health and comfort in general. A need must be satisfied, and expended energy must be replaced. Satisfaction calms unrest and a feeling of wellbeing takes over.

Selectivity and Protective Behaviour of Venus

The Venus function allows us to select and choose. Venus selects from what is available that which is good for her, what suits her nature or completes her. It is a kind of protective behaviour that avoids problems. She not only chooses things to possess them, but also people she meets until she has found the right ones that she can love. She would like to live the consonance of feelings with other people to get the most enjoyment out of a relationship. She reacts directly to contact and is responsive to the play of Eros in all degrees of sensitivity. Every detail must be right though. She experiences the least disturbance as unpleasant (the Princess and the Pea) and becomes unbalanced if something disturbs her harmony.

She is vulnerable in matters of love and pleasure, because she is open and totally adapts herself to the object of her affections. She closes up immediately if danger is in the air. This sensitivity is a natural form of protection to avoid getting hurt. That is why it is so important for her to make the right choice and to use what is good and right for her, even if it appears selfish. This natural primal instinct allows her to avoid all that is unpleasant and ugly.

♀

Art and Aesthetics

Venus has always been associated with art and artistic expression. Venus's good taste also extends to aesthetics. The ability to set aesthetic standards and to recognise the well-balanced gives her a good feeling for quality. The individual sense of harmony and what is suitable is what makes decisions for Venus. A strongly marked Venus in the horoscope does not necessarily indicate artistic ability, but rather the efficiency of aesthetic values. In this sense, aesthetic means seeing the harmonious interaction of energies in all things. She enjoys the good and the beautiful both in the earthly sense and in the aesthetic, cultural arena. In this way, the balance between body and spirit is maintained. If something gets out of balance, Venus immediately pays attention. She suffers from imbalances of energy and feels trapped in the polarities between beauty and ugliness, between harmony and conflict, between attraction and repulsion. This tension can be a strong motive for creativity. Dissonance is a pre-requisite for artistic creation. As soon as harmony is disturbed, Venus becomes resourceful. She looks for and finds ways to create a work as perfectly as possible. There is always something to touch up, to improve on until the creation resembles the inner image. The great, powerful works of art would not have been possible with relaxed balance.

Beauty and Harmony

It is obvious from the above that Venus signifies harmony and beauty in the horoscope and compensates for hardships. The sextile aspect that corresponds to Venus also releases or smoothes out tensions (red aspects). Venus balances, makes compromises, smoothes the roughness of life and tries to bring goodness and beauty to the harsh realities of everyday life. As the great life enhancer, she wants to make life brighter and more beautiful. Venus is not interested only in works of art; she also wants to make everyday life colourful and joyful. We are talking about the little things that that make life worthwhile, tasteful items and decorative and festive interior design. It is as if she enjoys the blossom on the tree of life. She serves no purpose other than a feeling of wellbeing and is grateful for any support and help. She always strives for balance and avoids any one-sidedness. She gladly gives back what she receives, on the one hand to serve the law of poetic justice, and on the other hand to maintain harmony and wholeness.

Politics and Peace

The harmonising, balancing function of Venus is more crucial today than ever before, when it is an important political task to encourage mutual understanding where war and conflict rule. The many efforts to create economic prosperity for all are ways to do this. Most negotiations around a table aim for peaceful co-existence, even if it still does not always work. The goodwill and willingness for it to happen are often present though. A cultivated Venus could make a melody from all the discord in the world; individual initiatives could combine to make a holistic, global effort.

The feminine plays an important role in this. Women must and will come more and more into their own in the world to balance out the masculine (Mars). Many hold the world of men, the politicians, responsible for most of the misunderstandings in our society. Much more can be achieved today with the ways of Venus than one would think. The balancing principle of Venus can be effective both in social commitment and in political power. Venus has never been without resources and has already achieved much that could not be changed with violence. As the ruler of Libra, she has already produced many good diplomats.

She knows how to appeal to men's honour, to awake in them the desire, to drive them to act and to get the best out of them. How many great men would be what they are without their wives? A true Venus wife knows how to get a great deal out of her husband. She is skilled in asking for, demanding and seeking understanding. The means she uses to reach her goals correspond completely to her nature. She manages to assert herself without violence, to improve things or to achieve something desirable. This is the secret of the Venus function. Unlike Mars, she does it without forcing. Venus is concerned with well-being, with the improvement of situations. She can wait, let time, things and situations mature, until the right opportunity comes along. She hardly acts at all, she lets others act and is a born producer.

Venus, the Feminine Libido

In the couple formed by Venus and Mars, Venus is the feminine human libido and Mars the masculine. From this point of view, Venus works in the graceful interaction of give and take, granting and withholding, tensing and relaxing. None can resist her when she turns on the charm. She is irresistible when she beguiles a man, when she tempts and promises satisfaction. In love, she experiences a state of wholeness that she cannot otherwise feel, and from this feeling she draws energy that gives her the strength to accomplish new things. In sensual pleasure she loves the moments of passion and wellbeing and would like to linger in that state of bliss. But after satisfaction the opposite often comes into play, and she then falls in the polarity of passion and aversion and gets into a conflict that she wants to escape from quickly. To do this she looks for the right way to restore balance. A well-positioned Venus possesses the art of adapting to circumstances and of being at one with herself, with other people, with nature and with the universe. This attitude gives her a harmonious existence and corresponds to her deeply-felt desire for reconciliation, beauty and perfection.

Choice of Partner

In man, Venus is any energy that leads to longing and searching for a partner of the opposite sex. Someone with a strong Venus is always looking for a partner, they check out other people to see if they are suitable or not. A man or woman on their own is incomplete and seeks a partner to make them whole. Venus uses time-tested feminine rules to select her partner. The soft and tender can best prevail over the tough by adapting. Her strengths are cherishing, discrimination, suppleness, empathy and also knowing how to listen and wait for the right moment to come along. She lets others act, while she discreetly finds out how to get her way. She uses sensory input to influence feelings, with elegance, bright colours and beautiful shapes for the eyes, with melody and music for the ears and with fragrances for the sexiness. She is a good listener and acknowledges good in others, she can tune in to her partner with her feelings. She enjoys bringing love and understanding and often asks quite naturally: "How would you like it?" Even cooking is one of the Venus arts; it is not for nothing that we say: "The way to a man's heart is through his stomach."

Soul Mate

In the choice of partner, Venus always looks for her other half. She believes in the platonic idea of the "soul mate" and thinks that somewhere there is someone who has always belonged to her and who is her other half. She must find this person whatever it costs. If she does find someone that corresponds to this image and who complements her, sensitively satisfies her wishes and with whom she gets on well, then she believes she has found her soul mate. This idea is at the back of her mind in every relationship, and it is the only way that she can feel completely united with her beloved and experience herself fully through this unity. Once she has experienced this fusion she wants to repeat it so that she feels the pleasure of wholeness over and over again. She lets the cycle of repeated performances become a regular lifestyle, and looks for a balanced, secure system in order to satisfy her needs. Especially in the fixed cross, Venus holds on tight to her partner; in the cardinal cross she makes every effort not to bore him and in the mutable cross she indulges her amatory skills.

Transcendence of the Venus Function

Even Venus has her negative sides, some of which are mentioned above. The compensatory reversal of the feelings is most obvious in the case of excess. Attraction becomes repulsion, beauty becomes ugliness and art becomes artificial. Loving design degenerates and becomes shoddy. Instead of real Venus conviviality and hospitality we find hollow, vain flattery, e.g. at parties. Natural sensitivity turns into hypersensitivity to criticism, even when it is well-intentioned. The fascination with what is contrary to her own nature can be so strong that strange relationships can emerge from it. For example, a gentle, soft giving Venus looks for a strong partner who bullies her. Very often there is an incapacity to perceive harsh realities, appeasement and the inability to deal with conflict. Venus can declare something to be good and beautiful, not because she finds it so but because it is easier to tell people what they want to hear. This is not lying, just adaptation. An adapted Venus wants harmony at any price and easily makes lazy compromises. She represses the truth and prefers to live in an apparently ideal world where everything is all right. Looked at in this light, Venus avoids conflict; instead of actively intervening in her own destiny, she prefers to remain in harmony locked up in her golden cage.

Another weakness of Venus is vanity and coquetry. She is dependent on feedback and does everything to be popular. This can result in narcissism and an overriding self-love, especially if Venus lies before or on the AC, the I-point in the horoscope. In the stress area of the cardinal axes, compensatory forces influence the planets. In the case of Venus, grace often turns into an affected pose, beauty into exaggerated make-up, elegance into sluttishness and lively sensual pleasure into formalism. Her influence is no longer natural and attractive but brash and often repellent.

The myths also show us a Venus-Aphrodite in a double form: firstly as one born from the foam of the sea and derived from a higher order and secondly as Aphrodite Pandemos, who belonged to the underworld. Keeping a balance in life is the art of arts and the definition of Venus. As Venus in Libra she is the goddess of pure, heavenly love; as Venus in Taurus she rules sensual pleasure. Love comprises both facets.

The Crises of Venus

Even Venus cannot always live in the full consciousness of pleasure. When developmental forces take her over, she also experiences crises, conflicts and problems in order to transform her from the "little ego" to the "higher self". How she copes with this depends to a large extent on her motivation. If the ego-motivation is still too strong, she looks for everything good and beautiful for herself alone according to the motto "only the best is good enough for me". After every transformation crisis, she makes her abilities more and more available to others. The good of her fellow men will mean just as much to her as her own. She creates a balance between inner will and external duty, which has a healing and beneficial effect on the environment.

This naturally also depends on her position in the three crosses. A cardinal Venus deals with it differently to a fixed or mutable Venus. As Venus lies under the fourth ray "Harmony through conflict", Venus learns how to use her harmonising energy where conflict or deficiencies must be eliminated. Conversely, her healing powers are only awakened when a conflict, problem or danger arises somewhere. Then she becomes active and can have a harmonising and balancing influence.

From the higher place, **the transformed Venus** is the wisdom of knowing how to behave and find one's way in the real world without getting hurt and without getting into trouble with people or things. She looks for appropriate solutions to existing problems, deficiencies and malfunctions and seeks to bring understanding of the connections of many things in the right proportion. She can defuse conflicts and show useful ways to settle them. She acts as an intermediary in the case of blocked opposition and builds bridges of understanding between warring parties.

Considered from a higher point of view, Venus means "pure reason", for she is incapable of injuring or hurting anyone, but brings love and understanding to even the poorest of souls. Alice A. Bailey calls Venus as the esoteric ruler of Gemini the "Planet of Flexible Synthesis". In her flexibility she is an artist of love, balancing, beneficial, and a mistress of the pleasurable arts. Venus can harmoniously combine space and time and is able to create what is called atmosphere. She knows how to live, to spread harmony, show goodwill and to facilitate and improve all kinds of human relationships with her friendliness.

Mars ♂

The Masculine

> **Affinities**
>
> Hard, Masculine Planet (right column)
> Sun and Pluto
> Ruler of Aries and Scorpio
> Days of the Week: Tuesday
> Metal: Iron
> Aspects: Square and Red Efficiency Triangle
> Cardinal Cross
> Fire Temperament
> Fighting Planet
> Masculine Libido
> Sense of Smell
> Motor Skills

When we think of the masculine principle, we imagine a manly, muscular, athletic body. Mars is concerned with physical strength and the ability to perform. Without Mars there would be little activity, movement and variety in our lives. Mars loves action and is responsible for drives, impulses, setting things in motion and achieving things that did not exist before. Mars is a driving force that acts when it is stimulated to do so. If there is something to be conquered or defended, it immediately provides the necessary energy with which to react. If it has to measure itself against others and outcompete or beat them, Mars applies 100% of its energies. It cannot resist the challenge to measure its achievements and actions against other people's and to outdo them. This motivation allows it to react spontaneously and forces it to participate, intervene and act. It cannot just sit still and wait for others to come to it, but takes the initiative itself.

Mars the Engine

Mars is like an engine that supplies us with energy and produces the adrenaline we need to move our muscles and act. Mars is also responsible for our ability to do things, to act. It is a dynamic force that releases energy and discharges tension. Mars therefore symbolises an important principle without which very little would happen in this world. It overcomes the inertia of matter and keeps the world turning. Overpowering anxieties are removed, obstacles cleared, conflicts settled and goals quickly achieved. Without Mars, our muscles would tire, things would stagnate and this world would be a boring place.

Activity and Impulse

In our interpretation of Mars energy, we assume that this driving force is used on all levels. Activity, impulse, lively movement and power all depend on the position of Mars in the horoscope. This principle gives us the urge for action, the desire to act and an entrepreneurial spirit. It is energy that can be transformed into achievement. We first have to find out what the vitality and movement are to be focused on. Its competitive spirit often makes it critical; in combination with Mercury it attacks adversaries according to the motto: "Attack is the best form of defence". Martian power can be implemented in a variety of ways. The goal and the motivation are important in the accurate interpretation of the influence of Mars in the horoscope.

The Athlete

Mars loves to participate in sporting competitions and is always ready to measure his strengths against other people's. He greatly enjoys being competitive; it spurs him on to surpass himself and to use his energy with intensity. For Mars that is really living! If it comes to the crunch, he gives his all and takes whatever risks are necessary. He wants to come first and to win under any circumstances. This motive requires all his strength. There is no way he will renounce what gratifies him. In many sports, Mars pushes people beyond their limits. Elite athletes are often fanatical, obsessed with success and put up with adversity, austerity and exertion, among other things. They refuse to give up and admit defeat, and do not let up until they have achieved their objective. We recognise this extreme behaviour when Mars is on a cardinal house cusp, especially the AC. In the cardinal stress areas, energy output is always extremely high. He compensates for this with sport, the urge to achieve, ambition and competitive behaviour.

The Warrior

Mars is the courageous dare-devil who faces his adversary without fear or doubt, and does not recoil from danger. He throws himself bravely into battle without looking left or right.

Mars the Warrior
Part of "De Sphaere, Sigle XV"

He risks all if there is danger afoot, as this sparks his defensiveness, fighting spirit and aggression. In a flash, he strikes and drives away all assailants. His tools are the knife, the sword, the dagger and firearms; i.e., all weapons of war. In mythology he is the god of war, who defends himself with a sharp knife and is right there in case of danger, ready to fight and win. It is said that he was wild and driven, that he easily lost his temper and fought like a tiger if anyone crossed him.

Primal Instinct

As a primal instinct, Mars is raw power, which is enforced brutally using physical superiority so that others are brought to their knees. As a driving force, Mars tempts people to throw themselves undeterred into battle, even if it is pointless. We can see this fighting power in action if we watch soldiers in battle or street brawls. Many fight because they are obliged to, or because there seems to be no other way out. Mars is not an intelligence planet; it is a blind driving force that can be very destructive, particularly in warfare.

Mars, the god Ares

Mars is not only the god of war, but as the Greek god Ares he was also originally the god of spring, the thrusting youth. So he can be used for both warlike and peaceful activity. As god of spring (ruler of Aries), he represents a team of young men that was sent out to conquer new lands and colonise new areas. His symbols are the spear and the plough. The latter represents the principle of work, achievement and earning a living. In the archetypal form, we find Martian strength in the catching of prey to eat. The hunter is driven by hunting fever, and finds gratification in killing game. The god of war only enters the scene in times of danger. So Mars does as he is done by. Martian energy is basically neutral and can be implemented very differently according to circumstances and the level of personal development.

Mars as the Sense of Smell

In traditional astrology, Mars is associated with the nose. We talk about a snooper, who sticks his nose in everywhere to find the right trail and who has a "good nose" for bargains. Mars reacts to sensory signals, upon which his body prepares the necessary energy. Mars on a house cusp confers "a good nose", a well-developed sense of smell. People with Mars in this position respond to the subtlest smells. He can use fine perfumes to arouse both the masculine and feminine libido. It is a known fact that fragrances increase the instinct of the sex drive. A good sense of smell is required in the preparation of food, in the choice of partner, but also in identifying enemies.

Masculine Libido

Above all, Mars represents the masculine libido. This term, which Sigmund Freud used for sexual power, is best understood as the sexual appetite. On this level, Mars represents the sexual energy that brings him closer to the feminine in order to obtain satisfaction. As masculine sexual power, it causes passionate attraction to the opposite sex, the insatiable craving to possess the female. Its position in the horoscope tells us the strength of this power, as do the cross quality and the temperament. In its own signs of Aries and Scorpio, it provides the necessary energy on all levels. People with a dominant Mars are strong and active. In fire signs it causes periods of increased drive, in which one is at the mercy of, for example, the sexual drive, the urge to achieve and act, or the hunting instinct.

Mars and Venus

Mars is the polar opposite of Venus, and when they meet there is a polarisation: attraction and repulsion, activity and passivity, tension and relaxation, conflict and harmony. This gives rise to the duality intrinsic in men and women. There are two forces that interact within a single person. Mars produces powerful drives in men and women to gain satisfaction. The restless, wild hothead is occasionally calmed down and pacified by Venus, its opposite pole. She can tame his wildness and relax him. With her he would like to transcend himself and experience refinement and Eros. It is interesting to note that Mars-type men usually choose wives who are pure Venus types. Mars and Venus form a couple, as sung and represented by Papageno and Papagena in Mozart's "The Magic Flute": they approach each other, attract each other and are playfully drawn to each other to become one.

The Daredevil

There is actually something youthful, carefree and naïve in Mars. He goes intrepidly towards his objectives, lets nothing get in his way, looks straight ahead and has only one thing in mind. He cannot wait; he is in a hurry and wants to achieve his objective as soon as possible. He does not look around himself as he goes, and has no care and no consideration. This lack of reflection, self-analysis and caution can cause many problems. In rare cases he can become a homicidal maniac, who guns down anyone who gets in his way. But he does not care, he goes straight ahead, and sets himself above everything according to the motto: "Shoot first, ask later". He lacks the necessary sensitivity and patience.

Misuse of Mars Energy

Power as a primal force can become dangerous if it is blind and undifferentiated. Every excessive impulse can destroy and tear down natural boundaries. Typical of this are the lawless who can only fight for survival and are unable to abide by laws. Others, especially the weak, are subjugated, mercilessly abused and assaulted. Brute force, as often seen on TV, is an abnormal Mars function. One could wonder whether television acts as a compensation for repressed aggression. People can live it out impersonally on the screen and distance themselves from it. They gain enjoyment as they condemn the actors. In the action scenes they experience the sensations, the angst and the power but they themselves do not take part and are free from guilt. It is a strange pleasure to watch murder and homicide, be emotionally moved by it and to remain physically unharmed by it.

Compensated Mars Energy

Compensated Mars energy has a different psychological interpretation. It is well-known that every repression or displacement is dangerous, because it appears elsewhere as aggression. If an idle Mars is robbed of its aggressiveness and overflowing power, the energy flow will be blocked. The powers stagnate and cause inner anxiety, convulsions, anger and temper, and conversely also lethargy and depression. Other compensations for Mars energy are to let off steam by betting and gambling or speeding on the motorway as a replacement for bravery. Here the Mars energy that can enable great deeds is misused indiscriminately.

The Three Levels

In the case of Mars as a primal force, it depends how it is used and on which level it is active. Everyone is already familiar with our three-dimensionality: the physical, emotional and mental levels. These divisions give us a concept to work with. On the material level, Mars is primarily physical strength, the sexual principle or lust. On the emotional level, it is the urge to go forwards, driven by passion. On the mental level, Mars provides the unshakeable certainty that one is on the right path, and the conviction of being the only one able to manage given tasks.

The Transformed Mars

Mars energy, which in its primal form is primitive living activity, must be refined and cultivated. We always use transformed Mars energy when we try to reach spiritual goals. Mars helps us to overcome inertia, tiredness, hunger, anxiety and pain. In the actualisation of goals it provides endurance, tenacity and moral courage; it forces us to keep going. It provides zeal and enthusiasm, the drive to work and get things done, an input of energy in dealing with difficult tasks. It bravely leads the way, setting an example, and even helps others to overcome their fears. It is tough and hard on itself and gives everything it has got. During a venture it supplies enough energy to keep going and reach the goal in spite of all difficulties. On the transformed level we proceed carefully with Mars energy, and do not dissipate it in mindless activity, preferring to use it where it is most useful. In this way we always have enough energy available with which to realise our ideas and visions.

A transformed Mars can sometimes be overenthusiastic, demanding too much from itself and from others. This is how it conquers selfishness, love of comfort and laziness. It gives its all without batting an eyelid if it is a matter of serving an ideal. On the spiritual level, Mars corresponds to the "crusader mentality"; home and family are abandoned for the sake of an idea. This is often a fighter for certain causes or political objectives. It can transcend itself and is able to give its utmost. Without complaining, it takes on the necessary work so that a task can be finished. According to Alice A. Bailey, Mars is subject to the 6th ray, the ray of "dedication and devotion".

Mars, Sun, Pluto

Mars, Sun and Pluto are in the masculine column of our planetary table (page 15). All three are capable of doing great things. Unfortunately they usually lack the necessary sensitivity and empathy. They have high aims, upon which all their strengths are completely focused. As such, they often demand too much of themselves and of their environment. They sometimes burn the candle at both ends, and in the heat of battle they do not care if energy is wasted or not. The important thing is to instigate a change of circumstances, to intervene actively to prepare the way for the new zeitgeist. Such pioneers are always necessary at the dawn of a new age. The transformed Mars provides the energy required to do what should have been done a long time ago. The transformed Sun feels obliged to do something to improve circumstances. Pluto gives dynamic motivation and the focused will to make a creative contribution to evolution.

Jupiter ♃
The Eye

> **Affinities**
>
> Neutral Planet (centre column)
> Mercury, Moon, Neptune
> Ruler of Sagittarius and Pisces
> Day of the Week: Thursday
> Metal: Tin
> Aspects: Trine and Blue Talent Triangle
> Mutable Cross
> Earth Temperament
> Sensory Alertness, Sense of Sight
> Abundance and Success
> Optimism
> Powers of Perception and Observation

On the surface of the physical planet Jupiter, there is a large red spot resembling an eye, which has been the subject of much discussion since its discovery. Nobody knows exactly what the meaning of the eye is, what it is made of and how it came into existence. For astronomers, the verdict is still open as to whether it is a vortex of clouds or a cluster of gases. The size of this red spot

Planet Jupiter with Eye

is fascinating: it is 26,200km long and 13,800km wide, roughly the size of the earth's surface. If we look at Jupiter through a telescope, the eye is immediately visible. It seems as if it is watching us and would like to pass on a secret message to us.

It is interesting that in astrology Jupiter is also associated with the human eye. It controls our sight and allows us to see the world around us through the gift of vision. It provides our brain with sensory impressions, coloured visual perceptions, beauty and ugliness. We watch and look around us, and want to know what the world is like. Sight is one of our most important senses. We open our eyes in the morning and do not close them again until we go to bed at night. Impressions of the outside world enter the windows of our eyes the whole day long.

The optic nerve works unceasingly as it records and stores the visual world. We are almost certainly unaware of how hard the eyes work. We catch only fleeting glimpses of many things, but they are still recorded nevertheless.

Impressive paintings can hold our gaze, but we quickly look away if we see something ugly or nasty. Our eyes shine when we meet someone we love. It is well known that with Jupiter we perceive and enjoy beauty, perfection and pleasure. Its abundance is a blessing; it gives us hope, confidence and a positive outlook on everything that is good in the world. It allows us to be happy and enjoy life. It is the planet of the love of life.

Sensory Perception

Jupiter represents all sensory experience. It looks for sensory impressions everywhere and is always ready to take in everything that is good for it. A Jupiter person radiates the inner contentment of a happy approach to life. He spreads joy, goodwill and encouragement. He enthusiastically lets his interior goodness and beauty flow outwards and takes pleasure in all who benefit from it. Jupiter shows us what a substance, an object or a person is really like. Close inspection enables us to determine its true nature. This develops the powers of observation and judgement, so that we can distinguish between colours: black, white and all the shades in between and we can see if something is good or bad.

The Lucky Planet

It is not for nothing that Jupiter is called the "Lucky Planet" in traditional astrology. We can only be lucky when we are in full command of our senses. Developed senses are necessary to keep us constantly aware and wide-awake. Someone who sleeps and goes around with his eyes half-closed misses out on a lot. He is not aware of opportunities for success and "luck" passes him by. However, a person with sharp senses immediately recognises the pros and cons of an opportunity and spontaneously decides to do the right thing. He reacts quickly and confidently and grasps the chances he is offered. We say that successful people are in the right place at the right time, find the right words and achieve what they want. They exude confidence and persuasiveness and gain the sympathy of their fellow men.

The Jupiter Person

A Jupiter person is honest, jovial and helps others, especially if they are ill-treated. His judgement is usually such that he treats everyone fairly, which is why people trust him. He aims for a superior, meaningful order where everyone has their place. Throughout life, order gives him a deep sense of the jovial love of life and a sense of basic trust. He lives according to the principle "live and let live". He encourages prosperity, organic growth and a meaningful self development because he attracts people who are well-disposed towards him, support him and can help him out in an emergency. A Jupiter person believes in the good in people, radiates serenity and has a kind of primitive joy, a real humour that comes from deep within. Jupiter people always have a positive attitude towards life, say: "Yes" to life, and believe in the powerful effect of a superior order that makes sure that all is well.

A person with a well-positioned Jupiter strives for perfection; he has the ability to see what is needed to make things whole and to make it available. He always looks for the best quality, the optimal and the worthwhile and feels himself to be the best, the kindest and infallible. He admires all that is noble, grand and beautiful and likes to act the complete gentleman who impresses everyone with his refinement. He is respected, revered and admired, and people believe in him because he acts in good faith and is not pretentious or excessive. A person like this is a good counsellor, who treats his fellow men with priestly dignity and wise indulgence.

Jovial Representative

Other representatives of the jovial principle are kings and aristocrats who used to lead luxurious lifestyles in castles. They saw to it that they had the best of everything, enjoying a comfortable existence mainly at others' expense. They could not tolerate any restrictions and insisted on what they saw as their inborn rights. They themselves had actually done nothing to earn the grand lifestyles that had just been bestowed upon them. Behind this lay an inner insecurity and emptiness that were expressed as false pride, arrogance or pseudo I, and were intended to hide the reality. Only someone who was truly noble inside and had character could survive in the long run without behaving like a ridiculous snob. Jupiter is often found to have assumed the place of the Sun in the horoscope [e.g. if there is a weak Sun - Ed]. Some people live this unrestricted Jupiter energy as their true identity and as an ersatz Sun, which makes them seem phoney.

Jupiter as God the Father Zeus

The fact that the Greeks considered Zeus as God the Father also shows how highly regarded Jupiter was. Zeus as God can do anything, he does not miss a chance, seizes every advantage in life and enjoys them as a natural right. Jupiter as Zeus stands above everyone, and sees to it that the heavenly order is kept and that whoever acts appropriately receives his favours and is appreciated. Those who oppose him are banished. For the sake of expediency, Jupiter can even make compromises and therefore become dependent. At the highest level, Jupiter is the preserver of ethical principles. He defends justice and is able to convince with real humanity.

Jupiter in the Horoscope

This positive effect exists when Jupiter serves the truth and is interested in helping others and not just himself. This of course depends on its position in the horoscope. The basic rule for this is: Jupiter is most beneficial in its own two signs (Sagittarius and Pisces); it likes blue aspects (sextile and trine) and has an affinity with the earth temperament. It also feels at home in the mutable cross. On the planetary table (page 15) Jupiter is in the centre, neutral column that is associated with the mutable principle. It is mobile and enjoys being free to relate to everything that interests it. This mobility links to a constant organic growth that follows the laws of development and produces practical, viable results.

Jupiter Aspects

Green aspects stimulate Jupiter's flexibility of perception, association, imagination and judgement. Red aspects diminish holistic perception and reduce it to a limited range, as do the fixed and cardinal crosses. Links with other planets can also be favourable or unfavourable. For example, a conjunction with the Sun is a desirable aspect, the successful aspect of traditional astrology. It is said that only "those whom the gods love" have a conjunction of Jupiter with the Moon. Trines and sextiles (blue aspects) also promote its well-being, and a "guardian angel motive" is attributed to a trine to Neptune or the Moon. Blue aspects can also bring too much Jupiter; its gifts then easily develop into overabundance, showing-off, gluttony, oversaturation and sometimes also in weakness. With Mercury it promotes intelligence; with Mars, activity; with Venus enjoyment and with the Moon, emotional intensity. Saturn imposes limits on its desire for expansion, but deepens the cognitive abilities and the philosophical tendency. The spiritual planets inspire its fantasies, imagination and dreams; they often confer visionary gifts, heightened perception and intuition.

Horoscope Reading

We also rely on Jupiter as sensory perception when we do a horoscope reading. We take in the whole chart pattern with our eyes. We look at a chart for long enough until it starts to affect us and, as it were, talk to us. This visual assimilation awakes the intuition, taking us to another level of communication and suddenly we know an amazing amount. We draw the horoscope in different colours on purpose to stimulate our senses and intuition. We can take in and perceive the whole chart with our eyes, so that it becomes a holistic show that has an affinity with Jupiter. You can read about this in more detail in *Aspect Pattern Astrology* (21).

Jupiter Crises

Despite the beneficial and invigorating effect that Jupiter can have, there is also a crisis mechanism here, which leads to a change of motivation and to the transformation from material to spiritual existential values. With Jupiter it is the crisis of meaning that spoils the enjoyment of life. If we have too many things, then the abundance and comfortable lifestyle become meaningless and boredom sets in. Rich people who lead a luxurious, carefree life often suffer from this crisis of meaning. Their lives become empty if they only strive for material satisfaction, prosperity and external success. Although they may try to give their life meaning with new sensory stimuli, fun and amusement, deep down they still remain dissatisfied. From this inner distress they eventually find the path to a transpersonal, spiritual dimension. They discover a new meaning in a holistic world view in which the above and the below, the within and the without, and the highest and the lowest become one.

The Transformed Jupiter

With its striving for expansion of consciousness, the transformed Jupiter provides us with a comprehensive picture of things, it gives us a large enough distance from which to stand back and gain an overview. It is easier for us to understand how everything belongs and works together if we look at time and space from a bird's eye view, from a certain height. With Jupiter, our sense of sight, we see first the whole wood and then the individual trees. We see proportion, how everything hangs together and the meaning and importance of a person, a thing, a destiny. We see that every organism, every person is an integral part of a greater whole and yet still remains a self-contained individual. Everything has its own place and at the same time converges coherently in the whole. To understand this, we have to understand the different qualities of relationship and perceive sensitively. Jupiter is a sensory planet; it gives sensitivity to the content of forms, to what is intrinsic. In its holistic overview, its judgement is always fair and gives justice to everyone. The expansive power of Jupiter takes us into contexts of transpersonal meaning and raises questions of philosophical and religious meaning. It finds answers in a spiritual dimension, thereby causing an expansion of consciousness.

Synthesis and Wholeness

Considered from another perspective, Jupiter reflects the law of inclusion, the law of synthesis, love and "as well as" thinking, which lead to the experience of wholeness – as opposed to the "either-or" thinking of the past, which separated parts from each other. Jupiter thinks in large, broad concepts, it is the evolving organic growth in man and in nature. It integrates everything belonging to it, and unites things in the right proportion so that they form a functional whole. The experience of wholeness also includes the integration of cosmic laws and the perception and taking seriously of apparent trivia. It is the hermetic principle "As above, so below, as within, so without", which is so important both for esoteric theories and for astrology and allows us to see the connections between the great and the small and thus the meaning and the importance of our existence.

Attribution of the Planets

A) To the Three Crosses

The three main planets correspond in principle to the three cross qualities. They are governed by the motivations of these crosses.

Planet	Cross	Motivation
Sun	Cardinal cross	Will and power
Moon	Mutable cross	Love and contact
Saturn	Fixed cross	Security and tenacity

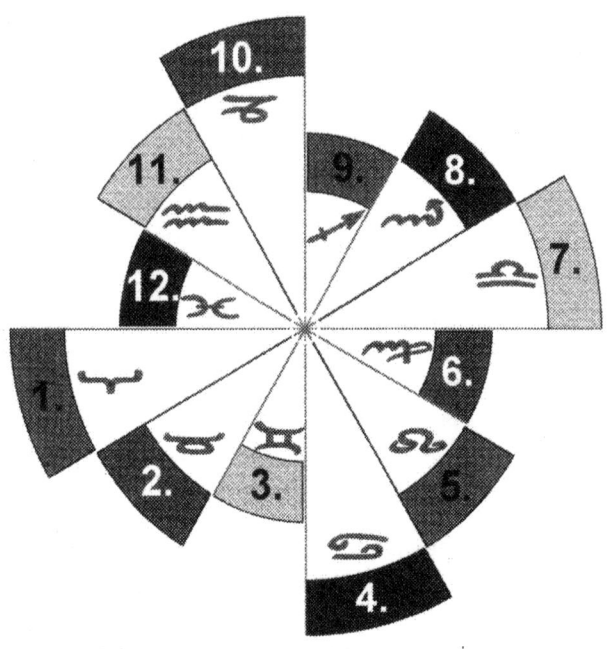

The Crosses

Sun in the Cardinal Cross

Aries, Cancer, Libra, Capricorn

The Sun corresponds to the cardinal principle. Will and power are its motivations. The stimulating, moving energy gives the Sun in the cardinal signs a strong will and the ability to exercise control over the environment.

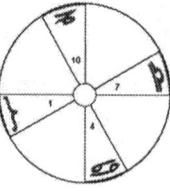

Cardinal Cross

Sun in cardinal Aries

The assertive power increases in the sign of Aries, and is augmented by the fire temperament, making Aries the prototype of this cross. Strength of will increases dramatically when the ego has to prove itself and wants to achieve something. These people can overcome limits, remove obstacles and win arguments.

Sun in cardinal Cancer

The water sign Cancer stands for the emotional world, which is why the Sun mainly uses its cardinal willpower for the fulfillment of its own wishes. It works on the environment until it gets what it wants. The will is used to do everything possible for the well being of beloved members of the family. Sun in Cancer also stimulates the maternal principle.

Sun in cardinal Libra

In the air sign of Libra, the Sun activates the mind. A Libra Sun can implement its own goals, plans and projects or those of other people with intelligent skillfulness and diplomacy. Its will is mainly directed towards the You, to the partner, to win their cooperation. They are often open to these strong-willed yet gentle influences for a long time, and this maintains harmony. The Libra Sun is completely commited to helping those to whom it is connected by love.

Sun in cardinal Capricorn

The earth temperament is added to cardinal energy. The will is directed towards concrete goals. There is a desire to control the world and find one's place in it. No effort is spared to get ahead and to do one's job to the highest standards. Capricorns do everything to reach the top; they acquire a skill that enables them to excel above others. They usually support people whose skills they respect.

Moon in the Mutable Cross

Gemini, Virgo, Sagittarius, Pisces

The Moon corresponds to the mutable principle; it is our feeling self. Relationships and contacts are indispensable for it, which is why in the mutable signs it is particularly open to any kind of contact and also suited to professions involving dealing with people. Chapter 6 is devoted to describing the Moon in the signs, so here's just a brief description of its position in the mutable signs.

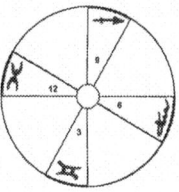

Mutable Cross

Moon in mutable Gemini

The air temperament strengthens the mutable principle. This Moon can and will relate freely to everything it finds interesting. Constraints or restrictions are hard for it to bear, so it avoids being tied down. It is very intelligent, is quick on the uptake and is well informed about many things.

Moon in mutable Virgo

In the earth temperament, the Virgo Moon's interests are directed towards concrete things. It likes to keep things in order and to immediately eliminate any disruptive elements. It can be used very successfully to achieve a certain perfection in relationships and in work. This is a serving Moon that is always ready to help.

Moon in mutable Sagittarius

Moon is in its element here too; the fire temperament makes it dynamic and flexible. It is in constant motion and never settles down anywhere. It loves freedom and independence, and avoids all constraints. It only takes self-imposed responsibilities and duties seriously.

The Moon in mutable Pisces

In Pisces the Moon's emotional temperament is combined with the mutable principle. This Moon lives at a depth that is barely accessible to outsiders. It is hard to pin down and evades control. Its love for all creatures allows it to share in a cosmic quality that makes it fascinating yet hard to understand.

Saturn in the Fixed Cross

Taurus, Leo, Scorpio, Aquarius

Saturn corresponds to the fixed principle, where the priorities are maintaining the status quo, security and tenacity, i.e. properties inherent to Saturn and which enable it to achieve stability. It has an affinity with the instinct for self-preservation that is particularly strong when it lies in the fixed signs.

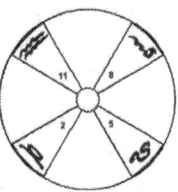

Fixed Cross

Saturn in fixed Taurus

Taurus is the prototype of the fixed cross, so Saturn as the form-creating principle is strongly placed here. Making life safe and eliminating all dangers are the priorities. Defence of the status quo, adherence to traditions and increasing property are characteristic features. This Saturn cannot let go of something once it is possessed, holding on to it tightly. It is conservative and sometimes stubborn.

Saturn in fixed Leo

The fire temperament of Leo corresponds to the inner core of the self. Here, Saturn is able to remain lively and balance out the crystallising forces. It can shield itself optimally from outside and be strong and invulnerable on the inside. Its private sphere is sacred; it protects itself from external attack. Its defensive attitude scares away those who want to intrude uninvited and welcomes those who approach it respectfully with open arms.

Saturn in fixed Scorpio

The addition of the water temperament unsettles Saturn. Although Saturn in Scorpio strives for stability, it is never quite sure if it will last. Feelings are hard to stabilise, they need something to cling to and use Saturn's limits, sacrifice and prohibitions to gain security. This reduces spontaneity and flexibility of the feelings and means that they follow emotional patterns or structures that seem inauthentic.

Saturn in fixed Aquarius

In the air or thinking temperament, security is achieved by creating stable and strong thought forms. Saturn in Aquarius has principles, dogmas or philosophies that he strictly adheres to, giving him backbone, authority and even power. He is not easily led and is suspicious of new ways of thinking.

B) To the Four Temperaments

Just as the three ego planets can be attributed to the crosses, the four tool planets can be attributed to the temperaments, which already reveal something of their properties. If these planets lie in a sign corresponding to their temperament, they are in their element and their specific abilities come into their own. These are listed below in the form of keywords.

Temperament Affinities

Planet	Element	Type
Jupiter	Earth	Realistic type
Mercury	Air	Thinking type
Venus	Water	Feeling type
Mars	Fire	Intuitive type

Jupiter in Earth Signs: Taurus, Virgo, Capricorn

If Jupiter lies in these signs, it has the following qualities: practical, realistic, economical, functional, beneficial, in touch with nature, alert, pleasure-loving, persevering, retentive, patient, thoughtful, lazy.

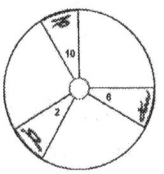

Mercury in Air Signs: Gemini, Libra, Aquarius

In air signs, Mercury's qualities are objectivising, theoretical, studious, awake, intelligent, comparing, value-free, critical, analytical-logical, intellectual, cultured, instructing, conciliatory, communicative, impersonal, adaptable, relativising, superficial.

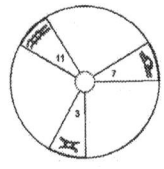

Venus in Water Signs: Cancer, Scorpio, Pisces

In water signs, Venus's qualities are selective, sensitive, subjective, feminine, fanciful, receptive, impressionable, healing, peace-loving, harmony-seeking, comfort-loving, sympathetic, devoting, in need of protection, anxious, vulnerable, cautious, observant, passive.

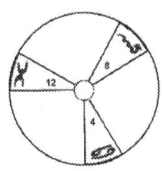

Mars in Fire Signs: Aries, Leo, Sagittarius

In its element in the fire signs, Mars is particularly active, masculine, dynamic, strong-willed, proactive, freedom-loving, risk-taking, combative, progressive, ambitious, selfish and individualistic.

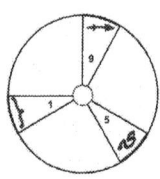

C) To the Seven Rays

The Seven Rays were published by Alice A. Bailey in two volumes as New Age psychology (8). It is very informative for astrologers to get to know this fascinating field that complements astrology. The Seven Rays are streams of energy which penetrate everything and therefore condition all life on our planet. In their combination with astrology they create the complex system that we call reality. They are relatively easy to understand and exist within us all as working energies and are related to the qualities of the ten planets. Without going into more detail about their individual qualities, the table below sets out their attribution to the planets. If you would like to know more about this, you can read the books of Alice Bailey or attend a suitable seminar.

The Seven Rays

		Primary Rays		
☉	♇	1st Ray	Will and Power	Cardinal
☾	♆	2nd Ray	Love and Wisdom	Mutable
♄	♅	3rd Ray	Active Intelligence	Fixed
		Rays of Attribute		
♀		4th Ray	Harmony Through Conflict	Water
☿		5th Ray	Concrete Knowledge	Air
♂		6th Ray	Devotion and Idealism	Fire
♃		7th Ray	Ceremonial Magic	Earth

3. The Three Spiritual Planets

Uranus, Neptune, Pluto
Transpersonal Essential Forces
• The Zeitgeist: Collective and Individual Effect •
• Collective Models •
• Expansion of Consciousness •
• The Esoteric Function of the New Planets •
• Transformation Model •
• Transformation through the Spiritual Planets •
• Esoteric Psychology • The Three Stages •
• Uranus, The World Improver •
• Neptune, Looking for Love •
• Pluto, The Superman (Master) •

Transformation of the Personality
Personal and Spiritual Psychosynthesis
• Strong and Healthy Ego • Interpretation Guide •
• House Position of the Ego Planets •
• Integration of the Personality •
• Psychosynthesis and Love • Wholeness •
• Developmental Tendencies •
• Transformation of the Ego Planets • Simultaneity •
• The Spiritual Path •
• Saturn Levels • Moon Levels • Sun Levels •
• Ego Fears and How to Overcome Them •

Initiation and Transformation
Esoteric Astrology
• Initiation in Antiquity • Initiation Today •
• Initiation Crises • Initiation Levels •
• Saturn/Uranus Transformation: 1st Initiation •
• Moon/Neptune Transformation: 2nd Initiation •
• Sun/Pluto Transformation: 3rd Initiation •

Uranus, Neptune, Pluto

Transpersonal Essential Forces

The Zeitgeist: Collective and Individual Effects

More and more people are becoming interested in the planetary configurations that currently influence humanity as a whole. These issues become particularly pressing in times of crisis. We want to know why catastrophes are reported on the news every day, why many people are ill and tired, why the economic climate is worsening and unemployment is rising. People have always looked to the heavens in times of need in their search for answers. Astrology is a good way of understanding current events. These are connected to the movements of the spiritual planets Uranus, Neptune and Pluto. These three planets symbolise the zeitgeist that influences human history and determines current developments. Many astrologers track their effects related to drastic changes. We read in astrology books that people reacted to the three new planets as soon as they were discovered. People noticed especially that significant changes in human events occurred each time a new planet was discovered or entered a new zodiac sign. The following table shows the movement of the three spiritual planets through the signs of the zodiac since 1955.

Movement through the Signs of the Zodiac

	Neptune	Uranus	Pluto
Scorpio	1955-70 (15 yrs)	1974-81 (7 yrs)	1983-95 (12 yrs)
Sagittarius	1970-84 (14 yrs)	1981-88 (7 yrs)	1995-08 (13 yrs)
Capricorn	1984-98 (14 yrs)	1988-95 (7 yrs)	2008-24 (16 yrs)
Aquarius	1998-12 (14 yrs)	1995-03 (8 yrs)	2023-43 (20 yrs)

For example, Pluto was in Scorpio from 1984 to 1996, where it brought about an intense purification on many levels. It uncovered undesirable developments and corruption in business, and many things that had hitherto been suppressed or secret came to the surface. Since Pluto entered Sagittarius in 1996, its influence has been more noticeable on spiritual and mental levels. In Sagittarius, it intensifies the search for truth and meaning; many people want to get to the bottom of things and leave no stone unturned in their search for the truth. Among other things, Pluto in Sagittarius has also caused an education explosion with a surfeit of courses for professional and personal training. These are just a few of the effects.

Collective Models

We proceed on the assumption that the three spiritual planets act as models and therefore have an evolutionary character. Since they were discovered, they have had a changing and transforming effect on both the consciousness of the whole of mankind and on that of individuals. From this point of view, they keep the evolutionary process going.

Discovery of the three Spiritual Planets			
Uranus	13.03.1781	22.30	by Herschel in London
Neptune	24.09.1846	00.00	by Galle in Berlin
Pluto	18.02.1930	16.00	by Tombough in Flagstaff

The French Revolution broke out soon after the discovery of Uranus (1781), and was interpreted as an effect of Uranus energies. Many people found the courage to climb the barricades to free themselves from oppression by the aristocracy. Following these and similar events, Uranus was associated with revolutions, unrest and also accidents. Neptune was associated with infections and deception and Pluto with war and disruption. Through no fault of their own, many people become embroiled in a collective destiny. With Pluto they get into political and social confusion and are unable to prevent it. Uranus involves them in accidents, sitting in a train that derails or an aeroplane that crashes, or then becoming mourners, without being able to do anything about it. Neptune can bring us into contact with illness; we become infected and are the victims of an epidemic. Pluto makes us travel, perhaps to a country in which war has broken out and where our own lives are in danger.

It seems that in such fateful situations, the people affected are mainly those who are unaware and have little self-knowledge. People who are already working on their spiritual development react differently. In the horoscope of someone with no idea of the spiritual qualities of Uranus, Neptune and Pluto, they remain latent and can hardly be interpreted individually. Having no concept of individual freedom and spiritual development, they easily become the victim of collective currents. This means that the spiritual planets can only work individually in the horoscope when we know their significance. We must therefore strive for their qualities, so that they can become effective within us as spiritual models.

Expansion of Consciousness

With Pluto in Sagittarius (1996-2009), we can be sure that the deliberate contact with the spiritual planets is intensified and is part of our spiritual and esoteric education. Sagittarius is known to be the sign of philosophy, expansion, search for meaning and reorientation. The stimulation of Pluto's energy makes us experience an expansion of consciousness affecting all areas of our lives. This expansion enables many people to advance into new dimensions of thought. We only have to think of the increased interest in spiritual and esoteric matters. People are becoming more and more aware of knowledge that was formerly secret, unfathomable and only accessible to the initiated. Rapid developmental processes are currently taking place, caused by all three spiritual planets not just by Pluto in Sagittarius. Whoever is open to them will experience a transformation of consciousness. Those who ignore them may be unable to escape the collective destiny.

Esoteric Function of the New Planets

To tune ourselves in to the new planets Uranus, Neptune and Pluto and to align our lives to spiritual goals, we should first adjust our consciousness to these higher functions, and for this we need a suitable and convincing concept. Now is the right time to experience something of the higher model function and the spiritual significance of these planets. Only then can we start to incorporate the true balanced spirit of progress of Uranus, the unconditional love of Neptune and the divine will of Pluto – if only in a fragmentary way – into our lives. When we understand the function of the new planets and reflect on, meditate on and research them, we slowly realise that they can aid our spiritual development.

From an esoteric point of view, they correspond to the higher triad, the monad or the higher self towards which we are all striving. According to Alice A. Bailey (8), and the psychosynthesis of Roberto Assagioli (6), the goal of human evolution is to expand human consciousness and become one with the higher self. The divine self or the monad works as the trinity of atma, buddhi and manas, which are associated with the three spiritual planets. The creative intelligence of Uranus corresponds to the manas principle, the higher love ideal of Neptune to the buddhi level and Pluto to the atma or will aspect. The ongoing transformation of the threefold personality by the higher triad in the cycle of life continues until all pseudo ego forms are transformed and integrated. This transformation of the personality (symbolised by ♄, ☽, ☉) corresponds to the first three initiations and to the spiritual function of the three new planets.

Transformation Model

The illustration "Amphora" on page 81 shows the overall structure of human nature, both as the threefold personality and as the higher triad. We can see a line in the centre running from bottom to top. The ego planets Sun, Moon and Saturn are arranged at the bottom of the line. The tool planets are available for use by the ego. Above this, Uranus penetrates the circle of the personality. We then go up into the neck of the amphora, which is framed on both sides by Neptune. Only when Neptune's unconditional love has been developed can we access the divine will symbolised by Pluto. This amphora is a transformation and development model, developed after many years of research by Bruno Huber. It serves as a foundation for astrological psychosynthesis.

Amphora

Transformation Model

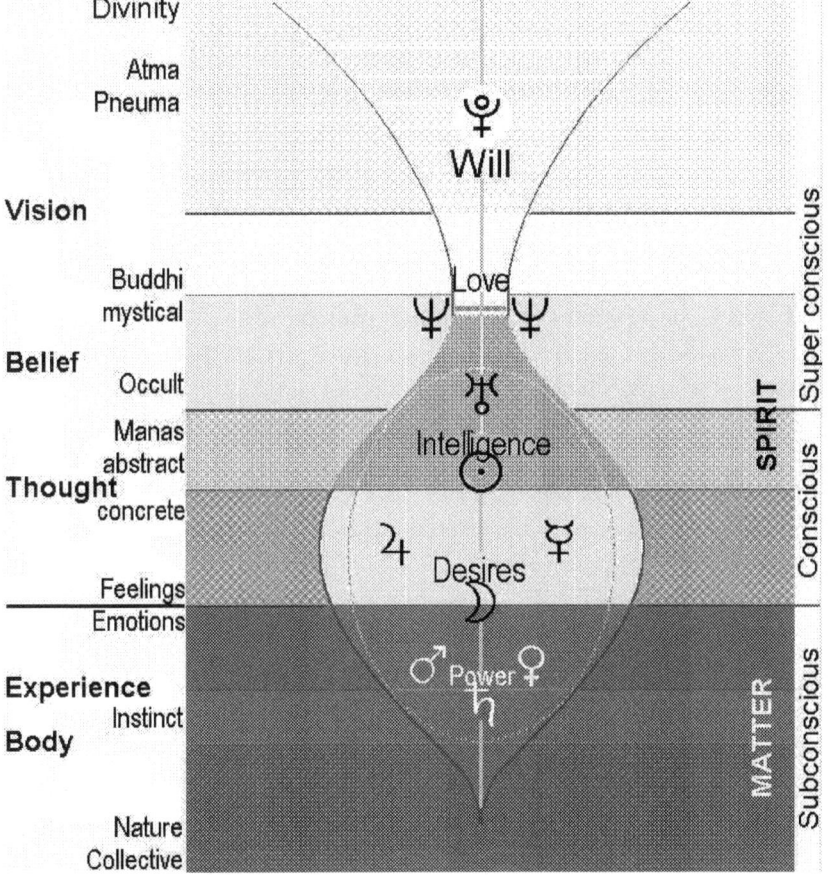

Stages of Development from Saturn to Pluto

> **Transformation through the Spiritual Planets**
> **Uranus, Neptune, Pluto**
> linked via aspects to Saturn, Moon and Sun.
> Outgrowing oneself.
> Activating inner strength.
> Assuming and fulfilling the spiritual mission.
> Visible in the horoscope as aspects and low point positions:
> a) The path inwards, reorientation and transformation.
> b) Experiencing the inner will, the threefold personality ☉, ☽, ♄ (structure, function, role) in the service of the Higher Self.
> c) The transformation happens as soon as motivation is aligned with the evolutionary plan.
> d) Through three great crises that lead to initiation:
>
> 1st initiation: Saturn/Uranus
> 2nd initiation: Moon/Neptune
> 3rd initiation: Sun/Pluto

Esoteric Psychology

Anyone who is familiar with the esoteric psychology of Alice A. Bailey (8) knows that the three spiritual planets act on a transpersonal level. These spiritual levels can only be safely entered after transformation of the ego powers. They lie above the ego sphere and dictate that there should be no I present there. The ego planets Saturn, Moon and Sun are transformed, elevated, refined and made permeable by the three spiritual planets, which as higher models of security, love and power provide the strength and potential to reach a specific developmental goal and to make a creative contribution to human evolution. But before we get to that stage, we must pass through other developmental phases, tests and crises. The esoteric term for this gradual process is "preparation for an initiation".

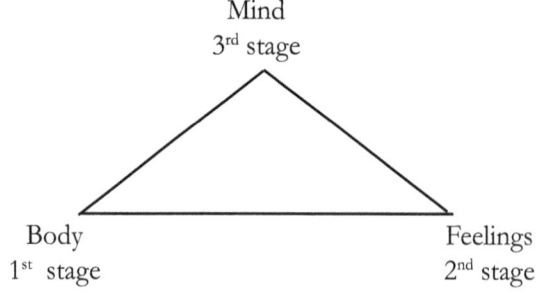

The Three Stages

The Three Stages

Trinity theory exists in many religions as the spiritual concept of wholeness, the bond between man and the cosmos. From it is derived the hermetic principle "As above, so below", "As within, so without", that forms the foundation of astrological and esoteric thinking. A holistic concept for the deeper understanding of the three spiritual planets enables a three-dimensional horoscope reading that is derived from trinity theory. As can be seen from the above, a person's level of awareness and receptivity are particularly dependent on these three planets. In the process, the distinctions between the three levels of human existence, body, feelings and mind are also indicated. Material changes take place on the physical Saturn level; wishes and imagination that lead to disillusionment are on the Moon or emotional level; and on the Sun or thinking level we assert our will so that we learn how to think correctly and identify our developmental goal. These three levels correspond to the three developmental stages for the three spiritual planets, which we have set out below.

Uranus ♅

The World Improver

Uranus, observing the heavens
Observatorium in Alexandria

Collective Effect

Uranus was in Aquarius for seven years from January 1996 to 2003. During the previous seven years it transited Capricorn, where Saturn's principle underwent a transformation. Many stable and often outdated structures were undermined and dispensed with. Old power structures collapsed. Uranus in Aquarius strives for a new quality of life for all through new ethical and humanitarian principles, with the emphasis on global communication, group awareness and mankind as a whole. Old hardened structures are declared to be detrimental and done away with. Better living conditions for all should not be neglected alongside the spiritual aspect.

On the physical level, Uranus, like Saturn, is concerned with striving for security. Unlike Saturn though, Uranus does not cling to old ways and prefers instead to seek security in the escape to the future. This is how Uranus impulses are directed to matter, resulting in the spirit of invention that the technical civilisation has produced. A Uranus person wants constant material improvement in life and is always looking for new ways of making life more secure, comfortable and interesting. There is a danger on this level that technology can take over; man can cease to matter leaving functionality as the be all and end all. Man would then just be a part of a worldwide machine. Such progressive thinking necessarily leads to a robot state, where security measures and strict regulations squash the living spirit.

On the feeling level, Uranus has a revolutionary effect, as has often been described in the literature. On this level, it generates unrest, nervousness and eccentricity. It causes a mood of dissatisfaction and agitation. At a certain point, the power to cause change becomes available and wants to make everything better at one stroke by tearing down limits and barriers and breaking new ground making it easier to solve problems. The [continental] Uranus symbol ⚲ – the dot inside a circle and the arrow pointing upwards – expresses this force. It is this arrow that wants to transcend limits and improve the status quo. Once the Uranus effect has started, there is no stopping it; everything presses forwards, towards change and liberation from chains and bondage. Uranus is the egg tooth with which the fledgling breaks out of its shell; it is the obstretrition present at a birth.

In the planetary sequence, Uranus comes immediately after Saturn, the last of the seven classical planets. Saturn shows the limits that will be overcome by Uranus. The boundary-breaking principle of Uranus is also oriented toward technology on this level. It does not just charge into a nebulous state, but actively seeks out new ways of actualisation. As a symbol of separation it strives to be free from unwanted attachments. It frequently plans ahead so that it can extricate itself from relationships immediately if they become too restricting.

On the mental level, Uranus represents creative intelligence. It has original ideas and is therefore also a reformer who looks for systematic ways of solving life's problems, one example of which is astrology. On the mental level, Uranus symbolises the power of the independent spirit that pushes forwards over the habitual boundaries of thought into the transpersonal realm, i.e. from worldly to universal thinking. Uranus brings insight that is not motivated by the will to survive but to become part of the Great Whole.

Uranus seeks knowledge for its own sake. It is the spirit of investigation that looks for suitable solutions to existing problems. Brainwaves happen on this level. Uranus breaks into the consciousness in the form of ideas that did not exist before, but that can change the entire situation at one stroke. The Uranus spirit is especially stimulated by opposition. No effort is spared to acquire knowledge, and resistance, obstacles and setbacks cannot hold it back. It can be fanatical though, and if necessary will stop at nothing to implement new things. So the creative intelligence can usually break through in times of need or problems, when it is required. That is why Uranus finds its greatest satisfaction in righting wrongs and improving conditions. Its deepest motivation is to bring about a perfect world in the future. On the mental level it is constantly striving for new things.

<u>Neptune</u> ♆

Looking for Love

Statue of the God of the Sea
Grand Master's Palace, Malta

Collective Effect

Neptune transited the sign of Capricorn until 1998, where its main effect was to transform the crystallising forces of Saturn so that everything that had solidified or was no longer useful for the future could flow again. One could say that Neptune destroys by dissolving. It changes and transforms things with a subliminal, almost subterranean and imperceptible action, and in so doing also makes a contribution to evolution. It hopes for redemption and evokes the longing for peace in a better time.

As it entered Aquarius in 1998, the principle of love and unity came to the forefront. Many people got together to fight for a better world. We only have to think of the chains of light in the big cities where thousands peaceably demonstrated for hours. Others united in alliances, unions and like-minded groups. For us, Neptune is the higher idealised love, and therefore a model that idealises, cultivates and transforms love and coexistence.

On the physical level Neptune has a boundary-breaking effect on relationships that are no longer viable. An effect like this naturally causes instability, confusion and chaos on the material level. This is also due to the erroneous belief that the Neptune experience must take place seamlessly in the existing concept of life, which is not the case though, precisely because Neptune represents a dimension that is outside our control and lies beyond our mundane existence. This is why there is often a desire to escape from reality and to give it another meaning. Harsh realities are avoided and refuge is sought in a fantasy or dream world, in pleasure, illusions or states of intoxication.

On the feeling level, Neptune's effect is particularly strong, as it finds congenial qualities here. It represents the accentuation of the Moon, which rules the feeling level. This second level is also concerned with the experience of love. When we are overwhelmed by Neptunian love, and our world is turned upside down, then all our previous material goals seem meaningless. That is why people decide to renounce material security in order to devote themselves to spiritual ideals. They want to surrender completely to love and are prepared to give up everything for it.

Others want to help those in need, to engage themselves socially, sometimes to an excessive extent. Sensitivity and the ability to love can also go beyond a healthy level. Neptune mostly causes an urge to outgrow earthly mediocrity so that we can find ourselves again in a different state of awareness. This includes the use of stimulants like drugs, alcohol, nicotine, etc. It is the urge to escape from the restrictions of material existence and share in a heightened state of happiness.

Neptune's identification with a state of ideal love can cause a breakdown of the ego's position; such people lose themselves to find themselves again in mystical union. On this level, many people enter a detached, unrestricted and often unstable state in which they lose their sense of self-reliance. This can lead to dependencies, mental disturbance and neuroses with strange addictions. Such people lose their grip on things and easily fall victim to all kinds of delusions. They depend on stronger people who use and abuse them. They then feel misunderstood by the rest of the world and are rejected and ridiculed. Others become scapegoats and the targets of blame and aggression. Many have a religious or mystical tendency to see the highest power in everything and give themselves completely to this ideal. Many become involved in caring for difficult or ill people who exhaust them, but whom they help anyway. They are unable to do anything for themselves because their spiritual aim in life is unconditional love. This causes the so-called helper syndrome.

On the mental level, there is a desire for universal love as the highest ideal. Neptune wants to transcend all the limits of earthly reality and to cultivate a new form of coexistence. On this creative thinking level, the gap that separates idealised love and the real world can be overcome. There is a heightened sensitivity and a refined awareness of communication (empathy) that breaks through all walls and flows from heart to heart. This is what Assagioli called "loving understanding". This Neptunian quality of loving and sensitive devotion has an understanding of human weakness and forgives everything; it is also called Christlike awareness There is an inner mission for salvation that provides a reasonable and effective Neptune experience on the mental level, also making Neptune the creative potential of love in action.

On the mental level, love as pure reason, as sensitivity, loving devotion and identification with all living things evokes the healer, the saviour. Subtle vibrations are perceived, the "secret floating between things", as Thomas Ring (11) refers to the Neptune effect, the invisible bond that unites everything is experienced as unity and is radiated as love. The sensitive response to these vibrations will lead to a new era of coexistence principally motivated by loving wisdom in all human relationships.

Pluto ♇

The Superman (Master)

The Ancient of Days by Blake

Collective Effect

Pluto transited Scorpio until 1995, during which time nearly everyone sensed something of its purifying effect. Much dirty washing was done; countless mistakes and scandals came to light and criminal behaviour increased alarmingly.

It was interesting how Pluto activated the qualities of Sagittarius in 1996. Its intensifying effect affected the thinking principle, the expansion of consciousness, science, education and information. Pluto in Sagittarius updates the whole Thinking Axis (Sagittarius-Gemini), which belongs to the mutable cross and is dominated by the principle of communication and contact. The intensive experience of communication between people thus entered a new era. Since then we justifiably speak of an information society. Information is gathered from everywhere, often with no unity of objective or purpose. We only have to think of the mobile phone, and how quickly it became popular nearly everywhere. New learning material, further education and transfer of knowledge became accessible via the internet. The worldwide web makes all information available to everyone, irrespective of the time of day, country, culture, race, religion or gender. We can no longer live without a computer; we need them to stay in touch with the world and to make contact. But even in these areas, Pluto is all about power and powerlessness, goal-setting and aimlessness. We must work out a new ethic with new rules that are valid for everyone. This will probably not be done until the period of maturity and testing in Capricorn from 2008 to 2024.

On the physical level, Pluto is always involved in problems of power. One calls for an unlimited reach of power, believing oneself to be the best, the greatest and the only one who is right. In the case of hardened ego powers this gives rise to megalomania or egomania, where a person thinks only he is right and everyone else is a novice ("Might before Right"). Power enables objectives and pretensions to power to be asserted and obstacles to be rigorously moved or talked out of the way. A lack of consideration for the demands of others and ruthlessness are the unpleasant side of Pluto on the material level. All its efforts are mobilised, it fights like one possessed for its property, status and power. Anyone who wants to contest this power will be labelled an enemy who must be got rid of.

On the feeling level, emotions are awakened and intensified, concerned with all possible types of partnership. A frequently narcissistic arrogance alternates with mostly unacknowledged depressive feelings of worthlessness. A strong tendency to show off is often developed to compensate for this feeling of inferiority, which is intended to provoke admiration from the You. In addition, Pluto demands absolute possession of the You. This demand can lead to slavish dependency and sado-masochistic tendencies particularly in sexual relationships. There are many examples of people who exercise power over colleagues or business rivals in their professional lives but slip into the role of masochist in their sexual lives.

Over time, these conditions cause processes of disenchantment in the consciousness, which can destroy everything previously held to be sacred. They are transformation crises, linked to strong doubt and anxiety. Although he recognises himself to be the causative ego, he is tormented by the anxiety that he is missing something or making some kind of grave mistake that can return like a boomerang and destroy him. He wants to be as perfect as possible and is convinced that he is the best. But it is precisely this over-estimation of the self and the anxiety about repercussions that cause mistakes to be made. A few people barricade themselves behind high expectations of those around them, others blame the world and the dear Lord for everything that they do wrong and have not achieved. In reality, Pluto sabotages false ego demands subliminally with its metamorphic power and has a destructive effect on the pseudo-I forms (split personalities) on the feeling level.

When the Pluto effect acts on the feelings as core energy, the motivation of the inner self starts to penetrate. This burrows into the feelings and undermines apparently secure connections. All safety measures and clever attempts to adapt are to no avail, and there are often transformation crises with high mental stress. We call urgently for help, look for a master, a guru a therapist, a group. Others appeal to the collective, to universal rights, and build a world image or a philosophy that is intended to give them the right to make claims. But these ideologies do not stop the nagging doubts; until finally drastic transformations of basic life motivation take place, which can give rise to temporary behaviour that seems like insanity to others.

On the mental level, Pluto provides insight into evolutionary laws and future developmental goals; it asks for perfection, not personal power. Its motive is the perfecting of the personality. Pluto contains a model that tells us what this perfection must look like. This imaginary image (imago) guides us. Pluto is now the image of the higher self, the pneuma, that wants to incite us to perfect our personalities; it radiates energy which penetrates to the very core of our being. This exciting goal acts like a fertilizer triggering the metamorphic transformation or growth process, and keeps it going until the goal is reached. It inspires the spiritual will, supplies the strength and energy required to survive all transformations and makes every effort to achieve the desired objective. Pluto is therefore an evolutionary planet.

This fertilization by the vision changes life motivation; it has a guiding role for the whole life, indeed for all ensuing lives, due to its evolutionary character. A "critical mass" has to be reached, at which point the transforming force of the Higher Self is released and instantaneously obliterates everything which opposes the evolving life. This is why Pluto is also often associated with death, in that it purifies and liberates. It leads to a transfiguration of the character with a fundamental change in the attitude to life, the life motivation. There is also a corresponding change in the environment. Pluto as the image of the higher self triggers an escalating dynamic that purifies, regenerates and allows the personal self and those of others to advance in alignment with the evolutionary goal. Synthesis is the new word for the unified will to grow and for the new age.

Transformation of the Personality

Personal and Spiritual Psychosynthesis

Below we link the transforming energies of the three spiritual planets with the development of the personality. As described in the previous chapter, the attribution of the three-fold personality to the planets Sun, Moon and Saturn is a useful astrological concept, which agrees with the findings of Roberto Assagioli's psychosynthesis and Alice Bailey's esoteric astrology, where transformation of the threefold personality is an important pre-condition for spiritual development.

In the astrological concept, Saturn symbolises the self on the physical level, it is physical awareness with its biological laws. The Moon is the feeling self that connects us to the world and its guises as a reflecting principle. The Sun is the autonomous self that works on the thinking or mental level as a self-conscious unit. The threefold personality is an undeniable reality. Everyone knows that they possess a body and feelings and that they can think. We can all distinguish between and understand the three levels. According to the laws of growth we are in a constant developmental dynamic on the three levels, leading to the unfolding and integration of the threefold personality. These growth processes are a preparation for spiritual development on the transpersonal level of Uranus, Neptune and Pluto.

Strong and Healthy Ego

It is common knowledge that a strong and healthy ego is required for spiritual development. For Assagioli it was important to make the sense of self strong and healthy so that it is able to function in the world on all levels; he called this personal psychosynthesis. In astrology, the positions in the horoscope of Saturn, Moon and Sun show how this ego is formed. It can be established quite quickly from the chart on which level problems exist, thus enabling them to be worked upon.

The following list shows which combinations of forces we have to work with in the assessment of the ego planets.

Interpretation Guide:
1. Planet quality (Sun, Moon, Saturn)
2. Sign in which the planet lies
3. Differentiation of Sign and House. The extent to which the sign in which the planet is situated corresponds to the house a) by cross and b) by temperament
4. House quality and background theme of the Sign (e.g. third house corresponds to the sign of Gemini)

5. House position of the ego planets (cusp, invert or low point)
6. Three zones in the House (cardinal, fixed, mutable)
7. Aspects to the ego planet (red, blue, green)
8. Is the planet part of an aspect pattern or not?
9. Axis theme (especially in the case of oppositions)
10. Development and transformation

House Position of the Ego Planets

We would like to deal with the house position one more time, because it contains important criteria for the transformation process. For example, for spiritual development there is a difference if an ego planet lies on a house cusp or on a low point. The Sun, as the symbol of a radiant, expansive self awareness, naturally prefers to lie on a house cusp rather than on a low point, where the effect is usually contrary and can even be the opposite of what the house, wants. This becomes clear when we know what the low point means. Here is a brief explanation to remind you.

At the low point (golden mean) in the twelve houses all energies are directed inwards. A planet in that position often does not even notice the outside world. For this reason there is no point making a big effort with these ego planets and trying with all one's strength to arouse an interest in the environment. It's a waste of energy because others do not react.

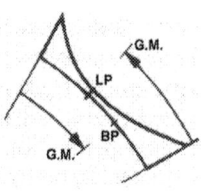

The low points in a house are "gateways to the inner being". These planets give us access to our souls, which represent the vital life principle and are symbolised by the central inner circle of the chart. There in the centre integrating energies are available, and can be perceived by low point planets. From the soul via these planets we gain pertinent guidance for our spiritual development. Low point planets should therefore be accepted and not unduly stressed. Instead we should learn how to heed our inner voice with them. When we are led from the inside out into life with these planets, we gather over the years sufficient substance to which the environment will react positively.

According to these criteria, we distinguish between strong and weak positions of the ego planets in the chart. An ego planet has success in worldly affairs when it lies on a house cusp, and in spiritual matters when it lies on a low point. A planet is particularly strong around 10°–12°, but weak at the beginning and end of a sign. You can read more on this in chapter 4 or in *The Astrological Houses* (16), page 96.

Integration of the Personality

Before spiritual development can begin safely, the integration of the personality must be worked on. This entails a dynamic collaboration of the ego forces on all three levels, with the aid of the soul in the centre of the horoscope. This requires a transformation of awareness and the knowledge that there is a soul that strengthens a person's positive side. Modern psychological healing methods work mainly with the recognition of people's good qualities and avoid drawing attention to their negative side. This is much more beneficial for self-development and wellbeing of the person concerned than working on their weaknesses. In modern education too, the emphasis on positive qualities leads to better results than did the old school punishment theories. If affirmation of the soul as the regulating inner entity is also involved, then ego problems can disappear quite easily. The integration of the personality depends on it.

Psychosynthesis and Love

Roberto Assagioli's psychosynthesis (6) also uses mainly positive methods for personal integration. He has described this process appositely as follows:

"One can only integrate what one loves and what is good for one, everything else is rejected."

We cannot assimilate what we reject and do not want, and do all we can to exclude it. So another task of psychosynthesis is first to liberate the unintegrated part of our personality from guilt and atonement before we can accept it as something positive. This challenge requires mental retraining and taking care of the good and constructive part of ourselves. In other words, that means that we must learn to love ourselves. It also means that we must love our neighbour as ourselves, and that we must love ourselves just as much as we love others. In any case, the universal concept of astrology helps to avoid the mediaeval concept of guilt and atonement and black-and-white philosophy. That is a possible way to self liberation. If we then want to go further, we can turn our weaknesses into strengths by reversing values through 180°. This reversal is actually a transformation, which leads to reorientation and new motivations. For example, if we give the ego planets a new, positive interpretation that is good and acceptable to us, then we are ready to integrate them and to assimilate them as belonging to us. For example, we could do this with Saturn.

Assagioli lovingly emphasised and affirmed these human strengths in his therapy. Love was his great quality. He always stressed that love is the only power in the universe capable of healing wounds. In our case, this means that our weaknesses can be healed by the awareness in our souls, because from the centre outwards everything is always fine. Only then can we experience self-worth, enjoy life and actualise ourselves and our ideals.

Wholeness

Perceiving our own integrity in the centre of our being is the first step on the spiritual path. As stated above, a healthy and strong ego is needed to be able to cope with spiritual energies. So our first task is to untangle and strengthen our personalities. The way to do this is not to practice selflessness, offer sacrifices and eliminate anything selfish. The selflessness that used to be so valued frequently proves to be a barrier to integration. If a person has too little self esteem, the ego first has to be developed and strengthened. For the spiritual path that we are to tread later with the three transpersonal planets requires an integrated personality that lives fully and consciously on all three levels. This needs a functional unit, a wholeness, and nothing should be excluded.

If a person starts on their spiritual path with a weak, limited ego, they will inevitably experience mental crises. Roberto Assagioli specialised in dealing with such cases in his work as a psychiatrist. In his psychiatric clinic, he noticed that many people became neurotic or mentally ill on their path to spiritual development. He said: "If there are non-integrated parts of the personality with lives of their own, the spiritual path becomes a path of thorns". This is an extract from Assagioli's writings: "Spiritual Development and Mental Problems", which were published in *Astrolog* numbers 28 and 29 (7).

Development Tendencies

It is obvious that the strength of the self-awareness depends on the position of the three ego planets in the house system and in the aspect pattern. However, this is never as perfect initially as we would like. The unfolding of our three-fold personality is never fully complete, it is constantly developing. Many people believe that this depends on external success, on "feedback" from the environment, and it is too often measured by this. They forget or do not know that spiritual development depends on how introverted our awareness is, and on orienting ourselves more and more to the centre of our being, to our soul. What is right for the worldly personality can be wrong for spiritual development, i.e. for the soul. Conversely, often what is important for the soul creates a crisis for the personality. In the horoscope, these crises are nearly always indicated by aspects of the ego planets to the three spiritual planets Uranus, Neptune and Pluto.

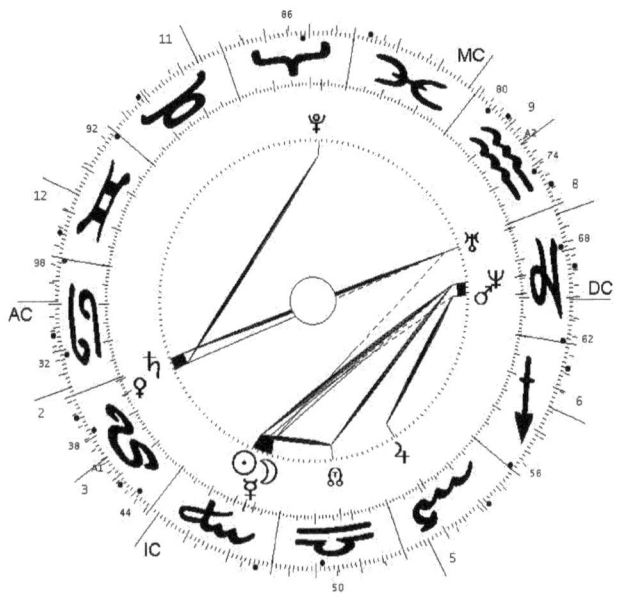

Leo Tolstoy, Russian novelist
28.8.1828 JC = 9.9.1828 GC/23.00 LT

In Tolstoy's horoscope we see all three ego planets Saturn, Sun and Moon linked by aspects to the spiritual planets: Saturn conjunct Venus trine Pluto, Sun and Moon conjunct Mercury, both ego planets trine Uranus and Neptune. Anyone who knows something about Tolstoy knows that transformations were a recurring feature of his life. People with aspects like these change throughout their lives. They want to grow spiritually and are not interested in the worldly success of their personality; all they need are answers to deep, vital questions. They transfer their consciousness to higher levels of existence and concern themselves with transpersonal matters such as the problems of mankind. In so doing they undergo ego conversions and transformation crises of awareness that change the personality structure through new life motivations.

Transformation of the Ego Planets

Spiritual development also involves the unfolding of the intrinsic, inner person, of his motivation, bringing motivation and approach into line with true humanitarian ideals. This is the lesser known ethical side of astrology, which is attracting more and more attention. The transformation of the ego planets mainly involves processes during which we gain a deeper understanding of ourselves, our life motivations, inner goals and spiritual principles. In these processes there is an ongoing conversion of the ego on all three levels: in every age phase, in every house, at every low point, in every sign and on all levels of awareness.

In simple terms, transformation of the ego involves conversion from a selfish person to a responsible, free individual who feels part of the whole and is capable of assuming responsibility for others. In this process, the integrated personality is guided by the soul and liberated from too much ego concentration and dependency on material success. It increasingly concentrates on larger tasks that concern society and do not just satisfy the "little ego". In the spiritual sense, we transcend ourselves by making a creative contribution to evolution as a free individual.

Simultaneity

An important feature of development is also that we do not always move up from one level to the next in sequence. On the contrary, it often happens that we find ourselves on different levels simultaneously. When we start on the first level, it is obvious that we cannot reach the next level overnight. Instead, the way from deciding to achieving is subject to certain time cycles. Everything needs time to reach maturity; the individual levels frequently blend into each other and can sometimes even be experienced simultaneously. It can be possible to start the whole circuit from scratch and then to have to repeat the whole journey because one still has not accomplished everything. There are always gaps and deficiencies, or some old accounts are still open that must be settled during the transformation process.

The Spiritual Path

Astrologically, this involves the transformation of the three ego planets to the level of the three spiritual planets Uranus, Neptune and Pluto. These are transpersonal essential forces that connect us directly to the higher self. If integration is achieved with the help of the soul, then the ability to act creatively is awakened in the inner circle. We come into contact with the laws of evolution and become creative. But this does not mean that some slight pain in our bodies can be wished away by the power of the mind, (which is incidentally also possible) but that a superior inner vision of the divine plan is revealed to us, and we mobilise all our strengths to put it into practice. Eventually, no other motivation remains in the transformation process. When we feel creative forces within us on this level, they are activated by the will of Pluto to work on the environment. Life motivation is adjusted accordingly; we want nothing more than to make a creative contribution to evolution. The spiritual planets are powerful transpersonal energy givers, working on the highest spiritual level as general principles and transformation forces. There is nothing of interest for the ego on this level. If there are still ego forces present on this level, they are converted and transformed, which does not happen without crises. So that people can establish exactly which level they are at and what they have to consciously focus on, we describe below the best known effects of the three ego planets on the three levels of human experience. We have also added brief descriptions of the transformation levels.

Saturn Levels ♄

Physical Level

The upper part of the Planetary Table from page 15 is repeated below as a useful introduction to the transformation. You can see Uranus placed above Saturn, Neptune above Moon and Sun above Pluto. The qualities of each in a pair are similar, the one working on the ego level and the other on the transpersonal level.

CREATIVE INTELLIGENCE	ALL – LOVE (Christ)	SPIRITUAL WILL
MOTHER ♅ IMAGO	CHILD ♆ IMAGO	FATHER ♇ IMAGO
Occultist	Mystic	Magician
Methodology	Mediation	Metamorphosis
Ideal of the perfect world	Ideal of unconditional love	Ideal of the perfect human being
Organising	Serving	Creating
BODY	**FEELING**	**MENTALITY**
Self-Confidence	You-awareness	Self-awareness
♄	☾	☉
Immunity Security	Sensitivity Sympathy	Vitality Mental capacity
housekeeping closing	learning opening	growing radiating
MOTHER heteronomous	CHILD ambivalent	FATHER autonomous

Ego Planets and Spiritual Planets

In the constitution of the personality, we know that Saturn represents the physical body and physical awareness. It controls matter. Everything that we can touch and see in the physical world is Saturn reality. If a person is mainly identified with his Saturn, he has both a strong physical awareness and a fascination with the world of forms, of existential values. This person tries to accumulate material assets to provide himself with security. He makes sure that he gets as much money, comfort, luxury and convenience as possible and safeguards the physical and material aspects of his life; he believes only in material existence.

On the first level we are at the mercy of Saturn or the physical condition. We are blind to spiritual values and all attention is focused on material existence. It is as if we are still children, existentially dependent on our parents. We cannot live alone and need protection and security. We experience this conditionality and the state of dependence psychologically when we start to strive for self-knowledge and further development. It takes a long time to break free from the inertia of matter, anxiety, inadequacy and loneliness. We are trapped by dependencies, calculations and material considerations. That particularly affects the disengagement process in partnerships and in contact situations or in the professional domain. How easily we let ourselves be distracted from inner goals because we are too comfortable and do not want to give up our material security. We adapt and stay on the Saturn level, not wanting to take risks and avoiding progress or change. We must recognise these factors as such on the way to our true selves or freedom, and slowly free ourselves from them. Most crises occur in disengagement processes that have not been fully worked out and completed, in losses of any kind, be it bankruptcy, robbery, illness or death of relatives, etc.

The second level always brings a situation of conflict. When we start to perceive something we enter a dual state. We recognise our conditionality and dependencies on material things and are painfully aware of our inability to do anything about it and suffer in a hopeless situation. Only when Uranus starts to work on Saturn do doubts arise as to whether what we have done up to now or the standards by which we have lived are really correct. This perception also causes great insecurity as we do not know what to do and feel trapped and stuck for as long as it takes to be convinced that something must be changed because our way of life no longer corresponds to our inner need for further development. Then comes the will to do something about it. The desire for change and liberation becomes stronger and stronger and a choice must be made. In this crisis, many people feel the irresistible pressure to run away, to leave everything, to abandon partnerships, security, money and wealth just to be free. This is the breakaway level.

The third level in the Saturn crisis is the undeluded perception of reality that can be termed real sense. Coming out of the conflict situation and richer in experience, we recognise that we want to create absolute clarity. On this level we strive for autonomy, we are now ready to take responsibility for ourselves, although despite this we usually remain dependent. Taking responsibility for our fate, and controlling our physical existence gives us the chance to respect and even to learn to love Saturn. That means that if we can experience and accept it as a useful vessel for personal self-actualisation, we can fully approve of it and become a "master of matter". On this level, our delusion-free sense of reality matures, we accept our physical existence as something positive and acknowledge its place in the evolutionary process. Recognising, accepting and mastering what is important in life brings the whole thing into proportion.

Transformation

The transformation process starts with the conflict in which we must overcome our blind, materialistic first-level mentality. Then we perceive material existence as a reality that must be outgrown. We assume responsibility for our physical existence, accept it for what it is, and then see it in a different way. We discover that the material form of existence is not the be all and end all, for when we die, we cannot take the possessions we have acquired with us. The transformation from Saturn leads to Uranus, which leads to a change in awareness so that it is able to turn to new things. The influence of Uranus brings creative intelligence that finds new ways of accelerating spiritual development.

Moon Levels ☽

Feeling Level

The emotional experience of the Moon level is well-known, as we all live intense emotional lives. The Moon rules the feelings. Like the moon out in space, it is only visible when the Sun shines on it. There is also a full moon, a new moon and all the waxing and waning phases in between. Our feelings are just as changeable. The Moon is known to be our contact self, the childlike feeling self that wants to be loved because it can only experience itself as an identity when it is in contact with others and gains approval through love. As the feelings are flexible and changeable, and the moon as seen from earth also has different faces and a constantly changing shape, the feeling self needs a long time to develop. Much patience and effort is required to liberate it. It invests a lot of energy in finding sufficient contacts so as not to be alone. It is always looking for people who are supposed to understand it, belong to it, support, love and take care of it. On the feeling level, the transformation goes from the Moon to Neptune, i.e. from subjective love to unconditional love, and there are three levels to pass through in the process.

On the first level (attributed to Saturn), the person starts out on the feeling level with a compulsive urge to search for the You. She would like the You, or the person she has a relationship with, to satisfy both her feelings and her need for love. This first level is compulsively blind, and does not realise that the love she has been capable of until now is actually just carnal desire. Everything is done from a selfish need to be loved and not to be left alone. She projects these desires onto the You and would like the You, the partner, the friend, the mother, the father, etc. to be just as she needs them to be. She then realises that it is just not that easy to make other people satisfy her wishes. Other people are not there to do what we want, they have other interests, other goals. This leads to disappointment, frustration, occasional anger and aggression, and ultimately to the second conflict level.

On the second level (attributed to the Moon), love can switch to hate or rejection. One is completely at the mercy of the law of polarity. If satisfaction cannot be found on the feeling level, the hunger for love is so great that one becomes unbalanced and starts to accuse loved ones and heap reproaches and blame onto them. People often even think that only they are capable of love and others are not. The associated jealous and possessive love that this leads to is well-known. They cling to their partner, suffocate and manipulate them with their wishes to such an extent that they are oppressed and driven into a corner. This leads to relationship problems in the couple. If a person gets stuck in this stage, she must learn through disappointment and heartbreak that what she thought was love is really just selfishness.

On the third level, as on the mental level, cognitive processes become possible. Here, the person becomes aware that she first has to give love before she can receive it. She recognises that love cannot be forced; it is a gift and follows its own rules. Love is a subtle energy field that cannot be evoked with possessive demands and projections. As soon as one tries to pin love down or demand it with force, it disappears. On this level, there are now various aids available as to how we can influence our own feelings and emotional reactions by our thoughts. It is important to realise that emotional love creates constant problems because it has nothing to do with reality. So we develop the will to no more be at the mercy of this eternal interplay and therefore to avoid further suffering. So begins the process of working on, improving, refining and cultivating our feeling level by trying to do good or to give love.

Transformation

The first level is home to the naturally-given desire of carnal love. On the second level we find that things do not always work as we would like, due to the polarities of love and hate, satisfaction and disappointment, sympathy and antipathy that represent the opposites at this level. On the third, more realistic level, the feeling area finally becomes permeable and sensitive due to the discovery and understanding of its own selfishness. It is reformed by great suffering and then finds that relationships with other people only work by giving love first, before it can be received. This then enables the transformation to Neptune, the model for universal love, to take place.

Sun Levels ☉

Thinking Level

The next level is Sun consciousness. The Sun is autonomous, it shines from itself and does not need anyone to make it visible. It is the symbol of the self-aware person who is free to connect with everything. The transition from the Moon to the Sun level takes place when the will is awakened and the person realises that he does not want to suffer any longer and can decide things for himself. This transition can be made relatively quickly if the tests of the Moon level have been negotiated successfully.

On the thinking level we do not just have wishes and expectations, as in the feeling self with its desires for contact and love. Instead the ego wants to be independent and achieve self-determination. On the thinking level we can move around much more easily and go where we want, there are fewer obstacles in the way; it is just the thoughts that come from the collective or from the unconscious that distract us. Our mental space contains all the thinking structures of the cultural environment into which we were born. Collective thoughts coexist in our mental space alongside our own personal thoughts. The stream of ideas coming from television, media or other sources constantly occupy our thoughts, so that images, ideas, philosophies and dogmas stimulate and fill our own thinking space. So where exactly are our own personal thoughts that we now have to develop? We find initially that we can watch all these thoughts running through our heads when we adopt the position of observer. Then we realise that "I think therefore I am". The next step is to advance further until we find the point of freedom where the I is able to say "yes" or "no" to life.

To do this, we have to realise that on the thinking level we are actually free and can choose whether we want to think certain thoughts or not. Unwanted thoughts can be rejected or ignored. Reading something in a book, learning something in a lecture or in a class opens up our minds. We can always decide for ourselves whether we want to accept the suggested ideas or not. Ideas are free, but we can only become aware of this freedom of choice when we start on our inward journey. Even when we have reached the thinking level, we still have three more levels of the evolutionary process to pass through.

On the first level, we want to fit in with everyone else, we think like other people and don't want to stand out. Anyone who thinks differently is ridiculed or attacked. This level is ruled by collective ways of thinking, clichés and patterns that we are attached to and by which we live our lives. Our thoughts are pre-programmed and prejudiced. Only what our parents, teachers and friends have taught and shown us is important. The influence of our upbringing and the educational system are decisive. Our minds are educated to be precise and clever, and literal, standardised thinking is developed. We just accept this indoctrination unquestioningly, because the first level corresponds to Saturnine blindness. On this level, many people do not think there is anything wrong with this at all. We realise only gradually that we actually have the ability to judge and to have our own ideas about relationships, about scientific discoveries, about beliefs, etc. Then the process of liberation from traditional thinking begins.

On the second level, the conflict level, we become unbalanced and polarised. We are usually let down by other people's promises and become suspicious. Serious doubts emerge regarding the validity of everything we have hitherto believed. Many people have a crisis of faith if they are religious, others become disillusioned with politics because they no longer agree with the power system. Others come into conflict with the education system or with the law. Many misguided ideas belong here too, in which people blindly follow some guru, philosophy or institution to find the truth. They go from one belief to another, and find that none of them can help in this crisis.

This level is comparable to the Faustian struggle for truth, where all Faust's collected knowledge did not help his despair and he cried out "Here I stand now, a poor fool, and am as clever as I was before." Only after the doubting phase do we realise that we are no wiser than a poor fool. It is then that we can really start to search for the truth, for the meaning of our own life, that can only be found in a higher transpersonal world pattern.

The third level is reached when we find that everything that we have learnt before is meaningless. We differentiate between what is important and what is not, between what is true and what is false, between death and immortality. In the transition to the third level, we give up and let go of everything that we have previously held to be true and built our lives around. That makes us see things in a completely new way and we suddenly discover our own ability to think creatively. Here we have the possibility to think and see the world as we want. We create new ways of thinking and a new world pattern is created, not out of some fantasy, but clear and in touch with reality. That is why a thinker on this level will not only be rich in ideas but also clever and wise.

Transformation

On the first level, we are forced to agree with collective thinking and don't dare to believe anything other than what we are told by the professor, priest, etc. On the second level, we come into conflict with prevailing opinion. We doubt everything, and enter a crisis of meaning that causes mental insecurity and conflict. Only on the third level do we become able to think for ourselves and experience the power of our own ability to think creatively.

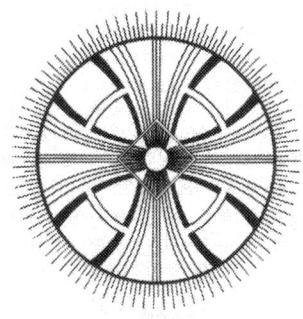

Ego Fears and How to Overcome Them

This gradual progression of the ego planets to the transpersonal level is always accompanied by fear. Someone who is in the grip of these forces makes drastic changes at every level. The habits of a lifetime are broken, old life motivations are now worthless, the devaluation of all values makes him start again from zero. Where there are aspects of the spiritual planets to the three ego planets Saturn, Moon and Sun, this feeling can last a lifetime. One could say that the spiritual planets, in their capacity of guardians of the evolutionary laws, indicate those parts of the personality that have to be changed in this lifetime by their aspects with the ego planets. The ego reacts to this transformation with fear and resists until it obtains security from the indestructible core personality. The ego is always afraid that it will be destroyed. The various types of fear are briefly described below.

1. Physical Self   Saturn ♄

Physical Reality, Security Motivation

Fear of physical pain, fear of the ephemeral, fear of letting go, fear of losing security. Fear of taking risks, of uncertainty, of constant change and transformation, i.e. fear of becoming part of the eternal flux of life. Fear of the unknown – of dying.

Transformation: Realising that beyond material existence there is an immortal self, a soul, which survives death, that there are other dimensions with their own laws, and when we discover this our feeling of fear is reduced. The expansion of consciousness of the soul and of the experience of being; finding security in the eternal, in the indestructible core, the self, anchoring in the eternal now.

2. Feeling Self   Moon ☽

Contact Level, Love/Hate Motivation

Fear of not being loved, fear of spiritual suffering, of rejection, of emotional coldness, of criticism, of being left alone. Fear of growing up, fear of becoming an independent person and leaving the security of the nest. But also fear of devoting the self, of being overwhelmed by others, of opening up, which is experienced as threatening ego destruction and dependence. Fear of the urges and necessities of existence, of finality.

Transformation: trust, forgiveness, reconciliation, striving for harmony, giving love, opening up and devoting oneself to the healing powers of one's own soul, divine love, the power of Christ within us, that makes all things new and unites everything, lets energy flow and gives the ability to be free from guilt, and security in togetherness, belonging to the great whole.

3. Thinking Self   Sun ☉
The Ability to Think, Rational Motivation

Fear of failure, defeat, inadequacy. Fear of reduced efficiency and vitality, of inability and weakness. Fear of losing the position achieved, control or power and losing face. Fear of those stronger than ourselves, of our plans being thwarted. The fear of dependency, of urges and limitation and consequently of subjugation. The fear of losing the awareness of our uniqueness.

Transformation: Realising that every individual is just a part of the whole, that we are all connected and interdependent. Above all, knowing that there is an evolutionary plan and that we are all on different rungs of the evolutionary ladder. We all have responsibility for ourselves and for each other. Tolerance and harmony of originality, searching for spiritual friendship, making a creative contribution to evolution. Taking responsibility for oneself and also responsibility for the whole, the group, the planet. Solving questions of meaning, becoming useful to the great whole.

The Zodiac

Initiation and Transformation

Esoteric Astrology

Initiation in Antiquity

In antiquity, initiation ceremonies were the focus of secret cults that took the candidates into transcendent worlds. They were usually put into a trance, their spirit was possessed by priests with magic powers, detached from their bodies and led from the material world into the spiritual world, where they experienced the continuation of life after death. In the Egyptian mystery schools, the induction into secret mysteries took place in established initiation ceremonies, in which the candidate had to lie in a coffin for three days in the first initiation in order to experience the immortality of the soul. In nearly all mystery schools, initiation ceremonies were celebrated according to secret, symbolic ritual, following strict rules. Candidates could then be accepted into a group of secret societies, occult masters in initiation societies, mystery schools, etc.

Initiation Today

Initiations still take place in everyday life today. According to Alice Bailey (8), initation ceremonies are being replaced by work that a spiritually oriented person can do for himself. The age of self-initiation has begun, and we can all decide for ourselves when and where we want to move up to a higher state of awareness. With suitable conditions and destiny, we can gradually evolve as required. Every transformation process involves initiation processes, which represent spiritual and psychological growth, so that the threefold personality is gradually integrated, coordinated and subordinated gradually to the soul and spiritual goals. The little ego changes through transpersonal and global motivations in the transformation process.

New age initiation is a process of do-it-yourself consciousness expansion. Every big life change causes a kind of initiation, be it marriage, parenthood, changes in professional life, becoming independent or illness. Whenever our lives change completely and nothing is as it was before, we go through an initiation. Initation is a fundamental part of the normal evolutionary development process.

According to Alice Bailey, the first five initiation levels relate to the five main periods in the life of Christ: 1. Birth in Bethlehem, 2. Baptism in Jordan, 3. Transfiguration on Mount Carmel, 4. Crucifixion on Mount Golgotha and 5. Resurrection and Ascension. We illustrate these initation levels with a new astrological concept in the following chapter.

Initiation Crises

In every big transition from one level to another and especially later spiritual levels, there is an intensive transformation of awareness, that the ancient mystery schools called initiation. The person caught up in these forces of transformation must make continual efforts to stabilise the changes in consciousness. That is why in times of moral crisis, there is often a magnifying effect, where everything unwanted seems much bigger than it really is. We are then convinced that we have made no progress at all, are quickly discouraged and can become depressed. Many people nowadays suffer from this kind of transformation crisis and do not understand what is wrong with them. To be able to deal with this, it helps to understand each crisis in more detail. The table below illustrates this.

Initiation Levels

Physical Level	Transformation	Saturn-Uranus	Damascus experience

1ˢᵗ Initiation "Birth"

♄ ♅	1ˢᵗ Level:	material dependency, physical conditionality
	2ⁿᵈ Level:	fear and letting-go conflicts
	3ʳᵈ Level:	undeluded awareness of reality

Emotional Level	Transformation	Moon-Neptune	Gethsemane experience

2ⁿᵈ Initiation "Baptism"

☽ ♆	1ˢᵗ Level:	demanding love, carnal urges
	2ⁿᵈ Level:	love and hate, purification of selfishness
	3ʳᵈ Level:	giving love, understanding, forgiveness, sensitivity

Mental Level	Transformation	Sun-Pluto	The Way of the Cross

3ʳᵈ Initiation "Transfiguration"

☉ ♇	1ˢᵗ Level:	programmed thinking, collective norms
	2ⁿᵈ Level:	doubt and searching for the truth, finding oneself
	3ʳᵈ Level:	individuation, creative thinking, will

The table features three levels: Physical, Emotional and Mental. Each is further sub-divided into three levels. For the sake of simplicity and to respect the system, we have used this division into three, although in esoteric literature there are always seven levels. Alice Bailey's theory of the Seven Rays (8) is well known, where each of the three bodies plus the soul lie on a certain ray and function accordingly. Below, we examine the three levels according to evolutionary ideas and how they relate to the ego planets and transformation crises.

Saturn-Uranus Transformation ♄/♅

1st Initiation – Birth of Christ in Bethlehem – Damascus Experience

1st Initiation

The transformation of the personality planets into the spiritual planets can be compared to the initiations in the ancient mystery schools. In the case of Saturn, we see the first initiation, which also began in the mystery schools in ancient Egypt with the overcoming and mastering of physical existence. As mentioned above, according to ancient tradition, the candidate had to lie in a coffin for a few days in order to experience the dying process. He found that the soul survived physical death, even when the body died. That was the result of this initiation.

The Experience of Death

One effect of the first initiation is that it changes our idea of death. How many people these days study life after death, the dying process, and read books about it and have inner experiences of it themselves? According to Alice Bailey, these days many people reach the first initiation. They are interested in ideas of reincarnation, believe in rebirth and in the evolutionary process. Many go through a dying process themselves and in this way learn something about the fragility of their body and their immortal soul.

The Birth of Christ in Bethlehem

The Saturn-Uranus transformation or the first initiation is, in Alice Bailey's opinion, connected to the birth of Christ in Bethlehem. As the baby Jesus was persecuted by Herod's myrmidons, so would the Uranian also be persecuted. In former times, it was common for astrologers, alternative thinkers, unbelievers and revolutionaries to be banished or burnt at the stake as heretics. Such experiences were often part of the transformation process from Saturn to Uranus. It is reassuring to know that astrologers and alternative thinkers are no longer persecuted these days!

However, some students of astrology do report that they are ridiculed by their relatives and not taken seriously. That is an after-effect of the persecution in the Middle Ages, and most people can put up with this slight hostility. Once Uranus has struck, and the limits on consciousness have been removed, there is no going back. Most people remain true to their new convictions and accept the downside.

Damascus Experience
From Saul to Paul

In transpersonal psychology, this crisis is called the "Damascus Experience". Just as Saul was touched by a ray of enlightenment and became Paul, we are transformed by the "lightning ray" of Uranus. Initially, Saul was against the new Christian religion, and later he contributed to the Bible. Such Saul-Paul experiences happen during this transition from Saturnine to Uranian thinking. For example, people who used to have no interest in astrology or esoteric matters are now among their advocates. This turnaround can frequently be seen during Uranus transits and especially during the age point transit over Uranus in the natal horoscope.

Uranus is also concerned with abandoning security. The Uranian impulses transform old familiar habits, hardened structures, scripts and materialistic attitudes. Many people are worried by change. People who do not adhere to tradition are attacked and criticised. A person who brings something new, who wants to free themselves from the trap of materialism or from relationships that have run their course, has to put up with being attacked by those close to him, frequently by his loved ones. For example, what courage it must have taken to climb up on the barricades and declare war on the aristocracy during the French Revolution. Uranus was discovered shortly before this time (13.03.1781 by Herschel). Crossing the Saturnine boundary sometimes means putting our life on the line. This should not be taken literally, but that is how this process feels.

Transformation Goal

In this transformation crisis from Saturn to Uranus, the person starts to realise that he is not only responsible for himself, but for all his fellow-men. Interpersonal relationships and social behaviour are his developmental goal. He learns by experience how to fit into the community, because it is the right thing to do. His changed awareness enables him to coexist with all living things and turn his physical body into an effective tool in the service of his soul, which is readily available for the varied tasks that life has to offer. The current popularity of Yoga and the focus on the body are a sign that many people are trying to do something for their physical bodies. They go on diets and training programmes to keep their bodies healthy and let their inner self shine through, and also to present an attractive appearance to others. This transformation corresponds to the modern attitude to the physical body in general. It is no longer seen as bad or impure, as it was in the Middle Ages, and is now experiencing a certain glorification, increased attention and even love. This leads to a lot of freedom in all areas, including health, love or transport, e.g. cars and planes. The world has now become so small that we can travel several thousand kilometres in a few hours, presenting greater opportunities for overcoming borders and distance, starting relationships and keeping them going. This is also part of the Saturn-Uranus transformation.

Changing the Way we Live

Another effect of this first initiation is that it makes us change the way we live. We no longer want to be the slave of our desires and resolve to control them. It is important to do this in moderation and not to become excessive. It is actually a question of overcoming greed and therefore dependency. This makes us more interested in a correct, healthy lifestyle and alternative medical healing arts. This enables us to live longer and allows many people a fuller life on all levels, making them much happier. Greater enjoyment of life in a healthy body is the expression of the first initiation. We no longer have to struggle for survival, we can enjoy life and even do something to reduce the suffering around us.

Trigger

These crises are usually triggered when the age point or a transit passes through Saturn or Uranus. Many people who have a Saturn/Uranus conjunction in their horoscope are sensitive to these transforming powers. In general, these processes take a long time and, if both planets are connected by aspects in some way in the natal horoscope, they become a life theme.

Moon-Neptune Transformation ☽/♆

2nd Initiation – Baptism of Christ – Gethsemane Experience

2nd Initiation

The second initiation is connected with the baptism of Christ, according to Alice Bailey. Baptism is a symbol of purification, where water is poured over the head. As befits our emotional body, on this level the purification is done by the tears we cry for love. From the developmental point of view, this means that we have to go through the passion and suffering of love that we have all experienced at some time in our lives. The next step to the third level can only be achieved by clear thinking; by learning to distinguish between pairs of opposites.

This necessarily brings a great crisis in the emotional body, called the esoteric "mystical death" or "the dark night of the soul", because the opposite poles are engaged in a violent battle with each other and for a long time we think that it is a battle of life or death between the two of them. The person experiences spirit and matter, good and evil, love and hate, joy and pain in one painful reality. He feels pulled this way and that between the two opposing forces and is temporarily unable to separate them clearly. He is attracted both by his internal spiritual goal and also by worldly and external validation. On the previous level, he discovered light and love within himself and now becomes painfully aware of darkness and hate. Because he wants to choose good, he must oppose evil. We are all familiar with these polarities, because they occur frequently in everyday life and cause many of the psychological problems that we encounter nowadays.

This is a purification phase, which can last a very long time. It is linked to the liberation and maturity of the little Moon ego, which is why the second initiation is the longest. We have to struggle for a long time before we are clear about our own feelings. The ego would much rather remain in a childlike state, chasing constantly after some idealised love or fantasy. The emotional level is situated between the mental and the physical levels, like a hall of mirrors, where things are reflected and appear as delusions. From an esoteric point of view, it is the astral world with its blindness and illusions, which is nothing less than a reflection of our psyche with its unsatisfied wishes and immature demands.

Woman as the Moon

Very many people, men and especially women, are going through this phase of suffering in love. For the past 2000 years, woman has been identified with the Moon and has been considered as an emotional being. She herself has continually identified herself as the emotional element. Not only because man shaped her that way under a patriarchal system, but because she herself remained in this childlike state and was convinced that she was dependent on men. By projecting her feeling self onto the man, her own sense of self-worth was always dependent on whether or not the man loved her and did not leave her. Actually it used to be that a divorced woman or an unmarried mother was ostracised. That is also why so many women now suffer when men leave them and have other women, mainly because they have made their sense of self-worth dependent on the man. The sense of self-worth that had previously been so dependent on men is currently undergoing a transformation on the collective feeling level. Women have been able to liberate themselves and gain self-confidence to such an extent that they have developed their own personality, and have just as much intelligence as men. For example, a lot more women than men study astrology. Our experience shows that many women have been helped by the universal wisdom of astrology to free themselves from old-fashioned thinking patterns. They have used it to create a space for themselves in which they are free, where they can retreat to and build their own world. That helps them to actualise themselves and thus to unfold their Sun ego.

The transformation level in the feeling area is never really finally completed; we fall back into it again and again. Even when we have achieved inner strength, selflessness, artlessness, mildness, the giving of unconditional love at some point in our lives, it happens again and again that we fall back into our old ways. From an esoteric point of view, on this astral level, the archetypal pattern of the Atlantean development phase in the planetary emotional body is also present. In Atlantean times, the astral or emotional body was developed, which still affects us now with the opposites of good and evil. When we look at evolution in this way, it is clear that we are still living out the karma of mankind. For each person who is struggling against the little, childish ego, against the need for symbiotic love, is in a way also doing it for everyone else.

Gethsemane Experience

In transpersonal psychology, the second initiation is also called the Gethsemane Experience. If we imagine Christ in the Garden of Gethsemane, we see him all alone struggling against his fear. All the young people are sleeping on the ground, Judas has sold him for 30 pieces of silver, Peter disowns him. Christ is left all alone, deserted by all his friends. In his anguish he cries out: "Oh Father, if you are willing, take this cup from me." After overcoming his fear he said "Lord, let not my will, but Thine be done."

The same thing happens to people who are preparing themselves for the second initiation, struggling with their feelings and suffering desperately in love. They feel deeply hurt, misunderstood, humiliated, disowned, beaten. During this phase, many are prosecuted and laden with guilt and embroiled in intrigues when they are actually innocent. The transformation to Neptune happens just as it is often described in books. Slander, intrigue, smoke screens, secrecy, addictions, we are spared nothing in one of these phases. Nobody understands us, no-one helps us, we are totally left to our own devices. This crisis goes straight to the heart, dissolves all boundaries, destroys all connections. Many people cannot tolerate it and crack up and take refuge in alcohol, drugs, madness. It was not for nothing that Assagioli called this phase "the dark night of the soul"; we feel deserted by everyone and there seems to be no way out.

There are countless literary examples of this process described in detail. It is a kind of comfort and may be helpful to let the people concerned know that it is just a passing phase. We really can say: "There is always daylight at the other end of the tunnel."

Letting Go

The solution is to let go, accept or abandon hope. The moment a person gives up his apparently legitimate demands or wishes, accepts what he is given and forgives his fellow men, he will find himself in a completely different situation. He experiences a warmth and love that are not of this world, but which accept and protect him in all his desolation. The suffering, injustice, losses and everything that caused him pain will disappear. That is the last step to initiation and leads directly to the energy of Neptune.

The only way to help such people is to make it clear to them that this crisis is part of their spiritual development. There are necessary stages of development that must be gone through in order to be a human being in harmony with the laws of development. This harmony is symbolically referred to in the words of Christ: "Not my will, but Thine be done." According to the evolutionary plan, all men have the longing for harmony within them, and a deep inner knowledge that it is important to put into practice the unconditional love of Neptune in this world. When we feel in harmony with these laws of spiritual development, we have progressed so far that from the point of view of the soul, nothing more can happen to us. We have come home. The source of a new life is to be found in this experience, and a new beginning, "See, I make all things new."

Transformation Goal

Discovering that love follows its own laws is the goal of this crisis. Its alternating ebb and flow, joy and pain imbue our entire emotional nature and everyone must follow this movement in order to receive any happiness that the Moon may have to offer. We must realise that life is eternal motion and that love is something that comes and goes and can never be pinned down. In other words, the realisation that living and loving are subject to the law of eternal change brings the right attitude towards life and love. They function according to their own rhythm and when the time is right, love strikes like a blessing. This is the only way to be open to the Neptunian quality that is achieved during the transformation process. We remain flexible, do not cling to anything, are always ready for love when it comes along. It is hard to explain how Neptune really works, but it shows us the higher ideal of love as a model on the highest level.

Trigger

Such acute crises often happen when Neptune transits an ego planet in the natal horoscope, or comes into opposition with one. They can also take place when the age point transits Neptune. When Neptune is aspected to an ego planet, there is generally a very familiar life theme. The type of aspect is not too important, although usually the crisis is greater for tense aspects than for a trine.

Sun-Pluto Transformation

3rd Initiation – Transfiguration – The Way of the Cross

3rd Initation

When the person has examined his emotional nature with the Moon during the second initiation, he can then go on to stabilise his awareness in the third initiation on the Sun level. The integration of the three-fold personality is now the goal. The personality is controlled from the mental level by thinking correctly, thus allowing the will to be asserted. The will power aligns and orientates all mental and physical elements of the personality towards the goal. The stage has been reached where one can do what one wants. Having an integrated personality makes for a successful life.

The Way of the Cross

Before we get to that point, we have to go through crises on the mental level. The life of Christ also helps to understand what is happening on this level. Controlling our thoughts is one of the most difficult things to do on the spiritual path. It is like a Medusa with many heads. As soon as one is chopped off, another one grows back immediately. This is what it feels like when we start to control our thoughts, to integrate the three-fold personality and create our own world image. This process is really like the Way of the Cross with many stations. Ideas from the environment are a constant disturbance, they influence and condition our lives, tempting us and making our good intentions disappear.

Temptation

On the mental level, it is relatively easy to see what has to be overcome and where we must insist in order to grow spiritually. But again and again we find that: "The spirit is willing but the flesh is weak." It is true that we know a lot and pick things up so quickly, but only with our heads. We do not know things "in our gut", and we do not manage to really change our lives. Although we see everything so clearly, there are unforeseen obstacles in the way. They come from the environment, from our social milieu, from our cultural background, and also from our own unconscious, the shadow area. We are confronted with old habits, with everything we have previously said and done. Esoterically speaking, it is the "Keeper of the Threshold" that stands before us and makes our lives difficult. We try hard every day to free ourselves from it and to plan our lives better. We put everything into raising our awareness to a higher level, but over and over again we are thwarted. We doubt ourselves, a magnifying glass effect occurs in which everything we do not want appears to be enormous. We think we have made no progress at all and feel worse than before. In this mental crisis things get out of proportion. Many people become deeply depressed and would rather give up.

The example in the life of Christ, when he went into the desert and fasted for forty days and prayed before he could experience the transfiguration, symbolises this process. According to tradition, Christ was tested three times by the devil in the desert, and each time he resisted. The three tests were might, matter and magic (the three "m"s).

Purification

On this level, we are constantly thrown off balance and fluctuate between underestimating and overestimating ourselves. Many are seized by a nagging doubt as to whether what they want is really right. This process is a purification by fire of the self motivation. The initiation crises are running continuously in the consciousness and on the mental level. That is why we should not stop believing in our spiritual goal and should continue to climb the mountain fearlessly and confidently. As on the Way of the Cross with fourteen stations, we drag ourselves along, joyless, discouraged; we would often just like to give up. But we are mercilessly chased on and can never rest. Sometimes the blows come from outside ourselves, sometimes from within. Exhausted, we finally reach the mountain peak. Here is the light of the Sun that controls the mental space and lets us see everything in a new light. It allows us to see everything important, refines our ability to differentiate and reveals the simplicity of all things. This is the initiation of the transfiguration, where everything is illuminated, everything appears in order and in divine harmony.

Transformation Goal

After the third initiation, the mental body is purified and fully developed. There is conscious freedom of thought, we become creative and find that thoughts can produce powerful changes. We experience for ourselves that: "A man is what he thinks in his heart". On the mental level, we perceive ourselves as thinkers who can make decisions about our own world. Here we are free to choose how we think, if at all. We can say "yes" or "no", we can make our own decisions and choices. We learn to implement the "Law of Rejection", as Alice Bailey described it in *A Treatise on White Magic*" (8). In this way, we are able to create a new world with the power of our thoughts. Now as teachers we can inspire other people with our knowledge and words, and bring about changes. Our maturity and spiritual potential allow us to influence others and lead them up the "mountain of enlightenment".

Paradigm Shift

There is also fallout from this transformation process in the collective. There are currently many changes afoot on the mental level, and a paradigm shift, in which old values are no longer important. They are doubted, questioned and rejected. Battles take place on the mental level, there is much discussion, doubting, criticising and verbal attacking of others. Some people can be so moved by doubt that they lose their grip and orientation in this mental crisis, they become fanatical and run the risk of enforcing their ideas. Their loss of ethical and human principles means that they get lost in relativism. All previous standards and values are trampled underfoot – religion, materialism, friendship. These people usually have no principles and are no longer interested in doing something for the good of the whole; they only want to enforce their own ideas. Nowadays, such conflicts are commonplace. Religious battles take place everywhere. We only have to think of racism, extreme right-wing radicalism and various types of fundamentalism.

Sun-Pluto Transformation

Evolution also provides the necessary compensation here. The transformation goes from the Sun to Pluto. When we have achieved everything we want and the little ego identifies with successful experiences, it takes what has been achieved as its own merit. The exaggerated Sun ego is then in danger of becoming overblown. The bigger it feels, the easier it is for Pluto to transform and reduce it, and the further it can fall. This transformation crisis involves bending oneself to the inner image of Pluto, the conscience, pneuma, divine will – and relinquishing the crown of the arbitrary Sun ego.

Cause

In astrology, problems on the mental level can be found in corresponding elements of the horoscope. For example: lack of air temperament, 3/9 tensions, Sagittarius/Gemini position, many green aspects (quincunx and semi-sextile), the ego planets Sun, Moon and Saturn combined with the intelligence planets Mercury, Jupiter and Uranus. Crises appear when the age point activates one of these planets or when transits by the slow-moving spiritual planets Uranus, Neptune, Pluto form a conjunction or opposition to them.

Month image from the Fresco cycle by Giotto

4. Rules for Interpreting the Planets

Introduction
• The Planetary Level • Energy from the Centre of Being •
• Tools for Self-Actualisation • Disposition and Behaviour •
• The Aspect Pattern • The Ego Planets •
• The Moon Nodes • Interpretation in the Zodiac Signs •

Planetary Rulers in the Zodiac Signs
• Sun in Leo • Moon in Cancer • Mars in Aries and Scorpio •
• Venus in Taurus and Libra • Mercury in Gemini and Virgo •
• Jupiter in Sagittarius and Pisces • Saturn in Capricorn and Aquarius •

Interpretation Rules
• 15 Points • Special Planetary Positions •
• According to Planetary Table • Aspects in the Columns •
• Unaspected Planets • Tension Rulers • 15 Point List (Einstein) •
• House Position • Sign/House Distinction • Four Main Criteria •
• Combinations • Example Horoscopes •
• Attribution of Planets to Aspects • Planets in Aspect Figures •

Aspect Colours on Planets
• Single-Coloured Aspects • Missing Colours •
• House Horoscope • Conjunctions • Three-Coloured Aspects •

Two-Coloured Aspects
a) blue-red, b) red-green, c) blue-green
• Sun • Moon • Saturn • Mercury • Venus •
• Mars • Jupiter • Uranus • Neptune • Pluto •

Planetary Connections
Interpretation in Keywords
• Sun Aspects • Moon Aspects • Saturn Aspects •
• Mercury Aspects • Venus Aspects • Mars Aspects •
• Jupiter Aspects • Spiritual Aspects •

Planetary Interpretation on Three Levels
• The Three Levels: 1. Body, 2. Feeling, 3. Thinking •
• The Ten Planets at the Three Levels •

Ptolemaic Planetary Sequence
• Year Rulers • Days of the Week •

Introduction

The Planetary Level

In the holistic interpretation of the planets, their position in the horoscope should always be taken into account. If we divide the chart into five layers, we can see immediately that the planets have a priority position in the inner circle. They connect our inner nature to our outer nature. Their central position in the horoscope means that they touch on all elements and layers. This is why interpretation of the planets entails knowledge and understanding of the whole horoscope with all its elements on different levels, plus knowledge of both the psychological and spiritual contexts. The latter becomes clear when we include the centre of being, the central circle, as the fifth level.

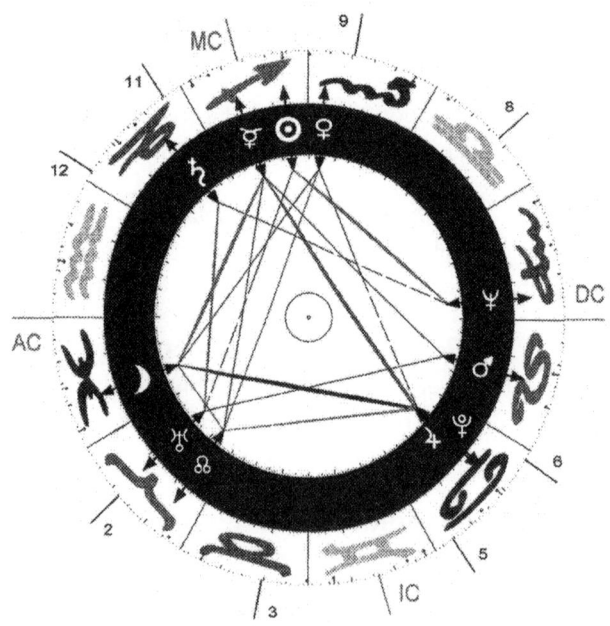

Planetary Level

Energies from the Centre of Being

Our centre of being is symbolically represented by the circle in the centre of the horoscope. Here the inner self or soul acts as the root of our being. This creative force gives birth to the personal self, sustains it during an incarnation and then draws it back into itself again. It can be compared to the hub of a wheel, where all the spokes – body, mind and feelings – converge. We always leave this central circle empty, thus respecting a level of freedom where astrology stops. We can imagine that life energies pour into the horoscope from this circle and stimulate and supply energy to the planets, which are then used by the self as organs of expression. For their part, the planets receive energies through the cosmic qualities of the zodiac signs from universal space, which they combine with the qualities of the individual itself and act on the environment through the house system. It is an eternally pulsating process of energy exchange. The planets are essential functional bodies with which we make contact with the environment and transfer the energy of the soul. They are our life organs that we use to perceive the world and experience and consciously act on it. They help us to develop and achieve our goals. We must use them consciously in order to achieve self-actualisation and success in the world.

Tools for Self-Actualisation

Looked at in this way, the planets are primary tools for self-actualisation. Someone who has studied the planets thoroughly and is interested in his own further development can achieve many things in life by consciously using the qualities of the planets. People's actions are normally determined by their environment and the necessities of survival. But the reverse is also possible, whereby we ourselves determine what we do and do not want to do. By focussing on a goal with complete conviction, we can use the planets to achieve it. With the necessary astrological knowledge, we can specifically and deliberately deal with the life tasks in the individual houses. We can even use our creative intelligence to change the world to conform to our own ideas, as long as our goals are in line with the will of our innermost nature.

As independently minded individuals, we are capable of recognising the demands and determinants in the houses. If they do not correspond to our own goals, we can change, renew or reject them. We have freedom of choice to decide for ourselves whether or not we voluntarily accept the duties, tasks and work required in each house. This makes us creative and the planets become tools for our individual development. As such, according to their qualities, they enable us to react independently in specific areas of life and to act according to our intrinsic nature. This freedom goes with the ability to take full responsibility for ourselves and our fellow men, and grows as we gain independence and take control of our own lives.

Disposition and Behaviour

This autonomous, self-contained individuality that is free to form relationships as it pleases, is also dependent on the distinction between sign and house, between inner will and outer duty, or disposition and behaviour. The signs of the zodiac indicate our hereditary disposition, what we were born with; the planetary positions in the houses show how we have been conditioned, the influence of our environment and behaviour patterns. They are two basic expressions of the planetary qualities that we must be aware of for constructive transfer within the houses.

Our dispositions, which are revealed by the position of the planets in the signs, give us all the chance to act as we see fit in the houses. A major part of this is the knowledge of how the different qualities work together. As long as we only listen to what the environment tells us and wants us to do, we cannot turn inwards to find out "who I really am, what do I really want and what am I really capable of?" Only when we ask ourselves these questions do we start to consciously make use of the planets as tools of our inner will within the houses.

The Aspect Pattern

The integration of the aspect pattern as a whole is also part of the self-actualisation process and holistic interpretation of the planets. Aspect patterns are formed by the position of the planets at birth. They represent the interrelationship of all the planets, and tell us something about the structure of our consciousness and life motivation. The aspect pattern is a deeper layer within us, situated immediately around the centre of being. We can access it by introspection and intensive psychological work on ourselves. This requires a serious and honest striving for self-knowledge, introspection, independent research and experimentation, the gathering of experiences and also the recognition of our own limitations and shortcomings.

If someone has already deliberately tried to use their planets, they will have suffered defeat as well as success and from that have learnt how to deal more constructively and creatively with these forces. They will have learnt a lot about themselves and realised from introspection the true nature of their being. The further inwards we go, the less we are able to abide by rules. This inner dimension is mostly closed to the intellect. Aspect patterns are formed by the groupings of planets and do not function according to the laws that we have learnt for the signs and houses, but to other laws. In *Aspect Pattern Astrology* (21), we describe the aspect pattern as a deep motivational level that leads us to the inner purpose of our being. Those interested can refer to this book.

The Ego Planets

The three planets Sun, Moon and Saturn represent an important ego-forming factor in the individuation process. These three planets are shown in red in the horoscope, enabling us to recognise the personality structure immediately. Their position reveals significant characteristics of the personality, e.g. whether it can assert itself in life, or will be controlled by external influences. The ego planets Sun, Moon and Saturn have a defining role in the aspect pattern and show their influence within the structure of consciousness. Some control an aspect figure and set the tone; others are not included in the aspect pattern, stand alone and are difficult to integrate into the whole.

The Moon Nodes

Although the ascending Moon Node is not a planet, it is shown in the horoscope as it represents a point of advancement for personal and spiritual development. We include it in the aspect pattern so that it remains active in the consciousness. Our book *Moon Node Astrology* (18), deals with the Moon Node and its importance in the horoscope.

Interpretation in the Signs of the Zodiac

As already mentioned, the sign of the zodiac in which a planet lies is always significant. The signs indicate hereditary dispositions and as such the deep inner pattern, which allows the planetary quality to react in a quite specific way. One could say that a Venus in the sign of Leo wears "Leo glasses", i.e. it expresses itself in the manner of Leo. How the basic character of a planet can be used in life also depends on its sign. For example, Mars in the fire sign of Aries will react fierily and spontaneously and always be ready for action; whereas in the water sign of Pisces, it is passive and observant. So the sign says something about how the basic planetary qualities are modified.

It simplifies things to define the sign in which a planet lies according to its cross quality and temperament. We know that each sign is a specific combination of cross and temperament. This combination can play an important role in the interpretation of the planets concerned as a motivation or a basic need. In the process, we should not forget that the sign position allows a first approach to the planets. It is helpful to know which planets rule which zodiac sign – when a planet is situated in the sign it rules, the latter is strongly emphasised.

Planetary Rulers in the Zodiac Signs

As you can see in the diagram below, all of the planets rule two zodiac signs, apart from Sun, Moon and the three spiritual planets. Claudius Ptolemy (25) described this system in his book *Tetrabiblos*. The axis of symmetry between Cancer/Leo and Capricorn/Aquarius is important. The planets are evenly distributed around all the signs. Following Cancer with Moon and Leo with Sun, Mercury rules Gemini and Virgo, then Taurus and Libra are ruled by Venus, Mars rules Aries and Scorpio, Jupiter rules Pisces and Sagittarius and finally Saturn rules Aquarius and Capricorn. On the outer edge of the circle, the three spiritual planets are situated in the signs to which they are attributed.

Planetary Rulers

These planetary rulers often lead us to talk about the Mars signs Aries and Scorpio, the Venus signs Taurus and Libra, etc. These characteristics of the signs are influenced by the planets as well as by cross quality and temperament. In the interpretation of signs, these three factors can be distinguished as follows: 1st the cross, which indicates basic motivation, 2nd the temperament, which determines behaviour, and 3rd the planetary ruler, which passes on some of its features to the sign. Ruling planets are therefore a third factor in interpretation.

According to Alice A. Bailey, every sign also has an esoteric ruler, which functions on the level of consciousness and determines the developmental goal of the transformation from the exoteric to the esoteric planetary ruler. You can read more about this in *Reflections and Meditations on the Signs of the Zodiac* (20).

Sun in Leo

The Sun reigns supreme in the fire sign of Leo. It feels as though the world revolves around it. A Leo Sun casts a spell on people to try out its charisma on them. It is self-confident and gives others its inner security and solar energy, especially those it loves. It is generally very popular, is respected and admired, and feels secure and strong when it can be effective.

Moon in Cancer

The Moon can give free reign to all its feelings when in the water sign of Cancer. Sympathy and antipathy, attraction and rejection come and go in a continuous rhythm. Like water and the phases of the Moon, the feelings are never still, but continually changing. This makes the Moon moody and dependent on the environment. It needs people who love it, whom it can trust and who belong to it. It feels safe within the protection of the family unit.

Mars in Aries and Scorpio

Mars is at home in both Aries and Scorpio. That means that the overall character of both signs has a Martian component. While Mars in Aries has a fiery temperament, and therefore greater assertive powers, in the water sign of Scorpio the emotional element is stimulated and activated. In both signs it strengthens the power of resistance, withstands danger and attack, fights for its rights and is capable of vehemently repelling those who attack it.

Venus in Taurus and Libra

In Taurus with the earth element, Venus functions more sensually and closer to nature, while in the air temperament of Libra it influences the aesthetic and artistic areas. This distinction is often compared to that between "earthly" and "heavenly" love. Or to put it more mundanely: "Venus in Taurus enjoys good food, Venus in Libra likes nice clothes."

Mercury in Gemini and Virgo

In the air sign of Gemini, Mercury has a temperament that corresponds to its intellectual nature. Here it is in its element and can implement all of its above-mentioned qualities. In the earth sign of Virgo, it is concerned with formal and concrete things. It confers analytical abilities, which enable every detail to be seen and everything that is not in order to be identified.

Jupiter in Sagittarius and Pisces

In the fire sign of Sagittarius, Jupiter can fully implement its expansive qualities. It seeks goals that transcend the mundane and reveal higher connections. In the water sign of Pisces, the emotional element of Jupiter imparts loving and all-comprehending insight. It puts itself out for those in need and usually finds a solution.

Saturn in Capricorn and Aquarius

In the earth sign of Capricorn, Saturn deals with harsh realities. It wants to conquer matter, can eliminate obstacles and possesses concrete abilities with which to achieve its goals. In the air sign of Aquarius, Saturn seeks stability in ideas. It constructs an intellectual model that gives it security. It holds on to this until Uranus, the new ruler, shows it the error of its ways (Saul-Paul effect).

Interpretation Rules

In looking at the rules for interpretation of the planets in the horoscope, we want to concentrate on the most important ones, which can be used by both students of astrology and amateurs. When we consider the position of a planet in the chart, we first define the special quality as described in the previous chapter. We already know that the specific ability that the planet embodies is influenced and modified by other factors, namely by the zodiac sign, the house and the aspects. For further differentiation, we can also ascertain strong or weak positioning of a planet within sign or house, as well as various other combinations and features which allow an individual reading. There are also other rules that enable detailed psychological definition, but these are mainly used by professional experts.

In the following we give an overview of how the 15 rules are used. The sequence corresponds to a systematic didactic syllabus. The horoscope reading generally starts with the aspect pattern, where as mentioned above, the planets are connected in special aspect figures that make a holistic statement. These points appear at the end of the list.

15 Points

1. **To which vertical column of the planetary table [page 15] does the planet belong?**
   Left: feminine. Right: masculine. Centre: neutral.

2. **Which level of the planetary table does it lie on?**
   Bottom: instinctive level. Centre: personality. Top: transpersonal.

3. **In which area of the horoscope is it situated?**
   Upper or lower, right or left.

4. **Which of the 6 axes does it lie on?**
   1/7 Encounter Axis, 2/8 Possession Axis,
   3/9 Thinking Axis, 4/10 Individuality Axis,
   5/11 Relationship Axis, 6/12 Existence Axis.

5. **Which Sign is it in?**

a) Cross:	Cardinal	♈	♋	♎	♑
	Fixed	♉	♌	♏	♒
	Mutable	♊	♍	♐	♓
b) Temperament:	Fire	♈	♌	♐	
	Earth	♉	♍	♑	
	Air	♊	♎	♒	
	Water	♋	♏	♓	

6. **Which degree of the Sign does it lie on?**
   a) Strong in the middle around 12°.
   b) Weak at the beginning or end of the Sign.

7. **Which House is it in?**

a) Cross:	Cardinal	1st	4th	7th	10th
	Fixed:	2nd	5th	8th	11th
	Mutable	3rd	6th	9th	12th
b) Temperament:	Fire	1st	5th	9th	
	Earth	2nd	6th	10th	
	Air	3rd	7th	11th	
	Water	4th	8th	12th	

8. **What is its position in the House?**
   a) House Cusp (HC), Balance Point (BP), Low Point (LP).
   b) Cardinal, fixed, mutable zone.

9. **What change does it experience from Sign to House?**
   a) Cross: cardinal, fixed, mutable.
   b) Temperament: fire, earth, air, water.

10. **Does it lie in an intercepted Sign?**
    The Sign has no House cusps.
    The environment cannot reach it, and it cannot get out.

11. **Does it lie in a Sign with two House cusps?**
    The environment is very demanding and it is often overstressed.

12. **With which planets it is connected?**
    Are they compatible or incompatible?

13. **Is it part of an aspect pattern?**
    a) Does it have an extra figure?
    b) Is it unaspected and alone?
    c) Is it a tension ruler?

14. **Which aspect figure does it belong to?**
    a) linear, b) triangular, c) polygonal.
    d) red, blue, green figure.

15. **Which aspect colours does it have?**
    a) one colour: red, blue, green.
    b) two colours: red-blue, red-green, blue-green.
    c) three colours: red-blue-green.

Special Planetary Positions

According to the Planetary Table

The planetary table on page 15 is a tried and tested aid to interpreting planetary positions in a horoscope. Every student should familiarise themselves with this table. It is a good idea to study it until it is firmly ingrained in your memory and you can recall it at will. It is a good guide to the different elements involved in interpretation

Aspects in the Columns

Planets in the same column are linked by quality and motivation. When connected by aspect, they complement or support each other, although they can also function and react differently. For example, if Saturn is conjunct Venus, the female image is coloured by Saturn and often corresponds to the mother image. This conjunction has a strongly feminine function, which allows all that is good and beautiful to be preserved and cared for.

Where planets form aspects to planets in other columns, you have to consider whether their qualities contradict or support each other.

For example, if planets from the masculine column form aspects to planets from the neutral central column, the contradiction can be strong. With a Mars/Neptune conjunction for example, Mars imposes qualities upon Neptune that are alien to it. Mars stimulates the ideal visions of Neptune and magnifies them, which is why in classical astrology this is called the "Idealist Aspect". In the horoscope of a woman, this conjunction can indicate dependency on the masculine principle, which causes problems in the process of self development. When there is a connection between planets, you should always check whether or not they are compatible according to the planetary table.

Unaspected Planets

Some planets are not aspected at all; they are not part of an aspect pattern. Such solitary or unaspected planets function autonomously, i.e. for themselves alone. They can evolve entirely according to their own nature without being influenced or disturbed by other planets. For example, someone with an unaspected Venus can be a particularly Venusian person whose character abounds with the main features of this planet. Women with an unaspected Mars are often masculine, but this planet can also be delegated to the environment. Usually they look for a man who "clicks" with this Mars (14). In an advanced stage of development, an unaspected planet aids spiritual development. It can bring a special talent that is visible to all and which contributes to the brilliance of the personality. Many artists have an unaspected Venus, writers an unaspected Mercury and politicians a solitary Pluto. (You can read more about this in *Aspect Pattern Astrology* page 54 (21).

Tension Rulers

In some horoscopes one planet is situated opposite the main group of planets. We call these planets "tension rulers". Empirical evidence shows us that such a planet dominates all the others; its influence is "superimposed" on them. When you discover a tension ruler in an aspect pattern, you should relate it to the life of the owner of the horoscope. This is usually very informative and enables you to learn a lot about astrology. However, you should understand the meaning of the planets that act as tension rulers on all three levels (physical, emotional and mental).

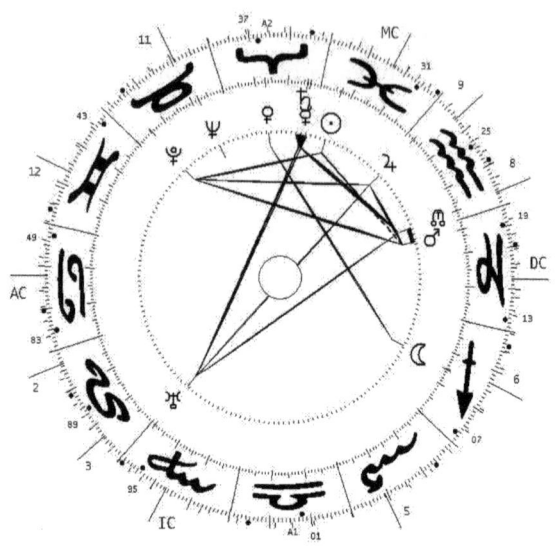

Albert Einstein
14.3.1879, 11.30, Ulm/Germany

In the case of Albert Einstein, Uranus is a tension ruler as it lies opposite the main group of planets in the upper space of the horoscope. It is situated at the balance point of the 3rd house, at the start of the sign of Virgo and in opposition to Jupiter. The 3/9 axis, the so-called thinking axis, therefore receives particular emphasis. The Projection Triangle also considerably strengthens Einstein's intellectual ability and Uranus as tension ruler allowed him to discover unforeseen things. His Theory of Relativity changed the world view of physics and philosophy. This venture into new dimensions of thought, signalled by Uranus as tension ruler, brought him worldwide fame. Here we can clearly see the powerful effect of a tension ruler in the horoscope.

15 Point List (Einstein)

For Einstein's horoscope, we go through the sequence of 15 points for the Sun.

1. **To which vertical column of the planetary table does the planet belong?**
   Right side, masculine.
2. **Which level of the planetary table does it lie on?**
   Middle level, Ego.

3. **In which area of the horoscope is it situated?**
   At the top in the Conscious space.
4. **Which of the 6 axes does it lie on?**
   4/10 individuality axis.
5. **Which Sign is it in?**
   Pisces   a) mutable   b) water.
6. **Which degree of the Sign does it lie on?**
   24 degrees Pisces, relatively weak.
7. **Which House is it in?**
   10th House   a) cardinal   b) earth.
8. **What is its position in the House?**
   Cardinal area 10th House, public efficiency.
9. **Which change does it experience from Sign to House?**
   a) cross: mutable/cardinal.
   b) temperament: water/earth.
10. **Does it lie in an intercepted Sign?**
    No.
11. **Does it lie in a Sign with two House cusps?**
    No.
12. **With which planets it is connected?**
    Masculine: Mars, Pluto.
13. **Is it part of an aspect pattern?**
    Yes.
14. **Which aspect figure does it belong to?**
    Talent triangle.
15. **Which aspect colours does it have?**
    Blue.

House Position

Point 8 "Its position in the House" is often ambiguous. We would like to explain briefly once more what the astrological houses really are and where they originate from in the horoscope (16). Technically they start at the ascendant, and the horoscope is divided into 12 parts going in an anticlockwise direction, with each one corresponding to a particular area of life. As you know, the ascendant is the zodiac sign that is rising on the eastern horizon at the moment of birth. To calculate the ascendant we need the exact time and place of birth. Based on this, the positions of the ten planets and the Moon Node are calculated and plotted on the chart.

To be able to judge whether a planet is in a strong or weak position in a house, we have to get acquainted with a few more rules. Most people know that it is through the houses that we are moulded by our environment. Here we learn to cope with life and to deal with a variety of tasks. The position within the house tells whether the environment helps or hinders us, or whether we get on well with others or not, so it is important that this position of a planet is accurately calculated.

Sign/ House Distinction

First of all we investigate the similarities and differences between signs and houses. We differentiate between the sign position as the hereditary disposition that we take for granted ("nature"), while in the houses we can change something through the influence of our education ("nurture"). Once we see acquired compulsions as unnecessary, we want to liberate ourselves from them. The zodiac signs can also be interpreted; they reveal our inner talents and signal basic needs that are deeply rooted within us and which strive for actualisation. They act on a planet in the house in which it lies and show how the planet will act in that house. This is why the planets are very important switch points in the horoscope, where the interior world interacts with the exterior world (Sign and House). This difference is very important in the astrological evaluation. When we notice that a sign fits easily into a house, this complicity gives an indication that the effect of this planet will be positive. When sign and house are not compatible, this planet must always overcome a certain inhibition. You can read more about this in *Astrology and the Spiritual Path* (13).

The education or conditioning of a planet occurs in the houses. For more sophisticated analysis, you should consider in which zone of the house it lies: in the cardinal zone (cusp to balance point), in the fixed zone (balance to low point) or in the mutable zone (low point to next cusp). You can find detailed descriptions on this in Chapter 5.

It is also important to observe if the planet is positioned on or near one of the three points of the house: the house cusp (HC), the Low Point (LP) or the Balance Point (BP) (see *The Astrological Houses* (16)). This affects its ability to act outwards or inwards. The position of a planet in the house system is established using the intensity curve on the next page.

Four Main Criteria

The following four main criteria should be borne in mind for a differentiated interpretation of the planets. There are other subtle distinctions that can be used to calculate the strongest ego planet and

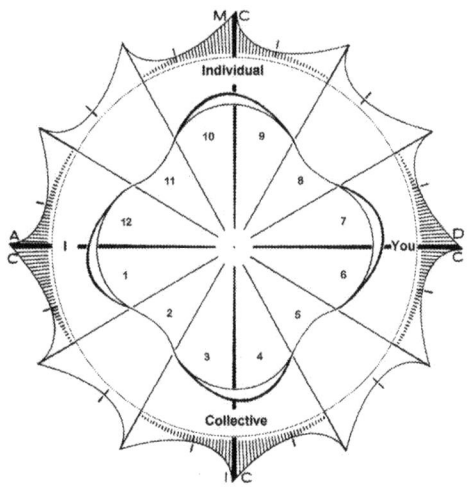

Intensity Curve

when there are integration problems, which are taught in the API School in special seminars. In general, the following main criteria are sufficient, in this order.

1st Criterion: House Position

Planets on a house cusp have the strongest effect on the environment and bring the ego the success it desires. Such a planet has a particularly strong reaction, perceives opportunities and can react accordingly. A planet on the low point is oriented inwards and is not easy to use successfully outwards. It serves the inner view and can reach the centre of being.

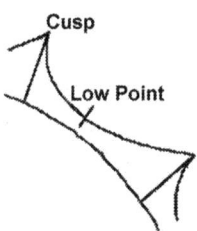

Cusp/Low Point

2nd Criterion: Sign Position

Planets near 12 degrees in a sign are strong; those at the borders of the sign are weak. The signs provide substance and hereditary disposition; they supply the planets with nutrition and energy. In the centre of the sign this effect is at its strongest, there is a lot of powerful genetic make-up, which intensively determines the character. The curve falls continuously and is at its weakest at the sign cusps. There the effect of the intrinsic nature is at its weakest, which is why other influences can have more effect.

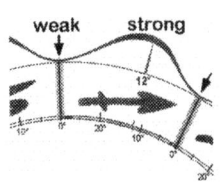

Sign Edge/12°

3rd Criterion: Aspect

For the third point, we look at the aspects that this planet makes. They are easy to see. The most aspected planet obtains all the energy of the aspect pattern. Of course, it is also important whether the colours of aspects to the planet are compatible or not. The following rule holds true: masculine planets are optimised by red aspects, feminine planets by blue aspects and neutral planets by green aspects.

4th Criterion: Position

The position in the horoscope is the fourth criterion. Unlike the other criteria, this is a qualitative distinction, not a quantitative one. The following rules apply for the ego planets: at the top the Sun is strong and Saturn is weak; at the bottom Saturn is strong and the Sun is weak. The central contact area of the horoscope best suits the Moon's nature. The other planets have special characteristics in each area.

Combinations

Strong and Weak Points in Sign and House

So, as far as the planets are concerned, we first evaluate their position in the houses and then in the signs. As mentioned above, the right house-sign combination is also important. First of all we determine whether the sign is compatible with the cross or temperament of the house, and secondly how the strong and weak points are distributed. We explain these combinations in more detail below.

Cusp and around 12° in Sign

Planets on the house cusp and also around 12 degrees in the sign have a strong potential; this is a strong position. A lot can be achieved with them; they possess sufficient energy and endurance and are noticed by the environment. Such planets can be successfully used to achieve goals.

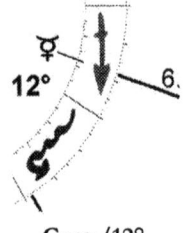

Cusp/12°

Low Point and Sign Border

A planet at the low point of a house and at the beginning or the end of a sign is in a very weak position. At the borders of the sign it receives little vital power and at the low point it can give little away to the outside. The environment does not notice it there; it is turned inwards. Such a planet mainly helps to orientate oneself inwards and to learn to listen to the voice of the soul.

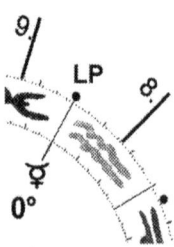

Low Point/
Sign Border

House Cusp and Sign Border

Another case is a planet on the house cusp and also on a sign border. This causes a certain excess stress: this person must demonstrate the ability of the planet although he does not have enough substance to live it convincingly in the long term. It can work for a while, but then it becomes stressful and unsatisfactory, and can lead to a breakdown.

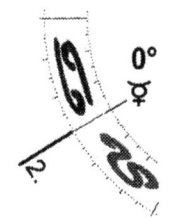

House Cusp/ Sign Border

Low Point and around 12° in Sign

This is the opposite of the above: a planet lies at the low point and in a strong area of the sign. This person receives enough energy from the sign for this planetary quality, but does not evoke an immediate response at the low point. However, he can withdraw into himself and get in touch with his centre of being. This provides him with energy and new life motivation so that he can confidently forego external success and set his own goals.

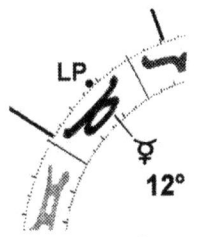

Low Point/ 12 Degrees

Intercepted Sign

A planet can also lie in a sign that has no house cusp. That affects all the house axes, because the opposite sign is also intercepted. If there is a planet there, its access to the environment is made more difficult. It can be used like a low point planet, i.e. for introspection. However, if one does aim outwards with it in order to gain approval, one will not be sufficiently noticed and will suffer accordingly. It is far better to use these planets for personal ends. We could even say that if this planet were protected and the environment could not access it, it would still be there for the self. In this way it quietly goes about developing its own interior world until its quality is needed.

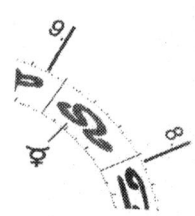

Intercepted Sign

Zodiac Sign with Two House Cusps

When a sign is intercepted, there are also always two signs containing two house cusps, which affects an entire axis. If there is a planet there, it will be in great demand by the environment. No sooner has it satisfied one end of the axis than it has to be ready to satisfy the other one. Such a planet enables the person concerned to do two or three things at the same time. If urgent necessities come up in the environment, he reacts immediately. Depending on planet and sign, he also feels overstressed and has difficulty relaxing. The planet's qualities will be very sought-after though, and can learn to cope with special tasks in the course of its development.

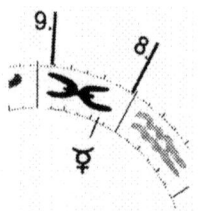

Zodiac Sign with two House Cusps

Example Horoscope

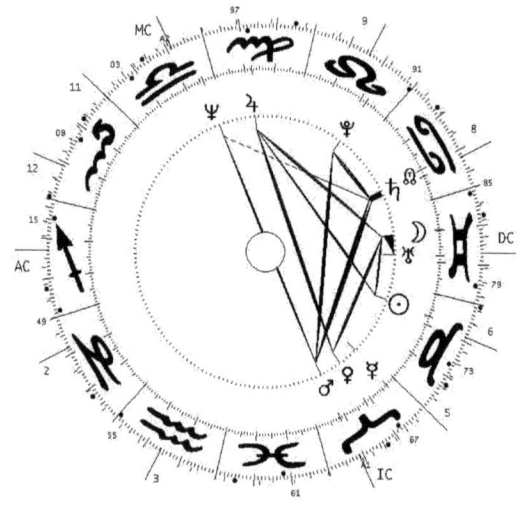

Psychiatric Nurse
13.5.1945, 21.30 St. Gallen/Switzerland

In the above horoscope there are several criteria to be considered. At first sight we are struck by the fact that all the planets are situated on the You-side. This is therefore a person who experiences herself intensively through the environment and is barely interested in her own self on the empty I-side. This person is selfless and does everything expected of her. She wants to make others happy.

Jupiter lies at the low point of the ninth house in the sign of Virgo, which has no house cusp. This planet cannot act directly outwards: first of all it lies exactly on the low point and secondly the sign is intercepted. Jupiter also has no great ambitions in the sign of Virgo; it wants to serve others, it supports and heals. It radiates three colours and is linked to the Moon and Venus by a learning triangle. The inner motivation, the serving of Virgo, can be directed very well towards others along this aspect. Jupiter, with its balancing and benevolent quality, can therefore be experienced via the planets connected by the aspect pattern, despite the intercepted nature of the sign.

The 4/10 axis has two house cusps, and great demands are placed on this woman there. The 4th house is particularly busy, occupied by Venus, Mercury and stressed Mars; it can be concluded from this that she is very active in this area in a clinic. Mercury is unaspected. This represents combinational reasoning and is not attached to the aspect pattern; it is therefore hard for the consciousness to control it. It reacts spontaneously and often uncontrollably.

The position of Mercury in the cardinal fire sign Aries increases the spontaneity and the stress area before the fifth house cusp does not allow Mercury to rest either. Here she wants to be creative and has trouble communicating her thoughts in a focused way. This is reflected in the fact that she talks at the wrong time; she interrupts others or cannot listen to them. The horoscope owner is a psychiatric nurse who has learnt how to give orders. Her Taurus Sun on the sixth house cusp incorporates her own character and inner strength in her work. Uranus/Moon on the You-point activates her contact-making, stimulates other people and gives her courage and new ideas. She gets very involved in her work and has helped a great many people.

Attribution of the Planets to the Aspects

Another attribution is the compatibility of the quality of the aspects with that of the planets. This corresponds to the Aspect Theory that we have described in depth in *Aspect Pattern Astrology* (21). To refresh your memory, here are the affinities again:

☌	Conjunction:	Sun/Moon aspect
⚺	Semi-Sextile:	Mercury aspect
✶	Sextile:	Venus aspect
□	Square:	Mars aspect
△	Trine:	Jupiter aspect
⚻	Quincunx:	Saturn aspect
☍	Opposition:	Saturn aspect

So, when Jupiter receives a trine, this aspect boosts its effect. If Venus receives a sextile, this likewise corresponds to its nature and augments its positive radiance. Conversely, a red aspect can provoke tensions and pressure to succeed that are alien to the Venus nature.

When sensitive planets like the Moon, Neptune, Jupiter and Mercury receive red aspects their original quality is changed. With the Sun, Mars, Pluto, Saturn and Uranus red aspects increase both productivity and enthusiasm.

One-Way Aspects

There are planets with aspects that are dashed on one side. Such aspects only work occasionally and are therefore weak. The cause of the one-sidedness lies in the orbs of the planets concerned. The aspect extends from the planet with the wider orb to the one with the narrower orb (e.g. a spiritual planet). That is why the aspect on the side of the latter is drawn as a dashed line.

Many people with one-way aspects find that they work when they feel well and strong. In situations of weakness such as stress, illness or mental problems, the aspect doesn't work at all. It therefore depends on the awareness of the person concerned as to whether a planet with a dashed line aspect is effective or not.

Planets in Aspect Figures

Most planets are part of some aspect figure. Here too the whole pattern and the associated planets must be taken into account in the interpretation. In a blue talent triangle, Jupiter functions according to its qualities, whereas in a red efficiency/achievement triangle it loses some of its beneficial effect and comes under pressure to succeed, which then changes its influence. This is why we have to ascertain whether or not a planet's qualities are compatible with an aspect figure.

We distinguish figures in terms of **colour** as follows:
1. Single-coloured aspect figures
2. Two-coloured aspect figures
3. Three-coloured aspect figures
4. Colour dominance
5. Missing colours

We distinguish figures in terms of **shape** and **colour** as follows:
1. Achievement figures are only red
2. Ambivalence figures are red-blue
3. Talent figures are only blue
4. Learning figures are red-blue-green
5. Irritation figures are red-green
6. Information figures are green-blue

You can read more about this in *Aspect Pattern Astrology* (21).

Aspect Colours on Planets

Aspect colours also influence the effect of the planets, so the planet quality can be strengthened, weakened or changed by the colour. The following list serves as a guide. The classification corresponds to the planetary table (page 15).

Sun, Mars, Pluto	Red aspects	Square, Opposition
Saturn, Venus, Uranus	Blue aspects	Trine, Sextile
Mercury, Jupiter, Moon, Neptune	Green aspects	Semi-sextile, Quincunx

In the first row we see the masculine planets, which react best to red aspects. In the second row are the feminine planets that suit the blue aspects, and on the third row are the neutral planets, which are compatible with the green aspects.

Single-Coloured Aspects

There are planets that are only aspected red, blue or green, which makes interpretation relatively easy. Red aspects are masculine and therefore geared to achievement, unlike blue aspects that are feminine-receptive and observant, whereas the green thinking aspects tend to be neutral.

Red Aspects   Square, Opposition

If a planet has only red aspects, the effect depends on correspondence with the above classification. A masculine planet can tolerate this dynamic well, a feminine planet is slightly irritated and for neutral planets red aspects cause contradictions. The sensitive planets can also experience increased sensitivity with red aspects.

A planet with only red aspects is often part of a linear figure, which has a cardinal quality and works predominantly as will impulses, even with a non-masculine planet. In a red efficiency triangle, many planets are also only aspected red; likewise in a red square. It also depends on the quality of the planets as to whether they can tolerate the pressure to achieve or experience a change in their quality.

Blue Aspects   Sextile, Trine

A uniquely **blue** aspected planet seeks harmony. Depending on whether it is masculine, feminine or neutral, either enjoyment, relaxation or adaptation will prevail. Blue aspects onto masculine planets (Sun, Mars, Pluto) diminish the performance level and readiness for action. A uniquely blue-aspected Venus heightens the need for harmony; it has trouble saying no and willingly does what it is asked. A solely blue aspected Mars is more circumspect in its activity, it reacts less to external impulses and requires an inner motivation to become galvanised.

Green Aspects   Semi-sextile, Quincunx

A uniquely **green** aspected planet informs itself before it acts. Too much hesitation can also bring insecurity or failure though. Indecision and waiting too long for better opportunities that often do not materialise cause projections and unfulfilled longings.

Missing Colours

To ascertain the effectiveness of a planet, it helps to start with the missing colours.

If blue is missing, this planet cannot relax, it is always full on and burns the candle at both ends. It gives off very restless vibes and has an irritating effect.

If green is missing, there is virtually no room for discussion with these planets. This person sees only two sides of a problem. Black and white thinking makes the exchange of ideas difficult.

If red is missing, the planet is less dynamic. According to the quality of the planet, it becomes sentimental, sensitive and sometimes unstable. It is almost completely lacking in drive and waits passively for opportunities to come from outside.

House Horoscope

Where there are missing colours and unaspected planets, the house horoscope should definitely be consulted. In the API school, it shows the background and the associated environmental influences. It is the horoscope that most clearly expresses the conditioning and behavioural influences of the educational collective (influence of the father, mother, siblings and environment). In this chart, the colours and aspects are often different from those in the natal chart, which shows that the person has acquired the corresponding behaviour. You can read more about house horoscopes and their interpretation in *Astrology and the Spiritual Path*, page 15 (13).

Conjunctions

If two, three or four planets are grouped together, we call it a conjunction. The qualities of these planets are latent in an embryonic state. They cannot act so easily by themselves; they need external help. They are often barely able to react to each other, which is why it is hard to tell them apart. They represent an embryonic potential in which much lies hidden; they are latent and can often lie dormant for a lifetime. To appreciate the extent of these forces, it is necessary to understand the functionality and meaning of these planets.

Interpretation is made easier by grouping the planets into masculine, feminine and neutral. If there are two masculine planets, the conjunction is considered to be red; with two feminine planets it is blue and with two neutral planets it is green. Planets from different columns can also form conjunctions. If, for example, the Sun forms a conjunction with Mercury, then the interpretation must be differentiated. When the Sun as an ego planet is in a close conjunction with the thinking planet Mercury, it will mainly be interested in things that directly concern itself and from which it can benefit.

If there are **three** planets, it is called a **bud** conjunction, because the number three is always connected with development and growth and allows something new to emerge, such as a particular characteristic.

Three-Coloured Aspects

A planet aspected with three colours has three possible modes of expression. The red aspect enables it to be active; the green enables it to reflect on its plans and to focus its powers on development. With the blue aspect it reaps the rewards of previous efforts. This constitutes an ongoing learning process. Planets aspected with three colours are involved in a developmental dynamic; they learn to perceive more and more sides of an issue. These planetary forces enable one to act cleverly and to do the right thing whatever the circumstances, particularly if they are part of a learning triangle. You can read more about this in *Aspect Pattern Astrology* pages 197-213 (21).

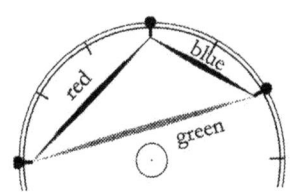

Two-Coloured Aspects
a) blue-red, b) red-green, c) blue-green

Sun

a) Blue-red aspects ☉
Trine, Sextile, Square, Opposition

With a blue-red aspected Sun, vitality is ambivalent; energy increases and then decreases again. In the "red phase", one is active, feels internal strength, can do the jobs that have to be done and achieve set objectives. This is followed by the "blue phase" in which the energy is interrupted. One should now force oneself to rest, in order to return to work refreshed with the red aspect. With a red-blue aspected Sun, it is advisable to live consciously by this rhythm. Depending on the sign, this works with varying degrees of success. In the cardinal cross, one uses up too much energy, in the fixed cross one has trouble getting things done and in the mutable cross the Sun's energies switch on and off more quickly, causing the person to feel slightly guilty and to use willpower to force himself back to work.

b) Red-green aspects ☉
Square, Opposition, Semi-Sextile, Quincunx

Blue is missing in this type of aspect, which we call irritation aspects. Such a Sun cannot rest, and can rarely sit down and enjoy life. It is always on the go and always has something to see to. This means that the vital energies are always working flat out and enables a lot of jobs to get done. But in the long term, one should not exhaust the vital solar energies too much as this can lead to a breakdown if there are no other blue aspects in the horoscope to provide a balance.

c) Blue-green aspects ☉
Trine, Sextile, Semi-Sextile, Quincunx

The self-awareness of the Sun is not strong; it is sensitive, shy, sometimes reserved and prefers to stay in the background. The sensitising effect of the blue-green aspect changes the Sun's self-awareness. Because red is missing, there is no necessity for a powerful demonstration of the ego. The person is modest and can also do things that others do not have the patience for. How self-awareness allows him to act in life depends largely on the cross and temperament qualities of the sign in which the Sun is placed; its place in the house system is also a factor.

Moon

a) **Blue-red aspects** ☽
   Trine, Sextile, Square, Opposition

The Moon is subject to a natural ebb and flow of the emotions, which is why blue-red aspects enable an active feeling of affection to very quickly change to the opposite. Sympathy and antipathy alternate, which is experienced as a continuous emotional roller coaster from one side to the other. This can lead to petulant and erratic behaviour in relationships, which is why the polarisation from active to passive should be experienced as a natural rhythm and care should be taken that this is acceptable to one's fellow men.

b) **Red-green aspects** ☽
   Square, Opposition, Semi-Sextile, Quincunx

We can quickly find out how this Moon feels by identifying the missing colour. That colour is blue, so this Moon cannot experience pleasure. It has trouble recuperating, as its emotional nature is overactive. This can appear as a frantic interest in the fate of others if it is on the You-side of the horoscope, but in a pronounced subjectivity if on the I-side, in which case interest revolves constantly around itself. The type of cross motivation is influential here too. In the cardinal cross there is constant emotional anticipation; in the fixed cross, one is greedy with the desire for possessions, and in the mutable cross one is constantly socialising and always on the go.

c) **Blue-green aspects** ☽
   Trine, Sextile, Semi-Sextile, Quincunx

Here the red aspect is missing; the Moon is sensitive, calm, passive and evasive. There is often no strong desire for conversation or human contact. It is observant and prefers to listen. If it lies in a cardinal sign, sensitivity has a favourable effect on interpersonal skills; such a person has an active interest in emotional matters, but the ego is not too demanding. In a fixed sign, it can even be perceived as being dull or boring, whereas in a mutable sign, the affectionate attitude to others makes for happy relationships. That is why such a Moon is suited to the helping professions, because it is more concerned with the needs of the You than with its own.

Saturn

a) Blue-red aspects ♄
Trine, Sextile, Square, Opposition

Saturn also reacts inconsistently to this ambivalent colouring. It can tolerate red well, as this helps it to cope with physical reality. Blue aspects can strengthen Saturn's tendency to stagnate, making one want to sink into inactivity and let inertia take over. Saturn's tendency to react with feelings of guilt gives the necessary push to return to the red phase. The red-blue aspect to Saturn often causes an either-or attitude in the demand for material security. Its active participation is dependent on the satisfaction of its demands; when they are met, it can engage itself energetically.

b) Red-green aspects ♄
Square, Opposition, Semi-Sextile, Quincunx

In the long run this irritation aspect can weaken Saturn. As it represents physical self-awareness, the exploitation of the physical resources can often affect the health. If our body is constantly running flat out, rest can sometimes only come with illness brought on by overexertion. According to the sign and house, the missing blue is an ongoing source of discontent, and can often lead to a weakening of the autonomous nervous system. The person works hard but cannot enjoy the fruits of his labours.

c) Blue-green aspects ♄
Trine, Sextile, Semi-Sextile, Quincunx

With the missing red, Saturn can become very refined. The sensitive aspect makes it receptive to the physical charisma of others. These people are unable to protect themselves adequately from everything that bombards them. They immediately sense the needs of others and understand their feelings. In the helping professions, they possess the ability to provide what is lacking. They not only react sensitively to physical needs, their own physicality is also invigorated by an awareness of health issues. There is often a deficiency of antibodies, which means that one has to take care of oneself.

Mercury

a) Blue-red aspects
Trine, Sextile, Square, Opposition

The ambivalent Mercury causes fluctuations in the mental process. It is usually polarised; either something is good and right, or it is wrong. It knows that there are always two sides to every story, which leads it to change its mind frequently. The red aspects make it active; it participates in the environment and is inquisitive and alert. When the blue phase sets in, it becomes calm, uninterested and tired. In the red phase, Mercury jumps to hasty conclusions and can easily make mistakes because it is too impatient to wait for results. These must then be corrected in the following blue phase.

b) Red-green aspects
Square, Opposition, Semi-Sextile, Quincunx

A red-green aspected Mercury constantly stimulates the mind. It is interested in anything and everything and is always collecting new information without going any deeper. It is into everything and can get on others' nerves. Because blue is missing, it cannot rest, must always have the last word and cannot wait calmly and level-headedly for the fruit of rational thought. There can also be occasional sleep disturbances, because it is hard to switch off from the mercurial circular thinking.

c) Blue-green aspects
Trine, Sextile, Semi-Sextile, Quincunx

There is no red in this case, so Mercury becomes very sensitive and receptive. Observation reveals that a neutral planet tolerates this type of aspect well, a masculine planet's dynamism is diminished and a feminine one feels particularly good. A blue-green aspected Mercury absorbs many things effortlessly; it is open but reacts mainly to external commands and not of its own volition. Depending on sign, mercurial thinking can be slowed down by the absence of red aspects and break down under pressure to achieve, particularly in the case of sensitive children.

Venus

a) Blue-red aspects ♀

Trine, Sextile, Square, Opposition

The ambivalent Venus is dependent on likes and dislikes. It feels more at home with the blue aspects as it can abandon itself and leave activity to other people. It can sometimes take a long time for the red aspect to take effect. Venus's need for harmony means that it does not willingly engage in conflict, as this red experience is unpleasant for Venus. Ultimately it will appreciate that it cannot avoid the conflicts of the red aspect, and instead has to learn to face them. By nature it wants enjoyment, is passive, likes comfort and shuns activity. Decisions and conflicts are put off until situations come to a head. This is why the ambivalent red-blue also causes moody behaviour, which can be difficult for others to understand. Venus's alternating activity and passivity can even be used for creative ends. Many artists have this type of aspect; although it puts them under a lot of psychological stress, it is precisely this contradiction that stimulates them to renewed efforts.

b) Red-green aspects ♀

Square, Opposition, Semi-Sextile, Quincunx

Venus with the irritation aspects goes to a great deal of trouble to surround itself with beautiful things. It puts a lot of energy into making sure that everything runs smoothly. As blue is absent, it is hard to satisfy. Its demands on other people, its activity and sensitivity produce unrest and conflict in the environment. Its need for cosiness, pleasure and comfort are never met. However, the over-stimulation of the aesthetic sensibilities means that the feminine cannot be enjoyed. It is always in a hurry to get what it wants, thereby causing friction and tension, which it then actively tries to eliminate. It very rarely manages to restore the harmony it desires though. A tendency to allergies has also been observed in the case of a red-green Venus,.

c) Blue-green Aspects ♀

Sextile, Trine, Semi-Sextile, Quincunx

This sensitive Venus aspect affects the aesthetic sensibilities and makes the person feminine and cuddly, even men. Such people are therefore suited to the healing professions where patience and sensitivity are required. They are content with small steps and do not expect spectacular success. Whereas blue aspects inspire great efforts to make things harmonious and beautiful, the green phase causes everything to be questioned again. Stability and the need for comfort, but also the attempts to be good and kind, are inconsistent and depend on environmental influences.

Mars

a) Blue-red aspects ♂

Trine, Sextile, Square, Opposition

With a red-blue aspected Mars, the flow of energy and the vitality are ambivalent. When full of inner strength and well-motivated, one's work can be completed. There then follows a kind of trough, where energies come to a standstill. One must then relax to be able to return to work fully refreshed with the red aspect. Absent here is the colour green, which would have been able to keep the energies moving as a kind of conscious connecting mental energy. Mars as engine and source of energy is also subject to the alternation of activity and passivity with this type of aspect. Mars has trouble tolerating this, which is why it still tries to be active, even in the rest phase. In relationships, the ambivalence causes one to fluctuate between being aggressive and peace-loving. According to the sign, in the case of Mars, the planet of drives, the "blue phase" means the enjoyment of pleasure until exhaustion sets in and the red phase comes round again. The relationship with sign quality, cross and temperament, must also be explored in interpretation.

b) Red-green aspects ♂

Square, Opposition, Semi-Sextile, Quincunx

With this type of aspect, the missing blue means that Mars is constantly stressed and producing new energies. It is unable to rest and is always ready for action. According to sign and house, it pushes itself to excel and its readiness for action enables it to master the most difficult situations. Mars the engine has a great deal of energy at its disposal. This is a very dynamic position that also characterises top athletes. But the lack of rest due to the absent blue can lead to unforeseen loss of energy or accidents.

c) Blue-green aspects ♂

Trine, Sextile, Semi-Sextile, Quincunx

With a blue-green aspect, Mars becomes calm and gentle, which means that it is well-suited to delicate work. Aspects like these refine the effect of the planets; hard, masculine planets like Mars in particular become calmer in certain situations and can wait until they are called upon. In the case of insufficient activity, debility can sometimes result from this type of aspect. At times, one lacks the motivation to do things and is left twiddling one's thumbs. In these phases, some people can only pull themselves together if there are really important things to do, or – according to the sign – their helping nature is called upon.

Jupiter

a) Blue-red aspects ♃
Trine, Sextile, Square, Opposition

Sensory perceptions are ambivalent. Sometimes everything is seen clearly and accurately, and other times the person is unobservant and does not really look properly. In the red phase, there is active and alert observation and evaluation of the environment; in the blue phase, Jupiter can be calm, comfortable and at times somehow switched off. Judgement is also variable with this type of aspect. What was previously found to be pleasant can suddenly be no good. The either-or nature of this combination of aspects often gives a tendency to opposing judgements. Here contexts can provide a benchmark and thinking should be holistically oriented.

b) Red-green aspects ♃
Square, Opposition, Semi-Sextile, Quincunx

If Jupiter lacks the blue aspect with which it has a natural affinity, it loses much of its pleasant, benevolent effect. Judgement is usually one-sided, this person places too must trust in subjective sensory impressions, which do not give him the whole picture. His judgements are usually rash and he is too quick to jump to conclusions that are inadequate as the blue aspect is missing. Mistakes or errors frequently occur, which he himself is unable to acknowledge or admit to. According to the sign, a red-green Jupiter can be constantly irritated and energetically defend its rights. Others are always seeking new sensations and are never satisfied.

c) Blue-green aspects ♃
Trine, Sextile, Semi-Sextile, Quincunx

With these sensitive aspects, the absence of red makes Jupiter refined and benevolent, understanding and patient. People really trust it, as they sense that it does not make rash judgements and is sensitive to other people and their weaknesses. It is not at all polemical, but flexible, wise and cultivated in its dealings with others. Occasionally it evokes caring feelings in appropriately disposed people around it who provide support and help.

Uranus

a) Blue-red aspects ⛢
Trine, Sextile, Square, Opposition

With a red-blue aspect, the revolutionary planet causes unpredictable activities and break-ups. There are rapid changes that are often reversed during the ensuing blue phase. What provides the courage for a breakthrough in the red phase can be regretted in the blue phase. As a feminine planet, Uranus has a basic need for security, which it wants to restore in the blue phase. "Two steps forward and one step back" would be a good definition. The environment is confronted again and again with this zig-zag movement, which it finds unsettling.

b) Red-green aspects ⛢
Square, Opposition, Semi-Sextile, Quincunx

Red-green aspects make Uranus very erratic and eccentric. It wants to deal with everything immediately and not put anything off. This person rarely deliberates for long and seldom experiences relaxation or enjoyment. The sensitive green thinking aspects can also be overwhelmed by the red aspects, which means that they too can act without due consideration. The creative thinking is often strange, sometimes brilliantly transcending the conventional, or it can be fanatical and one-sided. Some want to change the world at a stroke; they are very impatient and regularly overshoot the mark. Without a blue aspect they can hardly wait for their intuition to take effect.

c) Blue-green aspects ⛢
Trine, Sextile, Semi-Sextile, Quincunx

A sensitive Uranus cannot easily transfer the richness of its imagination because red is missing. But its creative, intuitive quality usually acts silently and the quality of its well-thought-out ideas is often astonishing. It "incubates" them until they are mature and then shares them with others so that anyone with a red aspect can put them into practice. It does not demand special treatment, but is generous and open. In many situations it is a catalyst that stimulates others to think and enjoys passing on its ideas. Many are only happy when they can sow seeds.

Neptune

a) Blue-red aspects ♆
Trine, Sextile, Square, Opposition

Neptune as the higher love ideal is uncomfortable with the ambivalent blue-red mindset. Neptune always wants to be in love and therefore finds red aspects hard to tolerate. Love is rarely compatible with pressure to achieve; the most it can do is want to help. This can be actively implemented during red phases, but it slackens off again during the blue phases. A blue-red aspected Neptune can only withstand demands to achieve until its strength runs out, which often happens abruptly in the blue phases as the ambivalent mindset is unrestricted by Neptune. Since Neptune is the principle that recognises no limits, it has trouble setting boundaries for itself; it is at the mercy of many things because it has no resistance to attack.

b) Red-green aspects ♆
Square, Opposition, Semi-Sextile, Quincunx

It goes without saying that without blue's calming effect, Neptune is subject to considerable stress. Its ideal of unconditional love leads it to devote itself to something or someone for a long time until all its energies are used up. This kind of dedication often brings with it a danger of overdoing it, which is why red-green aspects are also associated with Helper Syndrome. Many people burn themselves out and get to the point where they feel totally exhausted and exploited and do not even receive the praise they deserve. Their difficulty in setting their own boundaries leads to their reserves being used up and in some cases to a nervous breakdown.

c) Blue-green aspects ♆
Trine, Sextile, Semi-Sextile, Quincunx

These aspect colours are beneficial for Neptune; they promote its sensitive, healing influence. With the blue aspects it can dedicate itself devotedly to someone, listen to them and show its empathy. It can give love and act intelligently to alleviate the needs of others. The green thinking aspects indicate a high minded, idealistic desire for mankind's peaceful coexistence. These refined sensibilities are hard to put into practice in our competitive society, which is why it often feels misunderstood and powerless. But the longing for ideal love remains, even though it is more of a fantasy. This Neptune is very patient and forgiving, and even after disappointments can still open itself up to the basic principles of love.

Pluto

a) **Blue-red aspects**
   Trine, Sextile, Square, Opposition

   Pluto also reacts inconsistently to this ambivalent colouring. Red intensifies its willpower and strenuous efforts. Depending on the sign, red also increases the demand for power. Often Pluto can perform superhuman feats and bring about intensive developments. The blue usually remains in a state of rest; it is in a waiting position and strengthens Pluto's latent energies. In the blue phase, its demands for metamorphosis are often not noticed at all; only in the red phase does all that is repressed come to the surface and one is not left in peace until the change has taken place.

b) **Red-green aspects**
   Square, Opposition, Semi-Sextile, Quincunx

   Pluto has a particularly strong reaction to the irritation aspects. Red increases willpower and green provides ideas, motivation or information, which can accumulate thanks to Pluto's willpower. In many people this irritation encourages inner control and the readiness to obey a higher will. The irritation aspects strengthen the possibilities for metamorphosis. Pluto can direct its conversion energies like an arrow at that which is unwanted and which must be eliminated. That is why transformation crises are the order of the day for people with these aspects.

c) **Blue-green aspects**
   Trine, Sextile, Semi-Sextile, Quincunx

   Blue-green aspects make Pluto more sensitive and soften its intensity. Its demands for metamorphosis take place silently with no spectacular strokes of fate. It functions more according to the motto: "softly, softly catchee monkey…". This Pluto also radiates a gentle but constant conversion energy onto the environment, like a catalyst. The very presence of such a person can, depending on sign quality, have a metamorphosing or uplifting effect. Blue-green aspects usually leave Pluto in peace for a good while, and only when the age point projects a primary aspect onto it is one confronted with the metamorphosing conversion force and relatively old, ingrained habits can be discarded and changed because one has had the time to prepare for it.

Planetary Connections

In the list of planetary connections below, we have used keywords that should inspire you to work out your own interpretations. It applies not only to conjunctions, but to all types of aspect. A planet is often linked with more than one other planet, it just depends on the aspect figure in which it lies. The keyword-style listing is intended to give you some idea of the influence two planets have. You can arrive at accurate interpretations by considering the specific aspect and its colour, plus sign and house positions.

Interpretation in Keywords

Sun Aspects

☉/☽ reason and emotion, father-child-relationship
☉/♄ autonomy and responsibility, parenting
☉/☿ intellectual power and logic, expressiveness, subjective intelligence
☉/♀ awareness and aesthetic, warm-heartedness, need for harmony
☉/♂ vitality and energy, ego assertiveness and entrepreneurial spirit
☉/♃ expansion of potential, self-confidence and optimism
☉/♅ creativity, inventive talent, scientific and technical reasoning
☉/♆ commitment and love, understanding, readiness to help and to make sacrifices
☉/♇ will and power, professionalism, absoluteness and leadership qualities

Moon Aspects

☽/♄ anticipation and search for protection, mother-child relationship
☽/☿ emotional intelligence, psycho-logic, verbalisation of feelings
☽/♀ adaptation and love of harmony, creative expression, the well-adjusted child
☽/♂ compulsive love and courage, contradiction, anticipation and defiance
☽/♃ emotion and growth, interpersonal skills, benevolence, "*savoir-vivre*"
☽/♅ creativity and intuition, unpredictability, eccentric feelings, sarcasm
☽/♆ ideal love and belief in miracles, emotionally demanding, identification
☽/♇ claim to power over emotions, high anticipation, emotional rigidity

Saturn Aspects

♄/☿ objective intellect, the critic, mistrust
♄/♀ security and perfection, feeling for form, maternal feminine ideal
♄/♂ resistance and achievement, mastery of tasks, practical tests

♄/♃ harmony of form and content, demand for perfection, body awareness
♄/♅ the old and the new, Saul-Paul effect, destroying boundaries
♄/♆ reality and the removal of boundaries, idealisation of the mother, physical healing
♄/♇ tradition and renewal, spirit acting on matter, process of metamorphosis

Mercury Aspects

☿/♀ intelligence and harmony, balancing, artistic speech
☿/♂ judges and acts quickly, encouraging and loud speech, impatience
☿/♃ intellect and perception, holistic intelligence, symbolic thinking
☿/♅ intuitive, active mind, inspiration and imagination, seeing connections
☿/♆ deduction and intuition, sensitivity and dreaming of the future
☿/♇ intellectual power and rhetoric, demagogy, the power of words

Venus Aspects

♀/♂ readiness and initiative, male/female issues
♀/♃ holistic beauty, lust for life and pleasure
♀/♅ intuition and creativity, extravagance, artistic originality
♀/♆ devotion and desire to help, musical talent, transcendental art
♀/♇ perfection and synthesis, slavery and dependence

Mars Aspects

♂/♃ readiness to act, craftsmanship, achieving planned objectives
♂/♅ urge for change, impatience and hyperactivity, outbursts
♂/♆ desire to help and zest for action, inner guidance, idealist aspects
♂/♇ energy and power, obsession with achieving, stubbornness

Jupiter Aspects

♃/♅ abundance and originality, sensory alertness, looking forwards, sense of progress
♃/♆ development and transcendence, guardian angel motive and good faith
♃/♇ sensory acuteness and observation, keen insight and visionary foresight

Spiritual Aspects (Tasks for the Zeitgeist and Generation)

♅/♆ economy, business, technology, religion and the esoteric
♅/♇ spiritual male/female unions, global consciousness
♆/♇ personality and love ideals, synthesis, hippy or peace movement

Planetary Interpretation on Three Levels

It is an undisputable fact that we live in a three-dimensional world. Everyone has a body, feelings and a mind. We are aware of our personalities on three levels on a daily basis; the material physical level, ruled by Saturn; the emotional or feeling level, which corresponds to the Moon and the mental or thinking level that is experienced with the Sun. This is illustrated by the following diagram:

The Three Levels:

1. Physical (Saturn), 2. Feeling (Moon), 3. Mental (Sun)

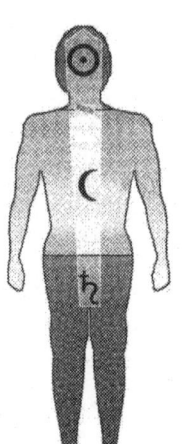

Spiritual Level
Thinking Self - MENTAL

Emotional Level
Feeling Self - PSYCHIC

Physical Level
Physical Self - BODY

Levels of Being of the Self

The Threefold Personality

This personality structure is very helpful for working on self-actualisation and integration, and was dealt with in depth in the previous chapter (19). This breakdown gives us a relatively simple but accurate key to interpreting a planet on the three levels of human existence. It makes a difference if a planet is interpreted as purely material, emotional or mental. The threefold pattern represents a process, an organic whole, which indicates an intrinsic coherency that gives life and meaning. There is always a development within it that we can identify with. Astrological statements about a person's character are more rounded, accurate, positive, harmonious and acceptable. This three-fold key not only makes us feel understood in our innermost being, but also more sure of how to interpret each planet.

Three Stages

If we look at a person's developmental journey, it is more meaningful to talk about stages rather than levels. In the interpretation of a planet, we can distinguish the **first stage,** in which the person is still largely unaware and attached to matter, which is why this is a blind stage as far as awareness is concerned, having an affinity with Saturn. The planet is undifferentiated and usually experienced as a drive. The **second stage** corresponds to the emotional level, the Moon, and is polar. Here the person is trapped in oppositions and learns the difference between black and white, positive and negative. Only at the **third stage**, the Sun level, can the person use their acquired ability to discriminate, enabling them to form accurate judgements about the planet and to experience its true nature.

There is another **fourth stage**, which anyone interested in spiritual development can reach. At this stage we mainly experience the transformed qualities of the planet, where it is placed at the service of the soul and used as a tool to put the evolutionary plan into practice. You can read about transformation of the ego planets to the spiritual level in more depth in Chapter 3.

The Ten Planets at the Three Levels

The following briefly presents the planets on the three levels of human experience, labelled 1st, 2nd and 3rd. This table aims to inspire you to do your own interpretation and does not claim to be exhaustive. It can be extended at will.

☉ **Sun**
1st I am unique, I am strong, individuality, egocentric, vitality, self-assertion, self-serving, obstinate
2nd Personal prestige, striving for success, self-knowledge, pride, ambition, competitive behaviour, arbitrary, strong-willed, ambitious
3rd Self-awareness, autonomy, intelligence, greatness, supremacy, authority, responsibility, creativity, enforcement

☽ **Moon**
1st Drive for social contact, emotionality, flexible, adaptation, dependent
2nd Changeable, moody, needs to be loved, cuddly, childlike
3rd Harmlessness, neutrality, openness, credulous, spontaneous

♄ **Saturn**
1st Material security, inflexibility, inertia, conservative
2nd Need for protection, defence mechanism, feelings of guilt, fears, negative attitude, pessimist, setter of boundaries, controller

3rd   Memory, responsibility, discipline, conscience, maturity, dignity, basic trust, endurance, reliable, well-structured

♀ Venus
1st   Comfort, narcissism, vanity, laziness, passive expectation, willing to compromise, libidinal, seductive
2nd   Love of harmony, kind, love of pleasure, docile, sense of style, avoidance of conflict, adjusted, "the beloved child"
3rd   Aesthetics, love of beauty, selectivity, striving for perfection, synthesis, awareness of value, culture, artistic, balanced

♂ Mars
1st   Engine, power output, energy, blind activity, aggression, argumentative, bossy, blind force
2nd   Combative, conflicts, overcoming barriers, cockiness, active devotion, fanaticism, gutsy, attacking
3rd   Dedication, pioneering spirit, boldness, heroism, commitment, courage, self-assertion, accomplishment

☿ Mercury
1st   Interested in words, quicksilver, inquisitive, gossip, misjudgement
2nd   Likes to communicate, chatty, curiosity, deduction, writing, resourceful, linguistic ability, informative
3rd   Mediator, intellectual brilliance, communication, powers of comprehension, messenger of the gods, learning ability, mental agility

♃ Jupiter
1st   Enjoyment of pleasure, sensual enjoyment, arrogance, rhetorical, satiety, pride, bossy, conceited, complacent
2nd   Joviality, righteousness, alertness, optimism, vitality, credulous, patronising, observant
3rd   Powers of judgement, sense of value, perspective, wisdom and ethics, finding meaning, philosopher, philanthropist

♅ Uranus
1st   striving for security, technical systems and backups, strategies, machinery, vision of the future, utopia
2nd   Eccentric, overcoming limits, obsession with innovation, subversive, erratic, fanatical
3rd   Creative intelligence, originality, spirit of research, intuitive flashes, inventiveness, striving for freedom

♆ Neptune
1st   Idealism, sorrow of love, devotedness, disappointments, delusions, belief in miracles, disintegrating boundaries, addictive
2nd   Devotion, healing spirit, self-abandonment, social conscience, ideologies, missionaries, helper syndrome, longing for Nirvana

3rd   Idealism, identification, unity, universal human kindness, mysticism, creative fantasies, bliss

♇ Pluto

1st   Masks, egomania, use of power, imposing the will, destructiveness, stirring up of what is suppressed, crises
2nd   Megalomania, drivenness, idols, conversions, crises, metamorphoses, purification and regeneration, death and rebirth
3rd   Spiritual will and motivation, single-mindedness, effective power, synthesis, creative contribution to evolution

Ptolemaic Planetary Sequence

This is used to establish the ruler of each year according to a seven-year cycle. It is a chronological sequence of planets that starts with the slowest, Saturn, and finishes with the fastest, the Moon. The new planets are not included in this sequence.

Year Rulers

♄	♃	♂	☉	♀	☿	☽
1993	1994	1995	1996	1997	1998	1999
2000	2001	2002	2003	2004	2005	2006
2007	2008	2009	2010	2011	2012	2013
2014	2015	2016	2017	2018	2019	2020

The days of the week are also calculated according to this method. The planets are arranged around a circle and joined by lines that form a seven-pointed star.

Days of the Week

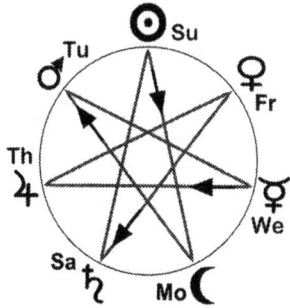

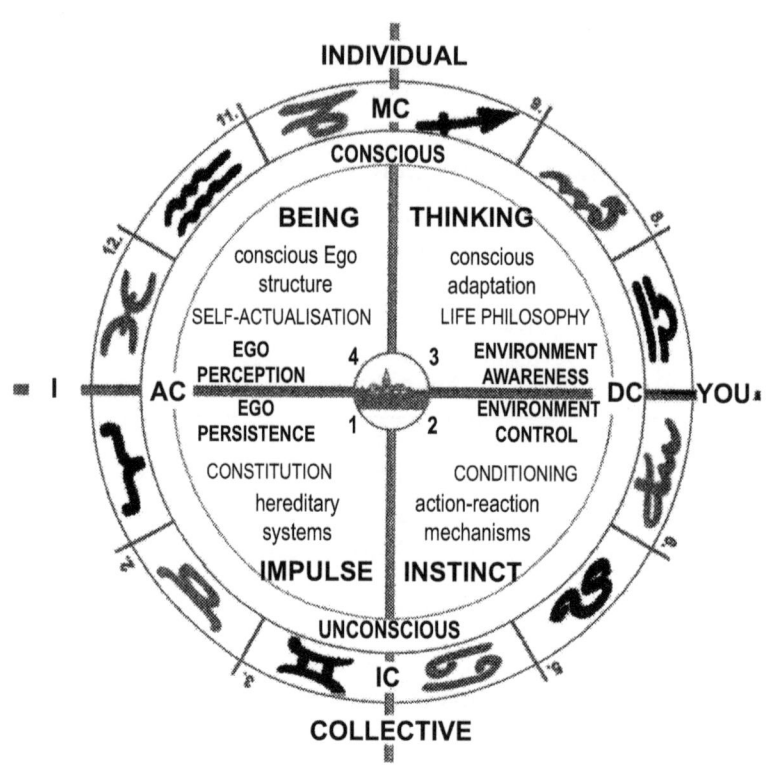

The Four Quadrants

5. The Planets in the Houses

Sun, Moon, Saturn in the Horoscope Hemispheres
• The Threefold Personality •
• Sun in the Upper Hemisphere •
• Sun in the Lower Hemisphere •
• Sun on the I-Side • Sun on the You-Side •
• Moon on the You-Side • Moon on the I-Side •
• Moon in the Upper Hemisphere •
• Moon in the Lower Hemisphere •
• Saturn in the Lower Hemisphere •
• Saturn on the I-Side • Saturn on the You-Side •
• Saturn in the Upper Hemisphere •

Sun and Saturn in the Twelve Houses
(Koch House System)

• Introduction • The Signs of the Zodiac •
• Three Zones in a House: Cardinal, Fixed, Mutable •
1st House • Sun • Saturn •
2nd House • Sun • Saturn •
3rd House • Sun • Saturn •
4th House • Sun • Saturn •
5th House • Sun • Saturn •
6th House • Sun • Saturn •
7th House • Sun • Saturn •
8th House • Sun • Saturn •
9th House • Sun • Saturn •
10th House • Sun • Saturn •
11th House • Sun • Saturn •
12th House • Sun • Saturn •

Sun, Moon, Saturn in the Horoscope Hemispheres

We first consider the effect of the positions of the three ego planets in the different hemispheres of the horoscope. As many people are interested in personality development, we also give an in-depth analysis of the positions of Sun and Saturn in the house system. To describe every planet in the hemispheres and houses would be beyond the scope of this book. It is not intended to be a reference work, but a thorough and detailed textbook dealing with the psychological influences of the planets in the horoscope. Students of astrology can then use their own knowledge of the houses to interpret the other planets for themselves.

The Threefold Personality

As we look again at the three ego planets in the hemispheres, it is important once more to distinguish between the three levels of life experience upon which our personalities are anchored, i.e. physical, emotional and mental, or body, feelings and mind (see also the diagram on page 154). At each level a focus of self awareness is formed in the course of the development process. Saturn represents the physical self, the Moon represents the feelings and the Sun the mind. A lot can be learnt about these ego functions from the positions of these three planets.

Their position in the horoscope mainly reveals the areas of life in which the personality can unfold, experiment and develop. There are general rules for locating the three ego planets in the house system, which enable us to make a basic qualitative evaluation. In the horoscope, they are particularly at home in locations where they can evolve relatively freely in their own way. For example, the Sun is well-placed in the upper hemisphere, Saturn in the lower hemisphere, and the Moon on the You-side. There are places where an ego planet is more or less restricted or blocked. These qualitative differences are described briefly below:

☉ Sun in the Upper Hemisphere

The Sun is naturally more at home in the upper hemisphere of the horoscope. This position also corresponds to the middle of the day, which is when it can shine at its brightest and be seen and felt all around. In the 9th and 10th houses is the area of individuality, where people can evolve until they are completely mature and become what we call an authority. Recognition, respect and influence are the result, and the Sun in these houses can, on behalf of the collective, take on

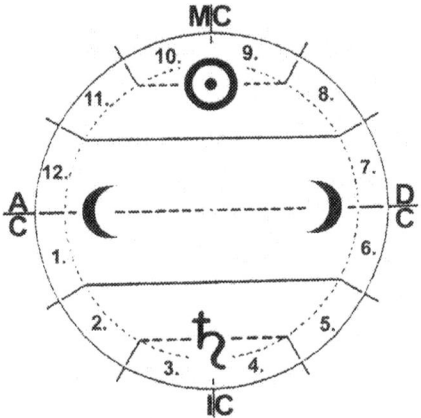

Horoscope Areas

the responsibilities and tasks entrusted to it. It can assess and deal with things correctly, thus achieving the success that a Sun definitely needs. Most people with the Sun in the upper hemisphere have the strength and courage to stand up for themselves and to give and assert their point of view. Self-assertiveness and self-actualisation are usually no problem. Also, as the Sun symbolises the father in the horoscope, this position suggests a strong father who was a good role model for developing self-confidence (unless the Sun lies at a low point). You can read more about this in Chapter 7 "The Family Model".

☉ Sun in the Lower Hemisphere

Here the Sun lies in the area of the collective and the unconscious. The 3rd and 4th houses have a particular affinity with family and social background. Once this Sun has accepted his roots, gained self-awareness, feels secure and finds stability and a sense of belonging, he can help the people he is responsible for and generally does a lot for relatives. He also benefits from the achievements of the family and the collective, for example, from the infrastructure of human society. He has access to it because he is a citizen of a country, a community. This is on the condition that he respects the norms of the collective, the written and unwritten rules. This Sun is particularly well suited to undertaking tasks for the good of the community, gaining its respect in the process.

☉ Sun on the I-Side

The Sun on the left hand side (1st, 2nd, 12th and 11th Houses) is actually just rising and must still struggle for recognition. It is strongly oriented towards the self, occupied with finding and developing itself. It has just begun to be an identity and for that reason is usually on the defensive. It uses a lot of energy to assert, and also to defend, its own ego, its living space and its own value. It is defensive and must construct its own private sphere. The ego needs a protected inner space that it can always retreat into, where it feels safe and can recharge its batteries and grow in peace. This space is protected from intruders and interferers. Only those who are invited in may enter; everyone else must remain outside.

☉ Sun on the You-Side

In the 6th and 7th houses, the person is strongly oriented towards the You. He needs others in order to find himself. That entails a dependency on the You that lasts until he clearly recognises exactly what autonomy and self-awareness are. Only then can a Sun share its entire inner richness with the You. It often plays a dominant role and many people admire it. This Sun usually experiences itself in its reflection in the You, so that it is often difficult to develop an individual profile and maintain the admiration of others. At the DC, there can even be a loss of ego which means that one loses oneself in the You and cannot live without it. The reverse can also be the case, depending on the sign, i.e. there is a strong desire to control the You, which represents another form of dependency on the You.

☽ Moon on the You-Side

The Moon is right at home here, for it is a sociable planet as befits our feeling self. On the You-side, it is always open to other people and ready to socialise. If someone approaches, it reacts spontaneously and sincerely. It engages quickly with the You and can therefore handle any social situation. But because the Moon is very open, it is difficult for it to set boundaries for itself. She feels many of the You's wishes and needs and they can weigh her down. That is why she has to learn to think of herself too sometimes and to consciously focus on her own wishes. Only when she finds a balance can she become an expert in social interaction on the I-You axis, the Encounter Axis of the horoscope.

☽ Moon on the I-Side

Even here the Moon is open to others. Although personal feelings react very subjectively to the environment, these people mainly embark upon relationships that their environment brings to them. The impulse is mainly external; they themselves are passive and prefer to wait to be approached. But then they become very clingy, and experience their own ego intensively in social situations and in love. They offer love on the same emotional level to all kinds of people, which sets off an exchange process that affects the whole Encounter Axis in social situations. They behave openly and naively even with adults, because on the I-side we experience the childlike in ourselves and in our loved ones.

☽ Moon in the Upper Hemisphere

The area of the 9th and 10th houses actually belongs to the Sun, and here the Moon has to take over the role of the Sun. This requires a lot of energy and can also create anxieties. People are afraid of not being able to satisfy the demands and expectations of the environment. This is why in the 10th house it is also called the 'Actor Moon', because it has to play the role of the Sun. Another term for this lunar position is 'Wanting to be popular'. It feels as though it is on stage and has to win the favours of the collective. The Moon is a reflecting instrument and needs people's constant attention, encouragement and feedback. That is also the main stress of the Moon in the upper hemisphere. It is always struggling for recognition and applause, irrespective of which house it is in.

☽ Moon in the Lower Hemisphere

The Moon can cherish and nurture emotional ties with people it is close to in the collective area. It is clingy, loving and adapted, and enjoys being with those it loves. It feels comfortable and safe in communal life and does all it can for others so that it is not alone. This lunar position often causes dependency on family and loved ones. While a person still seeks the security of the bosom of the family, she remains immature. Many miss out on the opportunity to grow up, staying in the family nest instead. They are afraid to step outside the protection of the collective and make their own way. On the positive side, the lower hemisphere is a place where belonging to the collective can be experienced and put into practice in active love by the feeling self.

♄ Saturn in the Lower Hemisphere

Saturn likes to be in the lower hemisphere, because there it feels anchored to terra firma. As the physical principle, it is looking for material security, and what better place to look than being rooted in the primordial soil, the source, the family and the collective? The primary function of Saturn is to guarantee security, both for itself and for those who belong to it and for whom it feels responsible. Saturn in the lower hemisphere mostly indicates a mother who could be relied upon and who was a good role model for the maternal function. Very frequently, such a person takes on tasks that stop him from satisfying his own desires. He cares for those weaker than himself, stands by their side through thick and thin and is prepared to share their load. This thoughtfulness creates a nice, secure atmosphere. This strong Saturn position enables people to cope with difficult tasks and relationships. He is burdened with responsibility from an early age because those around him can tell that he can deal with it conscientiously.

♄ Saturn on the I-Side

Saturn is responsible for its own security on the I-side of the horoscope. In the 1st and 12th houses, around the I-point, it is always trying to define its personal space. It is mistrustful of life, overly cautious and always expects the worst. It imagines how it will react or how it can avoid destiny. It often plans the future and prepares itself thoroughly to encounter possible strokes of fate. It must prove to itself that it is ready and work on being internally forearmed and strong. People with Saturn on the I-side find it hard to feel open and relaxed; they are naturally strict and closed. They work hard on improving their own ability so that they are prepared for anything. They are almost never satisfied with their own achievements and always find something to improve on. Self-criticism is very strong around the I-point, and these people are egocentric and self-oriented. Their own ego is surrounded by protective walls and it is not easy for others to get in. They set conditions out of fear of people coming too close.

♄ Saturn on the You-Side

Saturn is not a sociable planet; it is interested in physical security, and is dominated by a deep-seated fear and mistrust of other people. Its primary need on the You-side is therefore to structure relationships so that it can supervise and control them. Its willingness to socialise is also dependent on conditions and on whether it brings security or not. If the You observes and accepts its expectations, regulations or controls, it can open itself up. But if there is just one deviation from the agreement, Saturn clams up again. It is a mechanism that shuts down automatically if any danger looms on the horizon. It plans for the future, and only allows social contact when it corresponds to the plan. Saturn on the You-side is like a filter for the You, a control station that lets no-one through unless they know the password.

♄ Saturn in the Upper Hemisphere

As the planet of security, Saturn wants to be seen to be strong in this area. It is takes great care to function conscientiously and professionally, so that others will be convinced that it is a good, solid and responsible worker. In the individual area of the chart, Saturn mostly aims for a professional career that will impress others and ensure that it is treated as an authority and respected. The tasks that Saturn has to cope with in the upper hemisphere are mostly above average. Its personal security depends upon being the best and developing a particular ability or talent as much as it can, so that it can become a recognised authority. It tries to dominate others and sees to it that no one can contest this position. Saturn's fear up there is falling from a great height, which is what happens to many despots in the 10th house. That is why Saturn makes provisions and plans ahead for security and avoids mistakes and setbacks. Under no circumstances does it want to lose the position it has achieved. It is continually working on staying at the pinnacle of success, never allowing itself any weakness and always demanding the best from itself. If it loses control just once it has a bad conscience and immediately starts again from scratch.

Sun and Saturn in the Twelve Houses

Also appropriately applicable to:
Moon, Mercury, Venus, Mars, Jupiter, Uranus, Neptune, Pluto

Introduction

One of the most revealing factors in interpretation of the planets, especially of the ego planets, is their position in the house system. The four above-mentioned hemispheres are further divided into the twelve houses, starting at the ascendant with the first house and going in a clockwise direction around the zodiac (see diagram on next page). In psychological terms, the houses represent the influence of the environment and appear at the outer edge of the horoscope. There are twelve areas of life that we experience and are tested by every day. They represent environmental conditioning and show our acquired behaviour patterns, which we can consciously put into practice in our lives with the help of the horoscope. We do not have the space in this chapter to describe every planet in each of the twelve houses, so have limited this to the Sun and Saturn. The Moon's position in the twelve signs is described in Chapter 6. All three ego planets in the twelve houses appear in a series of the magazine *Astrolog* (numbers 20 – 40) (7).

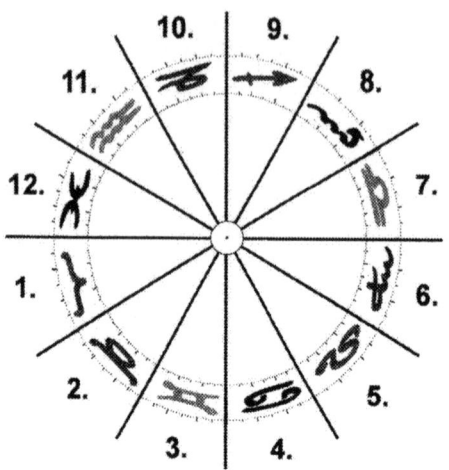

Zodiac Signs and Houses

The Signs of the Zodiac

The zodiac is composed of regular divisions of the Sun's orbit (ecliptic) into 30-degree sections, which are known as the signs of the zodiac. It is the Sun's orbit out in space, and is the cosmic framework that gives the planets a basic structure, which we interpret as hereditary disposition. According to the hermetic saying: "As above, so below", the twelve houses correspond to the twelve signs of the zodiac on a different level. It helps us to interpret the house position of each planet if we relate them to the twelve signs. The zodiac always starts with the sign of Aries, and this first sign has an affinity with the nature of the first house. The second sign is Taurus, and corresponds to the second house, and so on. The sign of Aries is not always in the first house, instead we find there the ascendant sign, calculated using time and place of birth. The possible combinations resulting from the comparison of sign and house should be considered in the interpretation process, as described in Chapter 4. For the purposes of this book, it is enough to know that *from a cosmic point of view*, Aries is always in the first house.

Three Zones in one House: Cardinal, Fixed, Mutable

We know from experience that it is not sufficient just to describe the planets in each hemisphere and house. We can only get an accurate picture of the planets if we further divide each house into three zones. This division was developed after years of research by Bruno Huber and is represented by the intensity curve (see page 133). You can read more about this in *The Astrological Houses* (16). The three cross qualities (cardinal, fixed, mutable) give us an idea of the nature of the three zones. The first zone goes from the house cusp to the balance point (house size times 0.382). This has an affinity with the cardinal principle in all twelve houses. Here the position of Sun is at its most influential, because Sun corresponds to the cardinal principle. The next zone, from balance point to low point, corresponds to the fixed principle. The fixed principle corresponds to Saturn, so here Saturn is at its strongest. The zone from low point to the next cusp corresponds to the mutable quality, which can be compared to that of the Moon. This is called the stress area of the house, because any planet placed there has to serve two masters. In the Huber School, we work with the so-called dynamic house system, in which the next house already starts at the low point of the previous one and therefore has a dual function until the next house cusp. You can read more about this in *Transformationen* (13), pages 79 – 140.

Overlapping

In the following descriptions of the planets in the three zones, you can assume that the described characteristics of each ego planet are partially also exhibited in the other zones. The boundary of each zone is not clear-cut and there is always some overlapping. Don't forget that the sign in which the planet is situated must also be considered in the interpretation, to see whether its temperament and cross qualities match those of the zone or not. Finally, the interpretation should be made and refined using the 15 points listed in Chapter 4.

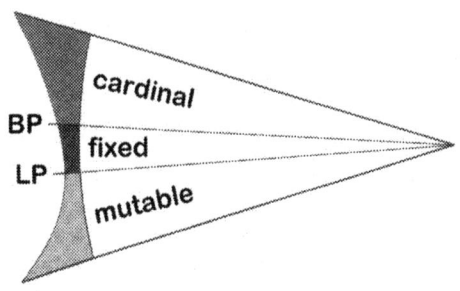

1st House

The first house begins with the ascendant, which represents the I-point in the horoscope. Life starts at the AC, as does age progression. Planets at the AC and in the first house often reveal the circumstances of our birth, how we entered the world. The sign at the AC or of a planet near the first house cusp gives an indication of how the person experienced their own birth, e.g. Saturn at the AC is an indication of a difficult birth, or that the soul did not want to be incarnated (refusal to be born). Such experiences mark the ego-pattern so strongly that the person can have problems with self-image throughout their life.

Jupiter at the AC has a positive effect on the ego. The baby is usually greeted with joy, and this conditions the ego so strongly that the person expects an equally warm welcome wherever they go later in life. If this greeting is not forthcoming, the ego is disappointed and it also has trouble dealing with conflict. On the other hand, Saturn usually toughens up the ego so that it is able to tolerate much more. You can read more about this in Chapter 7 pages 286-293.

The first house is also the place where the ego first makes an appearance. This cardinal house corresponds to the quality of Aries and has a strong drive that is intended to take the ego away from the protection of the mother into the outside world. For the ego, this natal push means self-preservation under any circumstances, making itself noticed so that it is not overlooked. The urge to be noticed creates a will to live, which guarantees survival under any circumstances for the newborn. Consequently, the purpose of the first house is the assertion of the ego, of personal identity. In the first house we dedicate ourselves to constructing a persona (according to Jung). It states something about how we want to be and how we want the world to see us. The ego can appear strong or weak in the first house, depending on the signs and planets involved. Our idea of our own self appears here. We have to live according to our own idea of ourselves. Our image is not immediately noticed by the environment, which is why we try to make an impression on others using the planets in the first house, to show something definite, to represent something in order to make ourselves feel good and reach out to others. It should now be obvious that this focus on the ego, the showing off, this "advertising sign" that we carry around with us our whole lives, is highlighted when ego planets are in the first house.

Sun in the 1st House

As the symbol of personal, autonomous self-awareness, the Sun must shine brightly in the first house. This Sun position makes us want to get the best from ourselves. We want to be good and are only satisfied when we have managed to complete all that is asked of us under our own steam. The Sun strengthens self-confidence and makes us optimistic, powerful and brave. We are convinced that we can cope with life and handle difficulties without other people's help. The Sun makes us autonomous and, depending on sign quality, we tend to take charge if others do not openly object. There is a strong emphasis on the self, we are self-confident and have a strong self-image and a sense of self-worth that cannot be challenged by others. We strive for recognition and take ourselves very seriously. Our appearance is authoritative and commands respect. If other people doubt our competence, we convince in any way we can (speech, actions or manipulation) that we are good, if not the best.

Anyone can be authoritative with a Sun position in the first house, so want their wishes to be respected and considered and make demands that are hard to fulfil. A Sun that wants to assert itself forcefully will be rejected by most people, because it hides an over-confident and pretentious ego. The more it insists on its demands being met, the more it gets on other people's nerves.

With this emphasis on self, especially with Sun near the AC, self-questioning is rare, and this lack of self-criticism can often be counterproductive. We only value our own thoughts and actions, and don't dream that we could ever be wrong. According to sign and house position, we think we are the centre of the universe and judge things subjectively. For this reason, we are often astonished when other people don't think the same way. This is especially true when the Sun is in a fixed sign (Taurus, Leo, Scorpio, Aquarius). In a cardinal sign (Aries, Cancer, Libra, Capricorn), we are convinced that we can handle life, that we are the best and can always achieve what we want. In a mutable sign (Gemini, Virgo, Sagittarius, Pisces), we want to impress others as a helper or to gain their love by teaching and guiding them.

As explained above, each house is divided into cardinal, fixed and mutable zones.

☉ **in the cardinal zone**, or just before the AC. Assertiveness and the drive to express oneself are heightened. Here cardinal energies are at their strongest: cardinal plus cardinal. This Sun cannot be ignored; it loudly draws attention to itself when it wants something. It has a strong will, sets its own objectives and gives its all to achieve them. Any

1st House ☉

opponents and rivals are fought off and eliminated. These people always feel that they must influence others in order to lead and guide them. They need a position in life in which they can assert their own will and where their desire for recognition can be met. This cardinal area also makes the Sun very charismatic, according to sign position, and gives it a powerful influence over other people, but means that they are not always treated sensitively. We would like our goals to be achieved overnight; there is an aversion to caution and prudence and a spiky reaction to resistance or criticism.

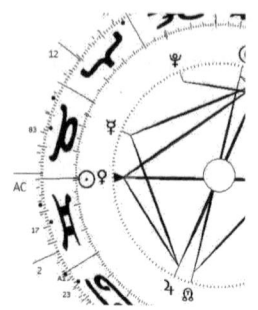

Richard Wagner, Composer
22.5.1813, 04.00 Leipzig, Ger
☉/♀ conjunction 1st House

☉ **in the fixed zone** of the first house stabilises self-awareness, and allows long-term goals to be set. The personality is strong, dominating and cannot be pushed around. Personal goals are achieved step by step and many things are left to mature in their own time. We must not forget that the priority of the first house is to ensure survival, which is particularly easy for a Sun in a fixed sign. Depending on the sign, the ego can throw itself wholeheartedly into a project. In the fixed zone, the sense of identity is often inflexible, but extremely stable. We are not easily persuaded, dislike adapting ourselves and prefer to tackle any problems rather than abandon our goals. We insist on our rights and reject any objections. Especially in a fixed sign, it is hard to yield and change. We cling to our legitimate rights and assert our own opinion.

☉ **at the low point** of the first house is introspective. It reacts hypersensitively to setbacks and is often offended. At the low point, the environment does not notice it and although it gives off positive signals, it is easily overlooked. That is why many are only considered as afterthoughts. This is often connected to a childhood trauma that the ego has interiorised, for example where a sibling was born at the time of an aspect from Age Point to the Sun and the parents had less time for us and we were no longer the centre of attention. That hurt the ego and reduced our self-esteem, leading us to retreat into ourselves and blame the environment if we are unable to succeed. Interestingly, this Sun position also attracts other similar situations again and again, where the ego has to hold itself back or where its personal identity rights are disrespected. Many avoid taking risks, play safe and hide their light under a bushel.

It is well known that a transformation can also take place at the low point, where we have to learn that we are not alone in the world, but that others have the same rights as ourselves. A Sun at the low point of the first house should become sensitive to the needs of others and should not always put its own needs first. This type of Sun must suffer until it acknowledges this fact. This often gives rise to masking behaviour, an obsessive compensative clinging to one's imagined authority.

☉ **in the mutable zone**, i.e. in the stress area before the second house, has to deal with two house themes: the self-presentation of the first house and the substance accumulation of the second. Self assertion often acquires a compensatory attitude. On the one hand, we are absolutely sure of wanting to achieve our own objectives, and on the other hand we are afraid of not being up to the job and of failing. This Sun must be certain that it is good enough and can cope. It puts a lot of energy into improving itself and accumulating substance, so that the value of its own identity cannot be doubted and can constantly grow. A transformation can help here: the first house gives strength to manifestation and assertion of the ego, and the second house delays this assertion until we are sure that the time is right. Many people have to wait a long time for that time to come though.

A transformed Sun is geared to making a success of one's talents, so that all tasks can be accomplished. It has a special inner strength and is not easily distracted. Other people can use it as a pole to swing around, to give them stability.

Saturn in the 1st House

Saturn's self-representation is quite different. Close to the AC, the self-image becomes saturnine, the attitude towards outsiders becomes cool and closed. Often birth was difficult and the child or mother had to fight for their lives. You can read more about birth circumstances and Saturn at the AC in Chapter 7.

♄ **in the cardinal zone** often radiates a calm security that others can rely on. Saturn is the protective function and embodiment of security and closes up the ego and protects it against external attack. Many refuse to let others near them. The boundary of the self is taken very seriously and many react very defensively to intrusions. They wear an impenetrable mask and do not let people look behind it. They keep their fellow men at a distance until they conform to their ideas and can withstand the scrutiny.

1st House ♄

♄ in the fixed zone makes harsh demands both of itself and of other people, which have to be met at all costs. Self-discipline and self-restraint, and the self-centredness that goes with them, are the effects of Saturn. Personal expansion is often restricted, the self image is worked on and much effort is put into personal perfection. That is why this person enjoys working hard. He takes life seriously, for him life is usually about carrying out tough duties or mastering self-imposed tasks. Playful amusement is not for him. He only enjoys working for others if it will show off his own superior knowledge or ability, which is also why he loves teaching.

♄ at the low point of the first house links the ego energies together, which often causes unfounded fears, mostly coming from the mother, which the ego holds on to and even encourages. There is a tendency to pay more attention to disappointments than to unexpected strokes of luck, which should be counteracted. This Saturn position causes pessimism; one expects the negative rather than the positive. Many people are turned in on themselves, closed and mistrustful, keeping others at a distance, which makes them unpopular. That is why it is important to cultivate faith in life and to take the occasional risk to break down Saturn's protective walls and free the inner being. People with Saturn at the low point in the first house are often very mature. They know how to handle matter, take difficult tasks in their stride and are efficient, reliable and responsible.

♄ in the mutable zone (stress area before the second house). The walls and blockades become more difficult to penetrate. The fixed principle affects Saturn and increases its fears, particularly the distrust of intruders. Here Saturn wants to hold on to what he has achieved at all costs. He cannot allow any losses at all, which is why in traditional astrology he is also called the miser. He takes great pains to defend what he has, be it possessions, people or a skill.

People with Saturn here start out with the fear that things will be taken away from them, which is why they are very good at building protective walls. In many cases there is a childhood trauma, either because personal living space was restricted, possibly by the birth of siblings, or the background was poor and deprived, and from the start they had to manage with very little. This kind of character trait is often visible throughout life.

The transformed Saturn becomes particularly mature here; it knows how to manage matter economically. It can be relied upon, it cares for others, it maintains and adds to what exists already and guarantees security for all those who are close to it.

2nd House

In the previous section, we talked about the ego planets in the first, cardinal Aries, house. Processes always take place in cardinal houses, so we can work positively on refining, cultivating and improving our self image. In the second house, the process of self development continues. Here we have to accumulate sufficient substance and secure our own existence. We have to define our own living space with boundaries, protective behaviour and defence mechanisms. So as the ego in the first house says: "Here I am, look at me, watch me", so that in the second house says: "Here is my boundary, you can come up to here, then my space begins and you cannot come in".

Sun in the 2nd House

The second house belongs to the fixed cross and corresponds to the earth sign of Taurus. That is why the central fixed zone and the low point are typical for the second house. Depending on the sign in which the Sun lies, the strength of self-awareness is dependent on the ability to protect the ego from being hurt and devalued, so that it remains invulnerable. It is the direct expression of the self, which declares that one possesses life substance that can be protected by setting personal boundaries. As well as the tendency to make things secure, the ego also possesses a natural and healthy self-defence. The rejection of outside influence can also lead to a conservative attitude, one-sidedness or obstinacy, i.e. self-defence as an exaggerated reaction to attack, in which a sledgehammer is used to crack a nut.

When the Sun is in the second house, the focus is mainly on personal self-worth. The person feels worthwhile when they have their own substance, their own means or possessions. A lack of possessions makes them feel less worthy than and inferior to other people. The fact that others have more possessions produces a burning envy that undermines their self-confidence and enjoyment of life. That is why this type of Sun will always strive to acquire things so that the ego can exist in the world. These things can be material, mental or spiritual values, or talents, or abilities, or personal skills or personal living space.

☉ **in the cardinal zone** of the second house enables the necessary resources to be acquired. Enough energy is available to be used purposefully to protect the person's existence on all levels. On the material level, they acquire the necessary finances, on the emotional level strengthen their emotional substance and on the mental level possess

2nd House ☉

talents and aptitudes. In the cardinal zone they measure their skill against other people's and become more competitive. The idea is to achieve the greatest effect with little effort. Loss of strength and substance rattle the self-awareness and are avoided at all costs or quickly compensated for.

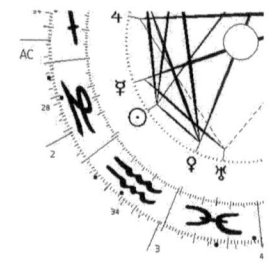

Telly Savalas
20.1.1924, 05.00 EST, Garden City/NY
☉ in cardinal zone 2nd House

☉ **in the fixed zone.** The tendency to safeguard and set boundaries prevails here. A person with the Sun in the fixed zone of the second house strives to acquire substance in abundance, to protect himself from losses and to stock up. He holds on firmly to what he has got and always wants more. He must always have a little more of everything than he needs, so that he has enough in times of need. Depending on the aspects that the Sun makes here, a tendency to hoarding or gluttony can also be observed. In the fixed zone, he is very economical with his energies anyway; none are wasted and he is keen to make gains.

☉ **at the low point** of the second house mostly results in the stagnation of outwardly directed efforts. The Sun is in a "passive position" and waits for opportunities so that it can acquire things without too much effort. It often waits a lifetime because its reactions are much too slow and opportunities come and go quickly. They often complain about missed possibilities and sit tight in their own prison sulking and embittered. The low point calls for reorientation and transformation. At low points, the Sun has to learn to listen to its inner voice, to concentrate on its inner centre of being where it can recharge emotional and spiritual batteries. At best, it can get in touch with its soul and acquire potential spiritual energies. It knows that it can use the hidden shadow of a day, that one day the time will come when the available substance can be used for a task of its own choice.

☉ **in the mutable zone** tries to lay down substantial stocks, to build on existing abilities and to analyse as accurately as possible – in the economical sense. In the shadow of the third house cusp, anxiety can cause compensative behaviour under certain circumstances. The combination of mutable quality with fixed principle produces contradictions, insecurity and fear of loss, which the person tries to counteract by hyperactivity or other compensations. They either try to eliminate life's dangers and avoid any risks, or hide and become a prisoner behind protective walls of their own construction. This type of Sun can acquire a great wealth of knowledge though, which can be put to good use later in a professional context.

A transformed Sun knows its own rights and the needs of others. It can share without being afraid of losing something. It gladly gives away its wealth. Taking and giving are in balance.

Saturn in the 2nd House

Here, Saturn gives a special relationship to things one has bought for oneself such as furniture and material possessions. It holds onto them for all its worth, as though they were part of its own body. "The house is like a second skin". All possessions raise self-esteem and support the need for security. What has been established and acquired is protected from all sides. There is a powerful need to delimit and protect personal living space and everything it contains. Nobody can cross this boundary without permission. Any danger that something can be taken away is prevented by appropriate protective measures.

♄ **in the cardinal zone** makes the person active. The priority is the defence of personal possessions and the physical body. A lot of effort is put into accumulating and holding onto possessions: the more one has the more secure one feels. Saturn itself comes with little money; it is frugal and can go without things if it has to. It is hard for it to share with others, as it is careful with money and does not give if it brings no personal advantage. Economic uncertainty and the possibility of loss can give rise to greed and miserliness. Money and substance are hoarded, so that there are enough supplies and therefore security in times of need.

As Saturn represents the physical body, the sense of physical self-worth is strongly marked. The person concerned is rather unapproachable, and their self-assurance depends on their physical integrity. This gives rise to defensive reactions and defence mechanisms that are intended to frighten away potential intruders. When there is physical injury or illness everything possible is done to get well again.

♄ **in the fixed zone** of the second house has a particularly strong effect because it corresponds to the fixed principle. Experiences often need to be repeated before something is understood. If a person acquires some specialised knowledge, he has to know everything about the subject and then some, so that he can be sure he knows enough and is a force to be reckoned with. In the fixed area, nearly everything is measured quantitatively. Learning processes are quantitative and classes often have to be repeated.

2nd House ♄

♄ **at the low point** of the second house makes habits very ingrained and one has trouble changing them. This often leads to a pronounced defensive attitude towards life. In particular, the fear of all kinds of loss, of health, money, people, position, etc. can become so strong that there is a tendency towards blocks and rigidity in social situations. The natural boundaries can turn into impenetrable walls, fortresses, in which treasure is hidden so that it is always safe. This is also kept secret; nobody else must know anything about this treasure so that there is no danger of it being lost.

♄ **in the mutable zone** makes the person insecure, irresolute, and often unsure of how to behave. On the one hand he is afraid of change and on the other his general outlook has to be flexible. He is confronted with the tasks of the third house and must undergo changes whether he wants to or not. He therefore adapts to the consensus, which makes him insecure. He seeks security in not attracting attention, not stepping out of line, and being like other people. He tries to talk the language of the collective and can then accurately communicate what conforms to the consensus. At best he can become a successful teacher.

The transformed Saturn in the second house is very good at thinking economically and helps others to make ends meet. It can get by on very little; it is thrifty and can do without things if it has to. People trust it because of its reliability; they know that it deals with everyone considerately, conscientiously and carefully.

3rd House

The third house is the mutable air house, corresponding to the sign of Gemini. Self-esteem is built on having a wide knowledge of many things. The more one knows, the better the personality feels. One can join in discussions and is also listened to when one has something intelligent to say. In the third house one often finds a special aptitude for languages and a pronounced receptivity. Communication and the transmission of knowledge are the principal expressions of the self. The third house offers positive possibilities, but one can also suffer from the pressure to think like everyone else. In this collective space, one is merely a part of the whole. Although the comparison with others motivates us to learn, knowledge of our own inadequacy or inferiority can be frustrating. In the third house there are powers that are greater than ourselves, which for example scare and threaten us with exams at school or fear at work. There are customs that must be respected and that is often not easy to tolerate for the ego that seeks independence.

Sun in the 3rd House

The Sun in the third house is mainly concerned with the gathering of knowledge, learning, further education, culture. The Sun likes to pass on the knowledge it has acquired. The more it knows, the more it is valued by the environment and the better it feels. Its own self-esteem is built on being in the know about everything under the sun and being able to talk to anyone about anything. That is why this position is good for teachers or writers. However, if someone with this Sun position is not able to demonstrate enough knowledge and education, he feels inferior and lost within the collective. The others with whom he often compares himself know much more than he does. So he does what others tell him to do and it is hard for him to develop an independent awareness.

☉ **in the cardinal zone** is always striving for recognition. The third house rules traditional thinking, and here the Sun is concerned with universal values, standardised ways of thinking and behaving that appear in literature, newspapers and the media and are taught in schools and universities. The vital self-esteem deals with all these things and picks up everything it is asked. Only when a person with this type of Sun can join in a conversation and has something to say and teach to others, will he feel worthwhile. That is why he should do all he can to get a good general education and never stop learning new things. He is usually quick on the uptake, can adapt to the consensus, and follow and take advantage of trends. In the cardinal zone of the third house, one has a particular gift for turning to the authority for the collective, be it a school teacher, the director of an institution or a company boss. One goes directly to those in power.

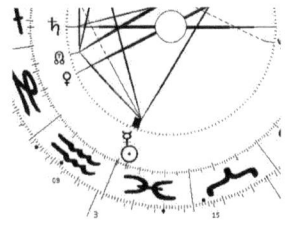

Erich Kastner, Writer
23.2.1899, 03.30, Dresden/Ger
☉ in cardinal zone 3rd House

☉ **in the fixed zone** strengthens the tendency to use situations or people for personal ends. A network of relationships is used with a view to gaining personal advantage from it. This Sun is suited to professions where communication is important. There is an effort to take advantage of every opportunity presented.

3rd House ☉

☉ on the low point reduces the speed of the mutable third house. The person reacts more slowly than in the other areas, but this gives more depth. They are often not supported by the environment, because the Sun is not visible at the low point. It is hidden, which frequently makes them think that they are not good enough; it is only later that they notice that they are just as intelligent as other people, and perhaps have to return to education to catch up. As mentioned above, the third house is all about intelligence, with the education of the formal, objective intellect, which is very highly valued in our society. That is why with this position of the Sun self-esteem also depends on how intelligent we are.

☉ in the mutable zone of the third house is "typical Gemini", because both correspond to the mutable principle. As a "stress planet" in the shadow of a house cusp it has to serve two masters, the mutable principle of the third house and the cardinal principle of the fourth. This usually gives rise to compensation mechanisms that must later be recognised as such and transformed in the individuation process.

The Sun in the stress area is very busy behaving as intelligently as possible and does all it can to play a role in the environment. It cleverly adapts to the needs of the collective, the family. In the shadow of the fourth axis, a great effort is made to get on with fellow men, with siblings, relatives and friends. Depending on the sign, this Sun would like to dominate them and tell them what to do. It knows that the whole collective is behind it and becomes its representative, exercising a certain power as the agent of public opinion. What "people" say goes, and many are not capable of forming their own opinion. But a person who changes their point of view too often is not taken seriously. However, in this "dual" zone, there is the urge to create an image of oneself. So one is always correcting oneself and has to readapt here and there, which is hard for the Sun awareness to do, striving as it does for autonomy and independence. Initially this is only possible by compensating, which inevitably brings with it difficulties and crises in the development of the personality. The Sun really wants to be in the fourth house already, in order to have the security of the nest or the collective. It strives for autonomy and individual freedom (particularly in the individual signs Sagittarius, Capricorn and Aquarius), but still has to fall in line with the status quo.

A transformed Sun always wants to help as many people as it can. In the third house it opens itself up to the zeitgeist and puts it in a form that everyone can understand.

Saturn in the 3rd House

As the physical self, Saturn only feels safe when it completely masters a subject or field.

♄ **in the cardinal zone** motivates (according to sign) the ambition and desire to learn through being with other people. One wants to be the best and to shine by mastering a subject. The necessary ability to concentrate is usually present, which allows what has been taught to be put into practice. Saturn strengthens the rational side of this house. Saturn is less concerned with ideas and abstract knowledge than how they can be used practically. Knowledge is only interesting when it is useful and can serve a purpose, especially when Saturn lies in a fixed sign. This purposeful and utilitarian attitude is the effect of Saturn in the third house. If it does not bring results though, one can easily give up and "throw in the towel".

♄ **in the fixed zone** causes a pessimistic attitude when there is a lack of success; one thinks that one is not up to it and gives up too soon. However, this Saturn position makes one ready to try again. Often objectives are only achieved after repeated attempts. However, too much should not be asked for at once, as Saturn imposes a natural boundary on the many-sidedness of this house. It therefore provides depth and the capacity for scientific thought. The small, day-to-day practicalities of life are taken seriously; sense of duty and punctuality correspond to the ideas of the collective. From the point of view of intelligence, Saturn is also our memory. In the house of learning and education, it is good at retaining and passing on what is learnt. Sometimes the ability to pass on knowledge and spontaneous reactions to opportunities are somewhat limited, especially in the fixed zone of the house.

♄ **at the low point** of the third house sometimes, where there are appropriate tension aspects, indicates speech difficulties such as stuttering. There are frequently problems adapting to new environments, and sometimes even signs of disorientation. Spontaneous social situations are difficult to handle, as one is rather mistrustful and requires a more formal approach.

♄ **in the mutable zone**, the stress area before the fourth house, is strongly linked to the thinking of the collective, hence an interest in the past, history, family tales or archaeology. Clinging to the old gives security and one is often the keeper of traditions and family inheritance. A lot of effort is put into this. Sometimes patriotism or clubbiness can also fulfil Saturn's need for security. Before the fourth cusp, one is stuck to the spot, does not want to move on and is dependent on home and mother, and cannot stop going back again and again. At best, this Saturn indicates a rootedness in the ultimate ground of being and a natural basic trust. There is often a constraining family background with responsibilities and duties that are not easy to shake off. We could also call it a family karma.

A transformed Saturn in the third house can pass on acquired knowledge painstakingly and responsibly. The thoughts of the collective are put forward persuasively and by standing by one's word, one is taken seriously.

4th House

The fourth house corresponds to the water sign of Cancer. This is the house of family and roots. Here we relate emotionally to our relatives, the home and the collective that we belong to. It is the nest we emerge from, the maternal space, protection, warmth and belonging. For adults, it is our own family that we create ourselves, that is to say our own home.

The fourth house is also the soil in which the seed of our individuality lies dormant. It is an important house for the development of the personality. Like the first, this is a cardinal house, in which the ego is reborn in a new way. In the first house the animal self is born, in the fourth the adult self. In this area of the horoscope we see the nature of our roots, which are necessary for a strong personality, so that the tree of individuality can grow tall and straight.

Sun in the 4th House

The Sun, our autonomous self, would like to shine in the tenth house or at the zenith, which is why it feels lost down in the collective space of the horoscope where it is at first forced to fit in with its surroundings. However, it is always trying, consciously or unconsciously, to dominate and play a controlling role. Hence with such a position there is great interest in family traditions, clubs, community life, institutions, homes, later also resulting in positions of leadership.

☉ **in the cardinal zone** wants to dominate at all costs, be it in an area of expertise or over people. At a young age, these people are often unhappy that they have to develop first before they can lead a group. That is why the Sun in the fourth house has two characteristics. The first is that such a person develops patriarchal needs, particularly men, of course. They have to be the head of the family, perhaps even heads of state. They identify with the state and in the cardinal zone are often very good at leading the collective and imposing their will upon it. In this respect, the behaviour and methodology of the fourth house is matriarchal, i.e. using role models and in a formal way. The strict adherence to this role model challenges the patriarchal dominance.

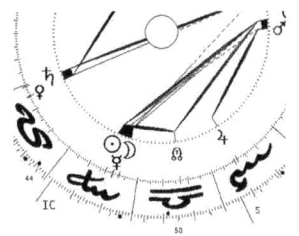

Leo Tolstoy, Russian Writer
28.8.1828 JC = 9.9.1828 GC
23.00 Jasnaja Poljana/SSR
☉ in cardinal area 4th House

This can often be seen in men, because they naturally identify with the Sun. They have always been entitled to be strong personalities, and feel that they have to be strong – even patriarchal – which is part of this focus on roles in their upbringing.

If the Sun lies in the **fixed zone**, then these people try to play the patriarch, although they are often soft and gentle inside. This is the classic case of the henpecked husband. Such men mostly have patriarchal roles and make very sure that everyone respects their role. At home they are upright husbands because in reality they are under matriarchal control.

For women it is quite different. They identify much more easily with the matriarchal aspect of the fourth house. In the **cardinal zone**, they work for the good of the family or the community. They are very interested in housekeeping and are very good at looking after and keeping the house or place of residence in order and devoting all their energies to ensuring the welfare of their dependents. In any case, the self-confidence of a woman in the fourth house is less than that of a man. In the **fixed zone** she is often shy, reticent, unassuming and sometimes subdued and intensively occupied with domestic affairs.

☉ **at the low point** and at the start of the mutable zone often causes compensative behaviour. For example, a woman can become a domestic tyrant; her self-confidence is built on over-valuing domestic affairs. This is a contradictory position for the Sun, which complicates the individual profiling process. It has to respect norms that have been prescribed by the collective. In order to actualise itself, it has to do what helps the collective on a large or small scale, which restricts the possibilities for self development.

☉ **in the mutable zone** of the fourth house: the influence of the fifth house can already be felt, which is why the Sun compensates its self-confidence. He often wants to prove to his father that he is also worth something. Mostly he leaves the nest at an early age to start a family of his own. He wants to have something of his own, to distance himself from his family and become independent. He tries to make a good impression on the environment, wants recognition for his achievements and wants to achieve things without depending on outside help. There is often a sphere of competence involved. He builds his own territory that no-one can enter uninvited. If anyone attempts to do so, they are rejected and fought as rivals.

The transformed Sun will learn before the fifth house cusp that others have the same rights as it does. This enables it to "change its spots" and to live in harmony with its fellow men.

Saturn in the 4th House

As the physical self, Saturn feels safely rooted in the ultimate ground of being of the fourth house. If family relationships are good there is a natural basic trust. Saturn is in a strong position here; it can live out its need for protection and motivation for security in the bosom of the family. One can close all the doors and enjoy feeling good all alone in the nest, and is not afraid of being alone. A Saturn self lives by its protection mechanism and by the success it strives for in life. The more protection and security it has, the better it feels. "My home is my castle" it says; it can even become aggressive if forced to protect the nest. It uses its own ability, tenacity and sense of responsibility and proudly renounces the fulfilment of its own wishes.

As Saturn has to do with the skin and the sense of taste, there is a strong need for physical contact, which may relate to the mother or to the whole family environment. To take an extreme example: a mother who gives too much physical contact becomes a mother hen, from whom the child is unable to escape when it grows up, because it still needs this degree of overprotection. The second case: a nest that is warm and soft develops a strong collective urge. This then produces people who always find it hard to become independent. They tend to cling to the collective or to groups, where they feel protected from danger. But this can limit development of the individual, which is also true for the first case. A person who is unable to break free from mother can never be independent. We often see how difficult it is to leave family or home when Saturn is in the third or fourth house.

♄ **in the cardinal zone** has strong, deep roots. Such people often see themselves as the guardians of family traditions, which they cling to, and they enjoy delving into the past. Historians often have this Saturn position. A sense of responsibility for loved ones is developed early on, and is hard to shake off. Care of the family is taken very seriously, which can be felt throughout life, even though it may no longer be necessary. One clings to the past and hardly notices how times change. Property and home ownership are often sought in order to settle down and provide security.

♄ **in the fixed zone** of the fourth house is hard to change, not only conservative, but even behaving as though life had never changed. Relatives are clung to with conventional, blindly loyal inflexibility; it is hard to make new contacts and anything new is rejected. One is also always talking about the past and judges the future by outdated standards. Although these people have an air of security, they usually have an old head on young shoulders and expect the worst. Saturn often makes them hard on themselves and on others, allowing little freedom. The same perfection and commitment they ask of themselves is demanded of others. They are often alone and their strictness makes others avoid their company. This loneliness can lead to premature aging and depression.

♄ **in the mutable zone** of the fourth house often shows the little-known soft and sensitive side of Saturn in the form of comfort and skin contact. But here in the shadow of the fifth house, Saturn has a dual influence. On the one hand, there is a curiosity about life outside the family unit, and on the other hand there is a fear of it, and the latter usually wins out. However, this stress area is well suited to the deployment of energy. With a conviction that one can do everything oneself and is good at everything, one does not willingly accept outside help. One cannot stand it if others are better at things; mastering practical skills is the foundation of self-control.

The transformed Saturn works daily on self-improvement. It takes on a maternal role, protects others, teaches them how to use matter skilfully and saves them from making mistakes.

5th House

The fifth house is a fire house on the fixed cross, corresponding to the sign of Leo. As with all fire signs the focus is on personal development. In the first house, the self image was formed, in the fifth the ego's influence is tested, and in the ninth we learn to think independently.

The fifth house is usually interpreted wrongly or one-sidedly. Love and eroticism, children, risk, adventure, speculation and art are

5th House ☉

mentioned in the books. Seen from the point of view of personality development, this is the house of self-testing, where we should learn how to behave so that we get on as well as possible with other people, while at the same time expressing our own individuality. It is a fixed, formative house, in which social behaviour is moulded. Planets in the fifth house indicate how we behave in intimate relationships and the way we present ourselves in social situations: attractive and likeable or stand-offish and unapproachable. It always consciously or unconsciously comes down to what impression we make on the environment, as to whether we are liked or disliked. From the point of view of behavioural psychology, it is the way that the ego imposes itself in order to create a place for itself in the world that is respected by others.

Sun in the Fifth House

As the planet of autonomous self-awareness, the Sun knows instinctively how it can make an impression on others using its charisma. There is a lot of self-confidence, but it is often dependent on how many people can be charmed and how much feedback is received, also in the sexual sense. The person wants to achieve a certain amount of self-determination and builds a personal "kingdom", a collective, which must be reliable: loyalty and absolute fidelity are required. He then puts himself out 100% for these people, in a way that also makes them dependent. Someone with the Sun in the fifth house takes possession of the people who are close to him; they belong to his "kingdom", thus boosting his self-confidence (as in all fixed houses). With the Sun we should aim for, experiment with and develop our creativity.

☉ **in the cardinal zone** makes a person successful in their own undertakings, they are dynamic, committed and enjoy taking risks. This Sun wants to experience things for itself and to be its own lord and master. This is the home of the competitive spirit that can also accept rules. He knows very well how to get the better of others and be the best in sport, business or politics. Adventure and games stimulate, and nothing ventured is nothing gained. Sun in this position usually makes the person ready to spring dynamically into action, giving entrepreneurial skills and an air of self-confidence.

This person has no problem winning over other people. When he puts his mind to it, he can charm many with his

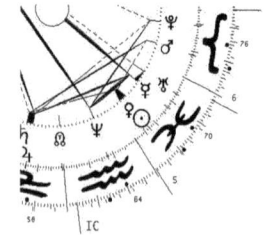

Karl May, German writer
25.2.1842, 22.00 LT,
Hohenstein-Ernstthal/Ger
☉ in cardinal zone 5th House

charisma. Once he knows he can do this, he develops a method, a way of imposing himself that works automatically. If this does not work for some reason, he quickly thinks up a new ruse in order to be successful again. Many then tend to show off in order to cover up failures. He cannot easily admit that he has failed, because he wants to save face at all costs. If the occasion demands, because he always wants to experiment in the fifth house, either he develops refined ways of dealing with people, ways that tend to be manipulative and are therefore fake, or real creative potential is released, increasing creativity and enabling true self-expression.

☉ **in the fixed zone** of the fifth house makes the person inflexible, depending on the sign. This is why the environment does not always react as they would like. Too much importance is often given to the need for personal security, clinging to old structures and believing that things must always be done in the same way. This is often related to a lack of self-criticism. Their self-image forces the environment to respect their own idiosyncrasies. They want to impress people and even to leave them awed and astonished. If this does not happen, they can be deeply hurt. They really want to be treated in a special way and be talked about. This is done with patterns and with ruses. In the fixed zone, these are practised until they become automatisms or reflexes that are followed compulsively. This is often experienced with their own children. The fifth house shows us our own children. There is a strong desire for immortality, we want our qualities to live on in them and that is why we are slightly possessive, and do not let the children (or also others who are close to us) go their own way.

☉ **at the low point** makes change happen. Possessive love is often trampled underfoot by the environment. Sun at this transformation point has to learn that it is not the centre of the universe, that there are also other people who have their own ideas. This Sun must become sensitive to the needs of others and must not force them to comply with its own demands. The more it refuses to accept this, the more it suffers. This often leads to masking behaviour, a compulsive, compensatory sticking to one's rights.

☉ **in the mutable zone:** questions of existence are brought up in social behaviour and in love. Over-compensatory behaviour can usually be observed in the shadow of the sixth house, which with the Sun is expressed as the pressure to achieve, often coming from the father. It wants to show him that it is not dependent on him and can manage by itself, and even that it is better than him. Some become workaholics; they act as if they can handle everything themselves and don't let anyone help them. The harder they work, the better they feel about themselves, so they often take on too much. To compensate, some develop a helper syndrome and worry that the help they offer will not be accepted.

The transformed Sun enjoys taking on duties and tasks for others. Their dedication to work is spontaneous and without ulterior motive, and they give what is needed without thinking about what is in it for them.

Saturn in the 5th House

Saturn, our physical self, is experienced in the fifth house by physical awareness and testing of physical limits, but also by physical fears (e.g. fear of contact). In the fifth house the body is an instrument used to make an impression. One also sees oneself as an erotic personality that is able to relate to others. But this body has to function and be trained. Saturn in the fifth house easily falls into patterns. Secure relationships are created for oneself and, when they work, held on to, consciously or unconsciously forcing the environment to fall in line with them. This is not demanded, but is done by waiting patiently; usually just a worried expression or a punishing look is enough to make people do what is wanted. Depending on the sign, this position gives a more or less secure self-image, which does not need to make a fuss. This makes disappointments all the greater if things do not always work out.

♄ **in the cardinal zone**: here the will comes into play, and we can often see that people are very interested in organising their own behaviour patterns, restricting and disciplining themselves. It is a kind of self-education and self-control of the reflexes and reactions that is often unconscious. Saturn nearly always indicates an extremely strong morality. One is restricted by everything that one should not do and self-esteem is often based on cutting back and denying oneself pleasure. There is the idea that self-denial on moral grounds improves the person. Depending on sign, Saturn can sometimes even take on a "saintly" character. This can be a kind of phoney showing off, though, as it is not at all compatible with the principle of the fifth house.

♄ **in the fixed zone** stabilises behaviour patterns throughout life. This gives security, but also causes anxiety and defensive behaviour in spontaneous social situations. This can include the so-called selective mechanism in sexual behaviour as well as all prohibitions, rebukes and moral restrictions from the mother. It is difficult to see through this later on in life, as the behaviour patterns acquired either alone or from the background and environment have become automatisms.

With Saturn in the fixed zone, the principle of security of this fixed house is expressed most strongly. That is why relationships are held on to even after they are no longer worth it. Jealousy is a pathological expression of the tendency to clinginess of this position in the fifth house. Strangely enough, there are often extreme behavioural tendencies. Saturn is at its strongest in this position, which can be called the "clamp effect". This means that the clinginess nearly always becomes obsessive.

♄ **at the low point**, the point of reorientation: Saturn switches completely. We know that moral restrictions are often fake, have nothing to do with the real life of the fifth house and also hamper self-awareness. If one realises that this comes from mother, for example, and one day sees through it, one goes to the other extreme; occasionally prostitutes of both sexes can be found here.

♄ **in the mutable zone**: there is again the danger of unconscious compensation. Tasks or other responsibilities are often taken on for other people, burdening Saturn with their problems so that it can complain about them. The person feels exploited and finds others ungrateful and increasingly demanding. As in any type of compensatory behaviour, only with experience do we recognise that our motives are misguided. To realise that we are selfish, we must be ready to change.

A transformed Saturn has overcome its fears. The person knows that they can take on social tasks with complete responsibility for the people entrusted to them. There is often the inner vocation to work with children.

The Curious Man
German Woodcut, 16th Century

6th House

The sixth house corresponds to the earth sign of Virgo. While in the fifth house we were still full of illusions and had to test ourselves out, the sixth house requires that we adapt to the realities of life. Here we have to find a place in society (You-side), a job we can do well for which we have studied, giving us financial security and enjoyment. The sixth house has always been known as the house of work in astrology. It is concerned with our ability to take care of ourselves, earn our daily bread and ensure our survival. This house is also traditionally associated with illness – if we do the wrong job for too long and work in the wrong place, we can't take it any more, take refuge in the 12th house opposite and become ill. Then other people have to take care of us instead. This psychosomatic mechanism must be taken into account in this house (also in the age point transit), particularly when one of the three ego planets is situated there.

Sun in the 6th House

In the sixth house the Sun, our autonomous self, goes to a lot of trouble to find a job in which it can develop and that corresponds to its talents. Mastery of existence, performance of duties, conscientious work and independent competence are the objectives of this Sun position. It identifies with tasks or work. Every day is almost continually occupied with fulfilling the necessities of life. If there is nothing to be done, it finds something. It sometimes makes a philosophy out of the needs of the autonomous self, i.e. using all its strength and being needed. Without work it feels bad. If there is no work, new jobs are found to be done to fulfil this inner need.

☉ **in the cardinal zone.** Here there is a need to play a leading role in any field of work, to lead others and tell them what to do. The ego gains reassurance when it is needed as much as possible by other people and is important to them. People with the Sun here often have a special talent for setting things up so that nothing works without them. This can be in a caring or serving profession, but is usually in a self-employed or managerial role. Such a person is naturally also convinced that they are the only one who is able to do these jobs properly.

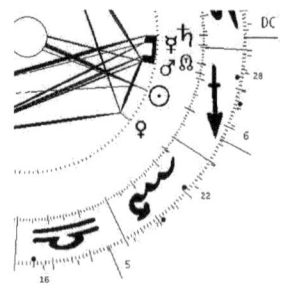

Voltaire, François, poet
1.12.1694, 17.30 Paris/Fra
☉ in cardinal zone 6th House

6th House ☉

☉ in the fixed zone tries to be moderate in all things, often feeling inferior and believing that others are better. In the sixth house, we are confronted with the needs and realities of life. It is not about creating new realities, but doing what has to be done. We must be honest and demonstrate a pure life motivation and genuine ability. There is no room for fibbing, bluffing, pretentiousness and hubris. For the Sun personality, this initially means reflecting on itself and its own abilities and possibilities. Because the Sun does not naturally like to be subordinate, for some this means "becoming smaller", limiting aspirations and cutting back. Here we are judged on the contribution we make by getting on with other people and serving them as we should. We are measured by our usefulness and efficiency. If we have nothing to offer, we are redundant.

☉ at the low point first has to demonstrate its ability before receiving the recognition it deserves, or finding the right job or profession. But usually (depending on sign) they suffer from being underestimated and used by others. At first the ego experiences this as a kind of defeat and for a long time battles with feelings of inferiority. However, as at all low points, this person has direct access to the innermost core of their being. Healing and helping forces can also be transmitted directly to the environment by the Sun ego, so that these people could well work in the social, caring and healing professions.

☉ in the mutable zone. Here we have the so-called "stress effect" for the Sun. There will be a certain ability to handle staff and subordinates correctly, when one evaluates the order of things according to function and usefulness. But if the Sun reacts too subjectively (which it does in nearly all stress areas), then the person does all they can to outdo others and be the best. The compensatory need to be unique makes them do whatever they can to be cherished and loved, and try to attract the attention of the You by overachieving (overcompensation). Depending on sign, favours are sometimes forced onto other people, so that this person becomes indispensable. When things go wrong, other people are blamed. This can lead to rivalries and friction.

For the transformed Sun in the sixth house, serving and helping others are basic needs. Helping others in ordinary life or in the field of social work, rectifying other people's mistakes, committing oneself to caring for the common good, always being there in times of need, are all the best qualities of a transformed Sun in the sixth house. They are ready to intervene where others have long since given up hope, which makes them very suited to the caring professions.

Saturn in the 6th House

In the house of work, Saturn uses the body as a tool and makes sure that it is not overburdened, allowing its efficiency to be maintained. Personal hygiene, fitness, the acquisition of manual or other skills are its fields of interest. Maintaining a good and healthy lifestyle is a priority. Saturn in the sixth house takes all the precautions it can on all three levels of human existence: physical, mental and spiritual, to guarantee survival. In the case of danger or failure, Saturn tends to blame other people, the circumstances, its tools, equipment, the weather, etc.

Effort is largely needs related; one works because one has to, and wants to successfully complete all the jobs started and earn enough to survive. Work is definitely not enjoyed for its own sake, but for what is gained from it; the only pleasure is in the end product, i.e. the sense of achievement and the practical benefits brought. That is also why there is an objective relationship with the You, colleagues, superiors and subordinates. Saturn manages and organises things according to planned goals, which means that both the boss and colleagues acknowledge one's efforts and find one indispensable. That is Saturn's main priority here. It is motivated by the need for security, protection and prevention, which will guarantee survival.

♄ **in the cardinal zone** has no trouble achieving its aspirations. A job is done carefully and thoroughly and deserved recognition is received. People with this Saturn position believe that others, work colleagues and superiors have to consult them. It is natural for them to demand attention and consideration for their activities, even welfare or care, often even by manipulative behaviour, whether in regard to nutrition, comfort, special favours, money or anything else necessary for survival.

♄ **in the fixed zone,** as the physical sense of self, is mainly concerned with personal security and health. Illness is seen as a possible danger, against which preventive measures are often taken based on a particular philosophy, such as eating correctly, vegetarianism, dieting, alternative healing methods, etc. The person is then very serious about sticking to these rules that they have created. They want to pass on personal experiences and insights to others, so people with Saturn in the sixth house are often connected to the healing professions, therapies, massage, etc. They can develop a missionary zeal in the process.

♄ **at the low point** frequently indicates concern for personal survival, health and physical well-being. For many this can take the form of a quasi-religious, puritanical theory or philosophy. Adepts include health campaigners or health fanatics who make regulations and compile rules as to what they have to do in order to stay healthy. In short, this is also the person who is always worried about their health, who always has something wrong with them, a typical hypochondriac. We have already seen this phenomenon with Sun in the sixth house.

♄ **in the mutable zone**, a learning area: one must always be learning something new so as to be always prepared for all eventualities, whether in professional life, learning new tasks related to the You or a partner, or in health-related matters. With Saturn in this zone, there is also a worry about providing for oneself; one must learn how to protect material needs and even life itself from the environment, in order to live comfortably. In the process, there can often be an excessive desire for approval and security.

Here, Saturn lies in the shadow area of the DC and has a compensatory effect, as do all stress planets. This means that it draws nearly all the energies coming from the aspect pattern into this area, so that it is equipped to deal with all dangers. With Saturn in the stress area of the DC, one is consciously or unconsciously prepared to use every means possible to make sure that a partner cooperates. One is desperate for all promises and agreements to be respected. Others are forced, often without realising it, to respect one's needs, relating to problems of existence and to one's own inadequacies or deficiencies. They are expected to bend the rules. In some cases this behaviour can escalate into hysterical manipulation.

The transformed Saturn in the sixth house overcomes its needs and anxieties by spiritual helping and serving. Its life is put at the service of others, providing them with security, foresight and support. It stops refusing to take responsibility for them and puts itself out totally for them. This allows it to recognise, and go some way to making up for, its own errors and those of others, in a caring, perhaps maternal profession.

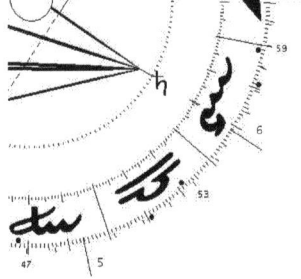

Jean Tinguely, painter, sculptor
22.5.1925, 05.30 Fribourg/Swi
♄ 6th House

7th House

The seventh house has always been known as the house of marriage and partnership. None of the twelve houses has been dealt with so superficially in the literature as this one. It is usually just the same old happy, unhappy or late marriages in the case of Saturn, luck in the case of Jupiter and separation in the case of Uranus. The field of the relationship to the You and social encounters is much richer and more important in the development of the personality than is commonly believed, which is why we should examine it more closely.

The seventh house can be compared with the experience of a sunset. The Sun moves towards fusion with the horizon. It merges into it. If we imagine a beautiful evening with no mist or fog, we can see the Sun set in a blaze of radiant colour. If we lose ourselves in this ambiance, we feel slightly melancholic, but also hopeful that the Sun will rise again the following day. We never feel that the Sun will disappear, but that it is absorbed by the horizon, which swallows it bit by bit. Something is always changing in this process. That is the basis of this seventh house. It is revealed in the relationship with the You in all its shades, colours and nuances, in all possible situations: joyful, painful, illusionary, fortunate, nurturing, noble, repressive. All possible kinds of relationship fill this house like the colours of a rainbow.

The ego planets are therefore also changed, developed and evolved by all You relationships in this area. There is always a strong orientation towards and dependency on others and on their feedback. Here we can only experience the ego planets through intensive partnership, in the collective experience of joy and pain, in the encounter and merging with the You, in doing things for others. The ego planets are characterised by the assuming of responsibilities or duties, by conflicts and fights within relationship, tolerance of injustice or the enjoyment of success, triumphing over others right through to romantic merging with the You. We try to describe the iridescent expressiveness of two of the ego planets in all their glory below.

Sun in the 7th House

There is nearly always a certain reduction in self-awareness when the Sun is in the You-area, particularly if there are insufficient opportunities for social contact. These are necessary here for self-affirmation, which is not at all typical of the Sun. The Sun should not have to rely on others; its self-confidence should come from within and not be dependent on the approval of the You. This is why a Sun in the You-area can often become a product of, and in a way a reflection of, its environment. Self projections and "great expectations" are projected into the seventh house. It is the house of the "echo effect", of wish projections, but also of the experience that "You reap what you sow". That is why a Sun in the seventh house seeks self-affirmation by doing things for other people. It is willing and also able to solve or take on other people's problems. It wants to matter to others; working with others to complete projects successfully raises its self-esteem. In business affairs it seeks out partnerships and prefers collaborations where it has to deal with people that it can influence or who are dependent on it. This Sun position makes one well-mannered and well-behaved with good interpersonal skills. According to sign and aspects, one is also able to avoid conflict or, if necessary, to handle it. One is prepared to face up to the You, to quarrel with them, to confront them and to learn more about oneself as a result of the confrontation.

The seventh house is concerned with the bonds that exist between people. It is not for nothing that it is called the house of marriage. We should also think of it as the house of the setting sun. It does set, but not for long. That is why the seventh house is also connected with temporary bonds, not with eternity. We believe too easily in the everlasting bonding force of the seventh house. We should not forget that the sun does not go down forever; there is a rhythm determined by cyclical laws of existence and relationships with the You, which have nothing to do with imaginings, projections or childish expectations of eternal happiness.

☉ **in the cardinal zone** gives a dominant will. This Sun has a special ability to manipulate and can make others do what it wants and what it thinks is right. It has a powerful influence on the environment and is therefore admired and respected and, according to sign and aspect, can also be feared because it can gain power over the You. It impresses the You, with which it therefore has a good

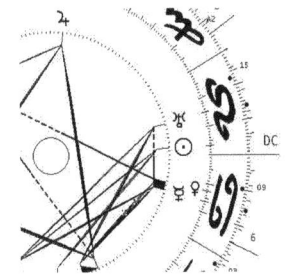

Carl Gustav Jung, Psychiatrist
26.7.1875, 19.20, Kesswill/Swi
Sun on 7th House cusp (DC)

relationship, is comfortable with all kinds of social interaction and loves to gain the You's absolute respect and to be admired and loved. By making a personal commitment to the well-being of others, one can often attract people who are weaker than oneself. It receives respect and admiration, but also excessive demands. Other people quickly notice that this is a vital strength that can be tapped into, which is where the struggle for priorities, rivalries, boundaries and preferential treatment begins.

☉ **in the fixed zone** nearly always has a firm idea of how it should be treated by the You. This rigidity causes one to be easily deceived by others or even oneself. If others do not behave "properly", one is usually personally hurt and it takes a while to realise that one has misjudged the You. Intolerance and misunderstandings in intimate relationships due to a lack of responsiveness are common. A partner irritates personal weaknesses and sore spots, which is found very unpleasant. Too much self-deception is a warning sign, because it means that one is basically completely unwilling to accept the truth. That is why demands made on other people are not met; one gets involved with the wrong people. A self-protective nature easily leads to feeling cheated. The person often wants more than they get, but in the house of balance and justice (as this house is also called), they receive what they are prepared to give (echo effect). That is why a Sun in the fixed zone will above all enter into relationships of mutual convenience and protect itself with contracts. Such bonds are taken seriously and the commitments are usually bona fide.

☉ **at the low point** of the seventh house will not be fully expressed. It is frequently misunderstood and its brilliance goes unnoticed. Many things that it does out of sincere conviction are misconstrued, misunderstood and do not catch on. The feedback, the echo effect, is lacking and many must give more than they receive. The Sun, the autonomous self, is introspective and should learn how to listen to its inner voice and correct its excessive devotion to the You by understanding its own motivations. Questions like "Why do I need the approval or support of the You? Why do I try so hard to get on with the You? Despite failures or setbacks, do I still believe that I cannot live without the You?" need to be answered. It is usually a question of correcting false ideas about love and partnerships, and admitting that one often acts out of self-interest. Here one has to find a point of support or rest within oneself, develop personal character and avoid ego projections by striving for truth and authenticity, in order to become capable of genuine coexistence.

☉ **in the mutable zone** of the seventh house, in the stress area, will at first compensate by an independent attitude. There is a desire to show the father or partner that one is strong and can exert influence and manipulate people. It often makes us proud when others dance to our tune. We show off, want to shine, outplay others, be the best and show everyone how good we are. Projections and compensations coincide here, which makes it more difficult for people to see us as we really are. Ulterior motives, unfounded fears and feelings of rivalry all play a role in relationships. In situations of cohabitation, frequent irritation at another's mistakes leads to conflict. Settling disputes can occupy us unduly and waste a lot of energy. We are constantly looking for balance and only achieve it when we acknowledge that we also make mistakes ourselves and that both sides are to blame.

The transformed Sun really helps partnerships to work in the seventh house: it knows what it is entitled to and what others' rights are. It is tolerant, fair and finds the happy medium. After many learning processes, crises and deprivations, duties and agreements are taken seriously and fulfilled. It enjoys making its contribution to the You, to the partnership, and so takes its place in the community. Wherever there is conflict, it builds bridges and tries to find a peaceable solution.

Saturn in the 7th House

The main priority of Saturn, the planet of physical self-awareness, is to protect us from danger, from external attack. It is not a sociable planet; its principles are those of delimitation and protection of function, i.e. guaranteeing physical and mental survival. That is why in the seventh house, the house of partnership and marriage, contacts with anything different and unknown are first averted and tested to see how dangerous they are. Saturn in the You-area always has a problem with unexpected contacts; it is a so-called "contact filter", a first-class selective mechanism. Social situations must be prepared for, introduced slowly and kept under control so that they do not become dangerous.

Anyone with this Saturn position first tests other people's sincerity, respectability, seriousness and usefulness before approaching them. Very demanding in choosing a partner, many "save themselves for Mr or Ms Right". It is not for nothing that Saturn is known in traditional astrology as the "late marrier". In fact, in social situations, he is a controller, an auditor, like the watchman at a factory gate. Nobody is allowed inside without some form of identification. This need to identify others can be very tiresome, especially in sudden encounters with people where rapid judgements must be made. One then makes bad judgements and hides behind regulations, time pressure or other excuses. Many opportunities are wasted. Saturn's security motivation can lead to a negative attitude towards the You due to contact anxiety and unresolved bad experiences, and form a blockade, an impenetrable social barrier. In dangerous situations, one forms the concept of an enemy, which in the house of the echo effect naturally produces hostility. But this is one's own fault and the situation must be resolved by treating the You fairly.

♄ **in the cardinal zone** lets the protective instinct come on strong. In positive cases, Saturn at the seventh house cusp looks on partnerships as a "project". It enjoys collaborating on difficult problems and "gritting its teeth". It is ready to make sacrifices, but also tries to get the most out of them. Saturn is not free from ulterior motives here. Most contacts that these people make are for a purpose and are also in some way rewarding in business terms. There is nearly always a reason for them, according to the motto "How useful can this person be for me and my goals?" That is usually the real reason behind the generosity with which Saturn treats other people. Once he has established a contact, he tries to control it, structure it and keep it safe. The You is often manipulated by conscious or unconscious feelings of guilt. Saturn sees to it that promises are kept. Many draw up contracts, regulations and prohibitions, and if previous commitments are not respected, they want to punish the You. They resort to anger or the withdrawal of affection in order to control the You.

Conversely, they also put themselves out for others who are being treated unfairly. They protect the weak and take care of them, mother them and sometimes reduce their responsibility by overprotecting them. In so doing they prevent them from maturing, despite meaning well. But this Saturn insists on receiving compensation in the form of devotion and gratitude, which are needed for personal reassurance and self-esteem and as a reward for its efforts. If these are not forthcoming, ways are found to punish those concerned, sometimes harshly.

♄ **in the fixed zone:** the effect of Saturn is strengthened. We are interested in the problems and tasks of the You and feel responsible for everything that happens to them. Those close to us gain reliable friendship, but also a tie. In all partnerships we want to achieve lasting security, which entails conventionalism and clinginess. We understand exactly how to reassure our partner by giving them what they want. We care about their concerns, which become our own, and work hard for them. We usually attract partners who need our input and skills. They are often still wet behind the ears and are looking for someone to support and help them to cope with life. But we tend to worry that we are being used or not getting enough back from the partner in return. Some hope that the deserved compensation will be on another level, and are happy with the promise of a reward in the distant future, getting by on their reserves in the meantime.

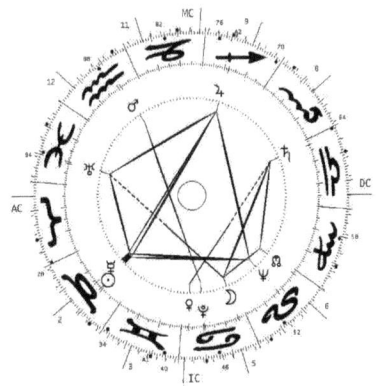

Louise Huber, API School Director
10.5.1924, 03.15, Bamberg/Ger
♄ in 7th House

Saturn in the fixed zone, and also in other areas of the seventh house, gives some people a deep-seated fear of being abandoned. Depending on sign and aspects, this can lead to power struggles, especially if they are devoted to someone or a separation is imminent. When this happens, it is a kind of threat to their whole existence, like a denial of their right to live. This is totally intolerable for them, so they try to prevent it happening. On splitting up with a partner, many people with Saturn in the seventh house tend to jump straight into another relationship, or even to have several in reserve.

♄ **at the low point** has a heightened effect, because the quality of the low point has an affinity with that of Saturn. Here it has an educational, karmic significance; we cannot avoid a transformation. All the above-mentioned concealed, selfish goals relating to marriage and partnerships are not achieved, or are corrected by fate. One often invests everything in a partner and receives little or nothing in return. The partner refuses to cooperate and it just does not work out. That is a tough test that causes many break-ups. During the transformation crisis (usually when AP transits this Saturn), crystallised ego wishes are dissolved and the ego's core is "cracked". Everything that was done for the You is shown to be null and void; it was worthless. This is a deep transformation and disengagement crisis; we feel powerless and have no more power over our partner, who does not react to demands and refuses to give anything in return. We are thrown back onto our own resources and do not receive the rewards we deserve. We have to get used to this, while still keeping the relationship alive. This makes us mature and grow until we learn that love and relationships have nothing to do with accounts, but mean being there for others without getting anything in return.

7th House ♄

♄ in the mutable zone usually makes one more flexible, but also more vulnerable to rejections and attacks. We allow the You no liberties that have not been previously discussed. We always want to be asked for permission first. If someone overlooks us or goes over our heads, we are offended and refuse to cooperate and plot for punishment or revenge. Here we feel the influence of the eighth house cusp, which is why we start to compensate and demand more from the environment than it is prepared to give. We cannot stand it if others have more attention, influence, rewards or devotion etc than ourselves. Depending on sign and aspect, we want to be indispensable or to hold an important, impressive role. We stop possible losses or changes with ruthless laws and inner or outer resistance. Spontaneous ideas are met with mistrust and rejection. But if we make the ideas or suggestions ourselves, we expect others to cooperate. We cleverly manipulate them by making them feel guilty and by including them in our plans.

From a psychological point of view, behind all compensative behaviour with Saturn there lies a deep-seated fear of life, a lack of self-confidence and security motives. Some will not win the battle in these separation crises and will be left by the partner, the You. Periods of solitude have a purifying effect, for here one is approaching the purification area of the eighth house with its conversion and transformation crises.

The transformed Saturn leads us to give up our defensive attitude and mistrust, and be grateful for every social situation, for spontaneous devotion and relationships we cannot control. In every house Saturn has a maturing effect. In the seventh this means the transformation of selfish tendencies in social interactions, partnerships and marriage.

8th House

The eighth house is a fixed water house, corresponding to the sign of Scorpio. The water temperament corresponds to our emotional nature, which is why we have to learn the Law of Love and Inclusion. For the ego planets, this means conversion, purification, transformation, renunciation of personal wishes and goals and material possessions, giving up selfish ideas about life in favour of further spiritual development. Hence this is the house of ego conversion for all the ego planets, linked with the unavoidable experience of the eternal cycle of death and rebirth.

Seen in this way, the eighth house is ambivalent, a house of crises. It is a space for conversion and rebirth – it used to be known as the house of death. Life and death rub shoulders here. It belongs to the fixed cross, with its motivation for security. From the point of view of behavioural psychology, this is the house of the structure of society, of the laws that regulate life in the community and guarantee security and continuity. All fixed houses are concerned with a regulated, standardised, fixed attitude. It is not an innate attitude, but one that is acquired, in accordance with conventional, practical and decent standards of acting, feeling and thinking. In the eighth house, it is our attitude towards society and the community in which we live. This does not mean a living model of society, but the structures, the laws for the protection of possessions, which mankind has developed during the course of its evolution. They are always strictly followed orders, unconditional principles, rights and duties, laws and prohibitions.

Sun in the 8th House

With the Sun in this position, one has to deal with the laws of society. We need them for self-actualisation, we have to bear them in mind, respect them and use them. If the Sun wants to benefit from the achievements of society, it must learn to know and live by the laws of the land. If this is not done, they come into conflict with established norms and can pay the price. For example, a criminal completely breaks out of the system and becomes an outlaw.

During the individuation process, some day we all get into situations where we must break free of the system, whether it be our own or other people's. If we want to continue to grow, we have to take risks. Even if we do not actually break free, we do experience inner crises and crucial tests of our strength. What is alive and growing within us cannot be permanently repressed. That is why the ego planets, and especially Sun in the eight house, are always involved in conflicts, in a battle between old and new, between functionality and creativity, between meaning and form, between life and death. That is roughly the range of development of the self in the eighth house.

☉ **in the cardinal zone** of the eighth house will devote all its energies to securing a position, a status in society where it can gain approval and be effective. It strives for social recognition, influence and protection. The best way to do this is to serve society, be it as an administrator, judge or civil servant, policeman, tax collector or similar. With the Sun here the You, the community, can usually be used to achieve self-actualisation. One can work one's way up to a management position in an institution or organisation, be given duties and responsibilities by the community, be appointed to look after law and order, fulfil functions and duties with conviction and do a job as well as possible. Everything seems to be in order.

But for the autonomous, quite individual ego needs of the Sun, there is not much room for its own creativity; it is confronted with the status quo and has to maintain it and commit itself to it, so that there

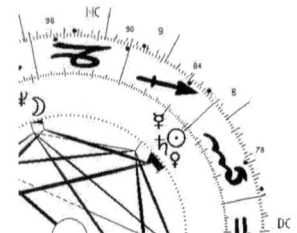

Dr. Franz Hartmann, Theosophist
22.11.1838, 14.30, Donauwörth/Ger
☉ cardinal zone 8th House

is little scope for the ego to develop freely. Depending on sign and aspects, this is experienced as a burden, pressure or stress, and some would love to be free of it someday so that they could eventually achieve independence.

☉ **in the fixed zone:** the expansive powers of the Sun ego are reduced by existing structures. The pressures and ties that often hold us back come not only from the community but also from strict family traditions. With Sun in the eighth house, we also talk about a dynastic mission, an inner compulsion to perpetuate what was inherited. In this fixed zone, there is confrontation between expansive Sun energies and inherited structure. We must deal with the societal or family structure and somehow use their help to get ahead and make something of our lives. This occasionally requires an unhealthy amount of adaptation, which can even lead to loss of identity.

☉ **at the low point:** here the conversion forces have a particularly strong effect on the expansive Sun ego. Depending on sign and aspects, this is experienced as a constant pressure, a requirement to "render to Caesar what is Caesar's". The person feels that their true self is not needed, they just have to fulfil a function and be a custodian of substance, goods and ideas. They therefore feel misunderstood and not accepted for who they are. The independently-minded Sun ego rebels and wants to throw off the burden, but it is unable to do so and falls back again and again into its old conventional ways.

The transformation process of the low point with the associated change of motivation does not take the pressure off the ego. Even if it feels dependent and powerless as a result of circumstances, the world or the father, it must undergo the low point conversion. That can cause the Sun ego great inner crises, because the whole world opposes its compulsion to be individual, original and unique. If this concentrated ego power then discharges explosively and the personality gets involved in the transformation current of the inner self (see also *Astrology and the Spiritual Path* (13) "Low Point Experiences"), the theme of death and rebirth overshadows the whole life. He always has to be ready to retreat, to quit, to let himself be underestimated and still feel an agonising fear that he can lose what he is rightfully entitled to. It is the impulses from the soul, from deep within the self, that allow us to realise the transience of all external material values, so a person with this low point Sun would be wise to face up to this conversion theme and accept it as the law that governs his life. For the more he resists the transforming forces, the greater his crises will be.

☉ **in the mutable zone,** the stress area before the ninth house cusp, indicates compensative powers. The Sun has to serve two masters, the eighth and ninth houses, which is why the crisis mechanism, the collision of intrinsic and extrinsic values, destabilises the ego. It can lead all too easily to a life lie, a misinterpretation of one's own motivations, inadequacies and insecurities. It tries to conceal this by any means possible, entrenches itself behind previous achievements and good deeds, blames others for its own failings, and accuses them or takes the credit for things it has not done. Here is a shadow area between what is forbidden and what is permitted, between the visible and the occult.

In the field of religion, there is an interest in the esoteric, the occult and parapsychology. The transcendental can also be a way to escape from standardised narrowness and pressure. This attempt is initially compensative and a lot of energy and concentration are required in order to find reality, one's own truth. Personality alternations can sometimes appear in the shadow of the ninth house because of a moment of sudden stress and irritation due to excessive activity caused by the repression of fears. However, this kind of stressful situation provides an enormous growth stimulus and intensifies the process of death and rebirth.

The transformed Sun in the eighth house is totally committed to its work, whether in the community, the family or for a government institution. It always serves the whole, and its influence grows as it devotes itself to and fulfils its inner mission, which is in harmony with the laws of evolution. If a spiritual planet (Uranus, Neptune, Pluto) is linked to Sun by aspect, there is an ongoing process of change and transformation throughout the person's life, the high-point of which occurs at the age point transit. In transpersonal psychology, this process is known as the Damascus Experience, in which Saul becomes Paul. This position allows the insights that have matured deep within the soul to come to light, and can produce a first-rate spiritual teacher.

Saturn in the 8th House

With Saturn in the eighth house security of status is a very important basis for personal well-being and protection. Saturn would like to have a firm place within society. It looks for concrete ways of protecting itself and enjoys working in established institutions that are solid and durable and can overcome transience. It takes pleasure in a civil service position for life, which if possible continues even after death. Duties and responsibilities are performed with the utmost care, boring as they may sometimes be. It identifies with work, taking on duties and functions as an important part of itself. It has a marked ability to go without home comforts and get deeply involved in difficult tasks that others are unable to handle, which makes it feel important and strong.

Saturn in the eighth house tends to cling to the old. In many things it is conservative, even pessimistic, and prefers to stick to what it knows rather than venturing into something new or unknown. It has the wisdom of the pessimist, who gives up at the outset to save himself from pain. It usually looks at the negative side of an issue, of a function, of reality. If someone emphasises the positive, it reacts suspiciously and angrily. It also suffers from a constant fear that something unexpected will happen so that the transience of matter will catch up with it, which it wants to avoid at all costs.

♄ **in the cardinal zone** undertakes social functions and roles with this in mind, feeling called upon to preserve the means and values of others/ the community, becoming the advocate of law and order. It wants to use its knowledge and skill to become indispensable, by taking on responsibilities and tasks that are too difficult for others to manage. Consciously or unconsciously, and depending on sign and aspects, with Saturn we are on the make, aiming to obtain some of the You's means – and we do all we can not to lose a source once it has been tapped. In this way, we make ourselves dependent on other people's means. The question for the eighth house is "What is mine and what is yours? How much can I have?" This is always the area in which karmic tasks are played out.

A particular feature of this Saturn position is a constant feeling of guilt. One is always bothered by conscience and has to deal with everything correctly, always remaining above board and beyond reproach. Conversely, one also likes to make others feel guilty and wags an admonishing finger at others' failures and mistakes. Attacking other people's integrity is a form of self-defence for Saturn. If others can be shown to be in the wrong, one is off the hook and has every chance of being successful oneself. When someone gains power in this way and only builds up his own ego without doing anything to serve the community, he begins a tightrope walk, for in the eighth house karma catches up with us. Here we have to learn that the small ego can still get by without status, possessions and power. With Saturn one is tested over and over again, either by strokes of fate, bankruptcy, redundancy or separations, until this maturity is achieved.

♄ **in the fixed zone** wants security at any price. It is only happy when it has a secure position in society, whether as road sweeper or general, where it can be supported, as it were, by the establishment: laws, structures and institutions. The price, which it is usually willing to pay, is dependency. People with this attitude like to be told what to do and to do what others want. Over time, they often lose the ability to make their own decisions and delegate responsibility for themselves to the company, to their boss or to a higher power. Such people are easy to manipulate with guilt and also to blackmail, when they react like puppets. Saturn's refusal to take risks, to take responsibility for itself or to give up its possessions, makes further growth impossible. This fear makes it build a strong security wall with an airtight seal all around it. This makes it even harder for it to handle life's natural changes.

♄ **at the low point** of the eighth house, which is also the low point of the whole house system, utilises the conversion energy that flows directly from the centre of being and wants to "soften" Saturn. Strokes of fate, setbacks, losses, economic crises, redundancy, family rows, bereavements and the like are required to instigate conversion and reorientation. Saturn's mission here is to mature. As mentioned above, in the eighth house it easily gets addicted to matter, routine, form and security. So there is a danger that the form of life suffocates and the objective handling of regulations, prohibitions and laws is given more importance than people themselves. On the one hand, one does everything possible to toe the line and not take any risks; on the other hand, Saturn at the low point of the eighth house is not on solid ground and cannot withstand the internal and external pressure for long. Life itself gets rid of any false security motivations and pulls apparently safe ground from under our feet; the floor gives way and the conversion begins. What happens is that existing protective boundaries are broken down by potential security, order and stability, upon which an independent self can be born. The interesting thing about this is that many people with this Saturn position do things either consciously or unconsciously that undermine their own survival. In the eighth house there are also self-destructive forces at work and it is not for nothing that it is also associated with suicidal thoughts.

♄ **in the mutable zone** gives the insight that we can also be ourselves away from the protection of the collective. The person becomes philosophical and understands more and more clearly that no protection or precaution, however thorough, has any effect against the wastage of matter, wear and tear and the inevitability of death. This also includes overcoming the fear of growing old and dying. A philosophy of life is developed, and often a sarcastic sense of humour, which reinforces or resists this process. Here in the stress area Saturn also demands the cultivation of physical awareness. It is certainly a good thing to do something about one's health and body from time to time, keeping it flexible and healthy and counteracting the crystallisation process.

The transformed Saturn in the eighth house must receive special care and attention. She should not let herself go and should be constantly trying to counteract the weight of gravity, inertia and listlessness. Health and enjoyment of life should be cultivated and encouraged so that Saturn remains flexible and is not afraid of life's natural destructive forces. She should not want to escape the vicissitudes of time, but should realise that there is real security in insecurity and in the constant changes of nature. She makes her own philosophy out of this, which sustains her and gives her a calm and responsible attitude.

9th House

The ninth house belongs to the mutable cross, which represents relationships, the principle of communication and contact with all living creatures. That is why people with planets in the mutable signs and houses are mainly interested in relationships. The ninth house activates the motivation to get to know human nature and the world in which we live, to see the connection between all living things and to understand its meaning. The ninth house is concerned with the expansion of consciousness, with the search for meaning. Banalities and truisms are not taken at all seriously but ridiculed instead; one knows better than that.

Temperament must also be considered in the development of the personality. The ninth is a fire house and is therefore related to the first and fifth houses and their corresponding signs Aries and Leo. They are concerned with self development. The quality of fire is concerned with the manifestation of the ego, or the self, i.e. with personal growth. That is typical for these three fire houses, which represent three different phases of this growth. In other words, there are three fundamentally different tasks in the development of the person: in the first house the I or ego is born and is driven to manifest itself, in the fifth house it tries to coexist with the You, and in the ninth it matures to autonomy, to the capacity for independent thought.

So the ninth house is concerned with thinking for oneself, i.e. the ability to think and live independently. Here one does not consult others or put forward their ideas, but rather possesses enough moral courage to express one's own ideas and to take full responsibility for them. Having an independent opinion is also the reason for many of the problems that crop up in the ninth house, for this easily comes into conflict with traditional values.

Sun in the 9th House

Behaviour in the ninth house is usually individualistic and takes little notice of what other people think, especially with the Sun, the symbol of the self-confident individual. People with the Sun here pander less and less to convention, and usually do their own thing instead. It is quite natural that this kind of attitude meets with resistance from the environment. They come into conflict with their nearest and dearest, i.e. with the third house. It's not always easy to stand by your own opinion despite the attacks of your closest relatives, siblings and neighbours. A person's moral fortitude depends largely on a strong inner core and is most effectively guaranteed by Sun in the ninth house. The three/nine axis is known as the Thinking Axis, so these two houses are both concerned with thinking: the third with conventional, received ideas, and the ninth with your own ideas. The third house lies in the collective area and the ninth in the individual area of the horoscope, so collectivism and individuality confront each other here. This is very significant for the ego planets.

☉ **in the cardinal zone** stands out in the environment by virtue of its own views. Self-confidence is strong; the individual is inwardly convinced that he wants to self-actualise. He usually attracts people who are happy to play by his rules. People with Sun in this zone of the ninth house are natural leaders who are convinced of their strength, vitality and charisma. They know themselves well and show themselves to the world as they are. Depending on sign and aspect, they are straight-talking and honest, caring little about what others think. They love their freedom and do not tolerate external pressures. They want to decide their own tasks and circumstances and find it hard to take orders. They turn out to be successful in life and are born leaders. Especially when the Sun is in a cardinal sign, some try to usurp leadership from others and to impose their opinions on them. They have trouble tolerating people who think differently from themselves. The central, autonomous personal will is oriented towards self-actualisation and self-assertion. Many think that only they know best and they always have the last word in arguments.

☉ **in the fixed zone** of the ninth house moderates the expansive Sun ego. Constant pressure weighs down on the Sun's need to assert itself. Although it wants visible and quick results in the environment, in this zone and especially at the low point, success does not come easily. Here it is necessary to acquire mental substance by reflecting a great deal on oneself and the world, by introspection and training the self-perception. In any case, we should learn to stand back, to explore the inner self, to be honest with ourselves, for only then can we be successful. The other people we want to influence will only take us seriously when we can show that we have character, have achieved something original and have created our own established worldview. If we have managed to pick up useful knowledge and skills, the environment will want them. There is usually pedagogical and educational ability, which is initially directed towards the self before the desired approval and appreciation are achieved. Someone who talks big will not be taken seriously. Only truly real, objective and comprehensive knowledge of a subject, situation or problem is willingly accepted by others, as they sense when there is a lot of substance and knowledge available, and have no problem following the suggested ideas.

☉ **at the low point** indicates a quite specific life task: it is necessary to define oneself clearly mentally and find oneself. So it is less about the outside world and more about personal spiritual experience. In other words, what matters here is being convinced of oneself as a spiritual entity. That is the task at the low point of the ninth house. There is less focus on material, physical success and more on intensively working out the laws of, and giving deeper meaning to, one's own life.

The conversion theme is also in operation at the low point, the transformation of the little, transient ego's perspective to a universal, comprehensive worldview. It is necessary to go deep within oneself

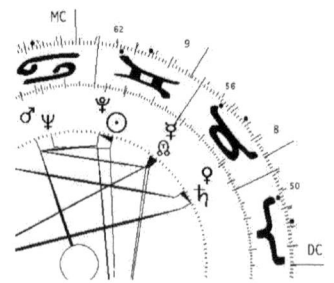

Jacques Cousteau, Marine Biologist
11.6.1910, 13.15, St. André-de-Cubzac/Fra
☉/♀ LP 9th House

and create a world model from personal experience that is not only valid for the little ego, but also for many other people by finding a greater and more universal life meaning. True philosophers can do this in the ninth house.

☉ **in the mutable zone** has an ambivalent effect, having to serve two masters: the ninth and tenth houses. This causes compensatory behaviour. Here I want to assert myself at all costs. Ambition and single-mindedness are the best compensations. I want to show my father and other people that I am the best, that I can achieve my objectives and know more than others. However, if the ego puffs itself up in the process and triumphs over others immorally, then the compensation will not be pleasant. Mental agility can be so great here that the boundaries are blurred between lies and wizardry, between truth and magic. The sensed expansion of consciousness exceeds the real possibilities, the consequences of which are self-delusion, self-adulation or even feelings of inferiority, combined with the fear of being exposed or unmasked. The person usually plays a role instead of being himself.

For the transformed Sun in the ninth house, the primary task is being honest with oneself, as well as admitting to mistakes and lack of knowledge. Conversion of motivation, abandoning selfish behaviour in favour of humanitarian goals, and focusing on the higher ethical meaning of life are part of this journey. It is necessary to outgrow oneself, be able to leave the little ego behind and devote oneself to transpersonal tasks. As a teacher, one can guide others and direct their interest to tasks that affect the world. This is how to gain the highest meaning from this Sun position.

Saturn in the 9th House

In the construction of the personality, Saturn represents the physical self. I am right to wonder what I want in the ninth house of thinking. As the basis of my philosophy of life, in the "House of independent thought, philosophy and the search for meaning", I create real, tangible ideas. In the ninth house, Saturn does not care whether it is understood or not, just whether knowledge gives it more security, truth and self-confidence. That is why it clings to previously established truths and lets them become principles by which it lives its life. It finds it easy to lay down moral and ethical guidelines by which it judges itself and other people. People who contravene these guidelines or who violate this self-established boundary are rejected and condemned.

From a developmental point of view, this Saturn position has a particular significance for the whole personality. In this house we realise how we can outgrow ourselves and the status quo. In a manner of speaking, this is the house of the expansion of consciousness. That is why this Saturn position is important for development, because as the limiting principle, it constantly makes us encounter our limits and challenges us to exceed them. Strokes of fate often trigger processes of self-knowledge that go to the limits of what is bearable, but which go on to lead to unimagined depth and responsibility.

♄ **in the cardinal zone** of the ninth house allows a more intense experience of the law of overstepping limits. Although we refuse to accept this law for very long, and stick to previous judgements and established circumstances as long as they work, we do let ourselves be convinced of the contrary by reality. We can sometimes change our opinion abruptly and astonish our environment by doing a previously unthinkable U-turn. Near the cusp, though, we ask other people to respect our judgements and our goals. When we have made a change of direction, the environment just has to accept it. People with Saturn in this position often cannot stand it if others decide things for them and do not let themselves be talked into things once they have reached a decision. Some draw a clear boundary between themselves and other people, become aloof and look down on the mediocre people below them, do not want to share their knowledge, strength or greatness of mind with them, and think: "they have to learn from their own experience".

♄ **in the fixed zone** of the ninth house deliberately limits us so that we do not have to grow. We do not want to change. We cling to the status quo and prefer to stay in a safe position rather than venture bravely forth. The crystallising out of my own truth, my own worldview, happens slowly. Ideas, my own as well as other people's, are questioned until they can withstand the tests of harsh reality. Saturn makes the thinking process rather ponderous, but thorough and deep. It can take a long time for it to reach the right results, and also a long time for it to pass them on. When someone with Saturn in the ninth house feels the need to communicate and to share his own thoughts, he will have to cope with the process of formulating them correctly. Depending on sign and aspects, that is hard for him to do and if he does not succeed, he prefers to keep things as they are.

Being afraid of one's own courage is typical of Saturn, because under no circumstances does it want to blame itself or make itself feel guilty. It is always afraid of compromises, surrendering and the knowing look. That is why it protects itself by holding back. It is typically secretive about its own problems, and does not like others to know it too well.

♄ **at the low point**: in mutable houses, the status quo reaches a point of dissolution that is never achieved in cardinal and fixed houses. That is why the areas around the mutable low points are also known as "points of greatest freedom of choice". Saturn must first recognise this freedom though, which is inherently difficult for it to do. It prefers to stick to what it knows. It has clever defence mechanisms at its disposal for use in dangerous situations. In its mind, it builds defensive, declaratory, argumentative walls around itself, so that it is not separated from its existing views.

In positive cases, Saturn brings the capacity for serious thought, perhaps even the mind of a true philosopher. It aims to bring its own substance to fruition, which often remains latent because it so often doubts its own abilities and is only actualised by internal or external crises. Some question their own ability to think for years. They prefer to listen to what others have to say and keep quiet about their own opinions until they are sure that they are right. That is not the solution though, as the search for one's own liberal point of view encourages one to let go of what is known and familiar, to make it possible to move on to new ways of thinking.

♄ **in the mutable zone** again gives rise to compensations. Saturn has to serve two masters: the mutable ninth house and the career-minded individualisation of the tenth. Saturn, with its close affinity to the fixed principle, finds it hard to handle the ambivalence of this zone of the ninth house. It is always struggling for security and compensates for its ability to commit itself, set boundaries and tie itself down with some kind of role playing or in an external function.

Depending on sign and aspect, the mutable ninth house is constantly calling into question Saturn's fixing quality, and the "truths" it has found are discredited in the process. Very often, maxims which one would like to rely on and be reassured by are proved to be false, leading to ambivalence. Sometimes the disintegrating effect of the ninth house becomes stronger, making this person more unstable in their thinking. At other times there is a search for an authority who can tell them what is right and what is wrong. Others cleverly feign their own ideological assurance, postulating pseudo-truths and principles with conviction. Whether these are true or not, Saturn must be proved correct so that it does not lose its footing. It cannot stand insecurity under any circumstances, which is why the effect of the ninth house is that: "I am always right". Here it is necessary to realise that mind rules matter, content must be more important than form and not vice versa. The insight must grow, that there are spiritual principles that develop within Saturn's matter.

The transformed Saturn in the ninth house is important for spiritual development. It develops the ability to recognise spiritual, meaningful connections, which enables greater security to be reached by crossing boundaries. The first step in this direction is the insight into one's own limited nature, the overcoming of arrogance and pride with modesty and humility. Here we should take Saturn seriously as the "Keeper of the Threshold", while also recognising it as the "Great Initiator", who will lead us from the hall of learning into the hall of wisdom. The Socratic tradition: "Wisdom only begins when I know that I know nothing", is a transformation experience that often occurs at the low point of the ninth house.

10th House

This is the highest point of the horoscope, the house where one can become an individual and mature personality. The description of the ego planets is therefore particularly important in this house, because the ego undergoes intensive training. People with ego planets in this house have a natural gift for showing themselves off to their best advantage, for attracting others' attention, setting the tone and playing a particular role. They often have a natural aplomb that cannot be overlooked.

The tenth house has always been associated with success and career, and corresponds to the earth sign of Capricorn. Planets here indicate how you can grow, and which goals you want to achieve. Like all cardinal houses, it is concerned with growth. In particular, it indicates the birth of the individuated person. Here one gradually grows into an autonomous and mature personality. Authority and reputation do not appear automatically; first of all they have to grow. Someone with a planet in the tenth house should not believe that this planet will enable them to succeed at everything in life, instead they must make an effort to achieve something that was not there before. As with all growth processes, the person must have a goal to aspire towards. Only then can they acquire the tools or special knowledge required to reach this goal. When they do manage to achieve it, they should not rest on their laurels; instead they should then work for the collective and make their own abilities available to others. These are the growth processes that the ego planets have to go through in the tenth house.

Sun in the 10th House

A tenth house Sun, especially near the MC, is always a sign of an authority in some field. I strive for a position in life where I have something to say, in which I matter, where I am important and can participate. Here I need a task in life that corresponds to the primary need to be unique, independent and to have authority. The dimension can be quite diverse here, i.e. I am either an authority in my domestic or professional life, where I know everything and have everything under control because I own everything. I am so independent that nobody can tell me what to do, I exercise a kind of power, am perhaps a prominent authority or an important political figure. To be an authority means being in complete control of what I am or do, and taking on the corresponding responsibilities and tasks. I must act on real knowledge and should not become dependent or be told what to do, but must make my own decisions and then also follow them through.

☉ **in the cardinal zone** of the tenth house is in its naturally most suitable place, because there is an affinity with the vital, catalysing principle on the same level. As a self-sufficient source of light, the Sun is the individual spark in the human consciousness, that certain something that constitutes a person's uniqueness. Its drive is strongly conditioned by a need for recognition from the environment. It has to dominate situations or people, take control and, depending on sign or aspects, fight off rivals.

With this Sun position, I feel called upon to take control. I know what I am capable of and cannot tolerate any competition. Depending on sign and aspects, I think: "I am the best". I am convinced of my own uniqueness, importance and competence. Weaker people usually follow my orders without resisting. I have little trouble in asserting myself and achieving my goals.

Most such people are taken seriously, are respected and have a natural authority. This is probably the easiest place for the Sun to express itself. These people feel they have a vocation for tasks that require all their Sun energy. They have a natural claim to leadership and can (depending on sign and aspects) recruit others for their own purposes relatively easily.

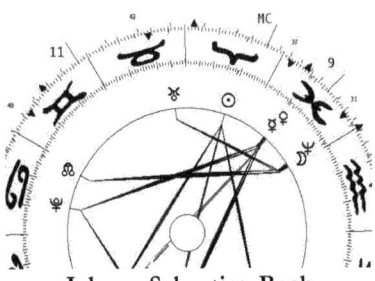

Johann Sebastian Bach
31.3.1685 GC 11.30, Eisenach/Ger
☉ in cardinal zone of 10th House

10th House ☉

☉ **in the fixed zone** of the tenth house looks for a position that guarantees as much security as possible within its own sphere of control. Many are very skilled at creating a solid position for themselves that they then want to build on and retain. They attract people and make them dependent in order to strengthen their own position and power. Others believe that the more people they have on their side, the more powerful they will be. But nobody can trust the collective in the long term, as its support cannot be relied on. It is the familiar experience: "Today they're singing his praises; tomorrow they'll be screaming 'Crucify him!'"

In the fixed zone growth processes are a constant challenge, especially when I believe I've achieved everything and have nothing more to learn. I should not trust myself. I slip all too easily into complacency and do not notice that life is passing me by. I should not stop working on improving myself, on acquiring things that contribute towards to the real substance of a mature personality. My own potential must be increased and worked on.

A person who does not work on their growth or maturity but blocks them, or thinks they are not important, must expect negative reactions from other people. They will meet with aggressive forces that emerge at some time in their lives, often at the age point transition, and bring them down from the heights they have achieved. No other house has such clear, rigid rules as the tenth, where the misuse of power sooner or later has a destructive effect on the ego.

☉ **at the low point** of the tenth house feels ignored, and without outside help it cannot be externally effective. Often it does not succeed simply because others are better, or just present themselves better. One feels misunderstood and is easily hurt when pushed into a corner by stronger people or not taken seriously. Self-awareness is very sensitive, especially due to a constant fear of losing charisma or status. Even the slightest competitive circumstances are often enough to provoke the fear of losing control of a situation. The individuation process is stunted if it pushes outwards and strives for power and status. The priority of someone with this Sun should be to free themselves from external dependencies and become autonomous. Here, destiny calls for introversion. They must go without external support, approval and prestige, set personal goals and follow the inner voice. But this alone is not enough.

In the individuation process, I need to be brave enough to live out my originality, to defy regulations or the dictates of the silent collective so that my actions are completely personal. Some have to do something crazy to liberate themselves from the expectations of family and tradition. For a while, some people go against their family in order to find themselves. This can last a long time until the personal or the original emerges. The reorientation of the low point Sun here means freeing oneself from the need for outside approval. When enough inner substance has been developed, approval is often forthcoming from others, precisely because it is no longer needed.

☉ **in the mutable zone** again has to serve two masters, the tenth and eleventh houses. To compensate, we "upgrade" our ego for no external or internal reason. We act as though we are superior, have elitist aspirations and hide our self behind imaginings and projections. We want our friends and those around us to treat us as if that is who we really are. We think we have the right to demand that the gates to social success open to us and set out to do all we can to belong to the upper echelons of society. If we do not succeed, we retire offended.

However, the eleventh house wants to lead our Sun-like nature to what is really important; creative processes are at work here that give a new form to the personality. But initially we resist this change and react by compensating. This can show itself by the Sun constantly demanding validation from the environment. It demands respect to which it is not entitled, gives itself airs, stands in judgement over others and moralises. With this Sun, we should instead first learn to show others more understanding, tolerance and due respect before asking for something for ourselves. We should also create something ourselves before we benefit from the creativity of others.

The transformed Sun radiates the strength and conviction of a mature authority who is followed by many people. It has natural leadership qualities and successfully completes the tasks it undertakes with a sense of responsibility. Other people respect it and are happy to follow it. Having the courage to act individually and responsibly enables exceptional performance. The Sun has developed its inner potential to full capacity and can achieve great things in fields of its choice. It shows the character and integrity of a mature personality.

Saturn in the 10th House

Saturn, the master of matter and form, wants to replace the Sun in the tenth house. But as it has no radiance of its own, it must pretend. That is why the tenth house Saturn is always looking for something that makes it shine: a position with status, a career, a sphere of competence, a position of external or internal power.

10th House ♄

In the tenth, as in all cardinal houses, growth processes are at work, working through all solidified forms and, over time, slowly dissolving them. Saturn fights this for all its worth. A person with Saturn in the tenth house is familiar with the experience of feeling more and more anxious the more their influence or external position of power grows. The more power they exercise, the more they are subject to the criticism of the collective. Deprived of the protective private sphere of the fourth house that lies opposite, this Saturn has to be available to everyone, to make decisions for them, taking responsibility for the community. It becomes the enforcer of collective wishes and visions and allows itself no personal freedom. Total commitment on its part is needed to maintain its position over the long term.

Someone who holds power has to do everything as well as he can, and cannot afford to make mistakes. He must hold on to what he has achieved, come what may. He cannot expose himself and has to save face and keep up appearances at all times. He is forced to overachieve, which either makes or breaks him. If the fear of failure gains the upper hand and he is forced to defend himself, he can become cruel and harsh. Then he can easily fall from the position he's reached. This is the law that Saturn represents in this position. Someone with Saturn here has to learn to respect this law, or it will turn against him should he misuse his power. Classical literature refers to several powerful men with Saturn in this position who were ultimately ruined, e.g. Caesar, Napoleon and Hitler. But not everyone with Saturn in the tenth house is a dictator. It is not important to what extent Saturn acts as the "Keeper of the Threshold" or as a boomerang. On a small scale, someone will usurp some kind of little piece of power from the collective space.

♄ **in the cardinal zone** of the tenth house leads one to make form and tangible matter more important than the spiritual, as in the stress area before the MC. It only values what can be demonstrated physically; everything else is treated as fantasy or superstition. At best, this Saturn position enables people to achieve excellence in a particular field and to stand out as a result of their special ability. By mastering form, they can use it brilliantly to their own advantage, or also for the benefit of the family or the collective, perhaps as a tribal elder, politician, scholar, scientist, company director or powerbroker in politics and business. Most people with this Saturn position are strongly tested at some point in their lives, in which spirit and matter, father and mother confront each other – and they have to find a form in which spirit and matter are in harmony with each other and can function perfectly together instead of against each other.

People with Saturn in the tenth house cardinal zone don't like others to comment on their affairs, and cannot stand criticism or excessive authority. Others are energetically rebuffed if they attack their authority or try to dictate to them. There is always a problem of authority, with open or hidden power struggles going on. Such people strive for self-determination and cannot tolerate rivals. Many frequently find themselves in some kind of competitive situation, either real or imagined due to fear. They have a special ability to lead others and to involve them in their plans. For a long time, they act as though their job and relationships must last a lifetime and have no concept of the possibility of failure or change. They stick firmly to a previously attained state and hold their ground.

Others are brilliant at borrowing power from the collective, from Sun-like personalities who lack the desperate craving for validation. As they themselves are unable to "shine", they use other people's light. Others delegate their aspirations to power to those stronger than themselves and bathe in their reflected glory. For example, in the case of a woman, this can be her husband, or in the case of a man, it can be working for a prestigious company. In this way they can champion good ideas, because they usually have enough authority (their own or that of other people) and ideas to be able to assert them with the people.

♄ **in the fixed zone** of the tenth house strengthens the motivation for security. It also tends to stunt growth. As already mentioned, all cardinal houses are concerned with growth. As the crystallisation principle, Saturn is not conducive to growth as it represents the final phase of development; it hardens existing forms so that they can last forever. Someone with Saturn in this zone easily adopts a rigid, authoritarian attitude where no further growth is possible.

Particularly in the fixed zone, Saturn will want to offer something equivalent to the vital radiance of the Sun that it can rely on. At best, it develops a skill at which it can shine and becomes a specialist in a particular field, an expert authority. If this does not work out, it has to borrow power from other people, for which it falsely takes the credit. This makes it dependent on the real skills of those more powerful than itself, so that it is constantly worried about what people think of it. It is afraid of the truth, of exposure and humiliation and of the possibility of losing its place in society. It keeps itself to itself and wants to avoid being exposed and people noticing its inadequacy and realising that it possesses no real inner radiance of its own.

10th House ♄

These people rarely receive the approval they think they deserve and are often convinced that their plans are thwarted and confounded by people stronger and cleverer than themselves. They have to learn that the difficulties destiny brings them can be a way of saying they are not yet mature enough to take on a particular responsibility. As long as their claims to status and influence are based on a false interpretation of themselves, they will fail.

♄ **at the low point**, the point of reorientation, conversion and transformation, will surely confound aspirations to power and bring ordeals several times in a lifetime. Here a person will finally learn to see that material power provides no real security. He repeatedly has to forego worldly success in order to obtain inner power from his own centre of being. He has to be seen supporting the family and assuming responsibility within the collective; personal power trips bring nothing. People with Saturn at the low point need strokes of fate or inner crises to make them grow up. It is precisely because they find it so hard to tolerate the loss of power that they have to experience it, so that they are continuously able to demonstrate their authenticity.

The lack of personal power at the low point can also manifest in a difficulty in understanding that other people can be more competent and better than oneself. In the event of ego problems, this can occasionally become a barrier that is hard to overcome. So long as he thinks he is the best or the only person to know something, he will fail and be rejected or avoided by others. A low point Saturn in the tenth house should never use illegal means of gaining power or usurp borrowed authority. Everything has to withstand the inner test for honesty of his conscience. Hence this position constantly demands that he questions his motives. Authority, aspirations and status should be in line with the inner character, the centre of being.

As always, a reorientation takes place at the low point, which in the case of the Saturn transformation crisis leads to the big self, the true self. A low point Saturn that is open to the vital energy coming from the centre of being will be able to function as a mature, sophisticated authority. The task here is to work on himself and his inner being, to enrich the inner character (saturate). The tenth house corresponds to Capricorn, the sign of initiation. Saturn as the ruler of this sign is both the "Keeper of the Threshold" and the "Great Initiator". In this regard, the Capricorn house also symbolises the inner conversion expressed in the esoteric seed thought of this sign: *"Lost am I in light supernal, yet on that light I turn my back"*. That is the inner task of such a self development problem. You can read more about this in *Reflections and Meditations on the Signs of the Zodiac* (20), pages 182-195.

♄ **in the mutable zone** of the tenth house, in the shadow of the eleventh house cusp, generates many kinds of compensative power forms. On the one hand, there are crystallised, dogmatic ideas about truth, human nature and the exercise of power; on the other hand, these people feel called to keep an eye on others so that they do not overstep their authority. Hence they are harsh critics of people who misuse power, judging them to be heartless and tearing them to shreds. Laws and principles are laid down that must not be violated. Should anyone do so, they act as judge and moraliser. The Inquisition in the medieval church is one example of this Saturn compensation.

As in all the stress areas, here too we can see ego-compensation in misconduct. It is usually his own guilt and mistakes that are being hidden and projected onto others. He constructs bogeymen so as not to realise his own inadequacies. In extreme cases, this attitude leads to fanaticism, intolerance and dogmatism. Such people are often stolid champions of rights, are authoritarian and look out for other people, which is why Saturn before the eleventh house cusp can also be called a "Nanny position".

The transformed Saturn in the tenth house symbolises the mature personality that is searching for a role in life with which it can identify and for which it can be responsible. These people often grow with their task, if exceptional difficulties have to be overcome. Away from claims of authority or the despotic exercise of power, they have to work out the true intrinsic value of the individual, i.e. being and growing and not formal rigidity. The aim of the transformation is the dominion of spirit over matter, and not the other way around.

11th House

The eleventh house is part of the fixed cross with temperament air, corresponding to the sign of Aquarius. This house is often misunderstood and nearly always judged superficially. The simple interpretation "House of friendship" is not sufficient. Combined with the three other fixed houses the eleventh is important because the ego/personality, here in the last space of the fixed cross, can assimilate and bring together a lot of valuable experiences. At best this shows itself in human maturity and dignity, in an ethic and humanity that can evolve into greatness.

In the eleventh house, we don't want to go on stage and hold forth, as in the tenth. Instead we choose a group of like-minded people with whom we feel comfortable and protected from hostile attacks by others who think differently. The motivation of all the fixed houses is "security at any price". Conflicts and pointless public debates are avoided where possible, for they create a lot of fuss and achieve little. Hence the circle of like-minded friends, the brotherhood, the elective affinity. This also includes secret societies, whose members enjoy the feeling of being one of the select few. The ego planets therefore tend to be exclusive in the eleventh house. An elitist awareness nearly always prevails; we want to be someone special and to stand out from the crowd. We insist on personal freedom and originality. We write our memoirs because we want others to benefit from our experiences.

The eleventh house means creative awareness for the individualised personality and therefore freedom from external and internal constraints. It is a natural goal of the ego to develop its individuality and to protect itself from strangers. Although it accepts that it is part of the community, it is constantly struggling in some way for individual freedom and independence. With the ego planets, we consciously or unconsciously resist interference. Here we are aware of our free will, which is why everything must be based on freedom of action. Creative expression can enable our originality to develop as far as possible. That is a basic demand of this area of life. It is concerned with human dignity, self-esteem and the right to be responsible for all one's actions. This develops into an ethic, a concept of the correct way to live that must absolutely be implemented. Freedom and respect for the individual are paramount in this house; they must not be questioned and under no circumstances be relinquished. Someone with the ego planets here would feel that as a betrayal. That is why the rights of the individual are tolerated and protected, not only one's own, but also other people's. That is the group consciousness of the New Age, which we hear so much about these days. In its highest form, like the spirit of Aquarius, it finds expression in the eleventh house as the "Harmony of the Original", the true brotherhood.

Another point that we must consider in assessing personality development in the eleventh house is the entire 5/11 axis, the Relationship Axis. In the fifth house we follow our spontaneous attraction to the You, here we get involved in experiences in order to intensify the quality of relationship. The fifth house is like a playground in which we are only capable of spontaneous experiences and passing fancies. Here we just enjoy being with other people. In the eleventh house we set conditions. We are guided by ideas about the You and about the world. We are selective and demand certain standards of character, social, intellectual or cultural status and high-mindedness in others. Anyone who does not correspond to this image or to our own status is disliked and possibly even rudely snubbed. The eleventh house is choosy and only allows contact with people it deems suitable. Thomas Ring (11) gives an apposite description when he says "there one is free from the compulsive agitation of the fifth house and can choose one's friends freely".

Sun in the 11th House

The Sun, our autonomous, self-sufficient self-awareness, knows itself very well in this airy house. We insist on individual freedoms and rights, have a high opinion of ourselves and do all we can to make others share this opinion. We want to appear broad-minded, which is why we have principles and clear convictions with which to judge the world and current events by sound standards. A certain charisma and image are important for this. That is why we are always thinking about creating an excellent reputation, making an impression and being noble and good. We often flaunt fairness and humanity. We like to teach others, because we feel called to propagate and defend human values. Depending on sign and aspects, we feel responsible for the state of the world and feel disgusted at everything that goes wrong. Some act as judges and criticise everything that is ignoble and imperfect. There is therefore nearly always a trace of fanaticism involved.

Particularly nowadays, the eleventh house, which corresponds to the sign of Aquarius, reflects the new spirit of the Age of Aquarius. That is why a person with the Sun in this position is in tune with all aspects of the spirit of the age. He has a feel for the conditions and opportunities of the modern-day aspiration for success; many also feel a vocation to contribute to the improvement of social conditions. Most are oriented towards the future, but some remain stuck with utopian ideas of improving the world.

☉ **in the cardinal zone** enables us to function autonomously. Many occupy managerial positions within organisations, businesses, corporations and associations. They are loyal bosses, honest and optimistic. People with a cuspal Sun dare to take liberties with remarkable *sang froid*, which other people would never contemplate. They don't worry too much about what others think of them, which is why they are successful at work – they react appropriately to general needs and expectations as they come up. People with the Sun in this zone easily find the right place in society; for many the doors to success open automatically. Some have a definite ability to acquire direct

11th House ☉

access to those in charge. Relationships, friendships or belonging to an association, a party or a trade union are considered to be a smart route to social advancement, so that they usually really do get ahead and become successful. But once they "arrive", they should not become proud and look down on others, or else they get trapped in the ivory tower of the eleventh house and lose touch with reality, isolated in a utopian illusory world.

If they pursue their own interests, these people know how to use their influence and contacts skilfully to their own advantage. Some people's loyal attitude then turns into a charade, role-playing, "just for show", so that they are respected and admired. Here they all too easily conform to worldly standards and are concerned with thoughts of prestige, rivalry, who is the best and morally superior. In its negative form, the eleventh house also causes technocratic categorisation with the associated inhumanity that goes with it. Fellow men are degraded to mere numbers, to faceless beings who are treated impersonally and heartlessly.

☉ **in the fixed zone** strengthens motivation for security, so someone with this Sun position looks for a group of people who share their interests and with whom they feel understood and comfortable. Principles and guidelines are drawn up together, which it is essential to respect. This can include groups of political activists, know-alls, or fanatics. Such groups can be bound together by either idealism or mutual interest. The unwritten law is: "You scratch my back and I'll scratch yours". Giving and taking are part of the image, the self-worth. Patronage is also a possibility, depending on financial background and social position. Some people with this Sun position become protectors of people and animals, perhaps becoming patrons and trying to win friends with their generosity. But in the fixed zone, boundaries are also drawn up between those who belong to the group and those who do not (chauvinism). An elitist attitude with group egotism is always based on a hardened, crystallised self-centredness.

Protectionist thinking is a safety function, a source of mutual protection and support providing the security of belonging. Depending on sign and aspects, one abides by principles and rules that often turn into dogma. Because ideas merge easily with one's own here, one identifies with spiritual issues and becomes an agent or champion of these ideas. Some people hide behind a powerful ideology and want to belong to an intellectual elite, protecting themselves with an ostentatious dogmatism, as do some church representatives and sect leaders.

☉ **at the low point** finds it more difficult to be taken seriously. It suffers from setbacks and low self-esteem, so some people compensate by seeking refuge in pretentious ideas of themselves, feeling that they are called to greatness but that the world just does not realise it. They cut themselves off and punish others with their contempt, become aloof and break off ties for no good reason. They are consequently often loners. Other people with this Sun position like to bond with a group of like-minded people. Hiding themselves behind an elitist aspiration to be appointed, they get stuck in the obsession that they belong to the chosen few. This usually causes them to be unable to act and suffer from feelings of neglect.

As at all low points, this is an ambivalent situation, which brings about a personality change. It is necessary to look inwards and develop one's own character. Here, this means forgetting personal importance or lack of it and being happy to serve a thing or a group.

☉ **in the mutable zone**, in the shadow of the twelfth house cusp, is again an indication of compensatory behaviour. The insecurity and tendency to dissolve of the twelfth house affects all apparently stable friendships and their associated demands. This can lead to an anxious clinging to people one is completely dependent upon for approval, while at the same time doing all one can to demonstrate the extent of one's independence. This is a real contradiction, and claims to originality and greatness often alienate the people one likes.

Compensatory behaviour can lead to misunderstandings and break-ups, and in some circumstances even to a "throwaway mentality". When people to whom we feel connected by love and friendship "fail" once and do not satisfy our demands, they are dropped – and simply thrown away. That is why in like-minded relationships these people find it hard to make friends who stick by them through thick and thin and are still around when they are in trouble.

A transformed Sun in the eleventh house will simply advocate and protect human interests and rights. Its high ethical standards and broad-mindedness are undeniable. Its high-mindedness causes it to automatically reject negativity. It can work unchallenged with a pure motivation for the improvement of conditions. Such a person cultivates a real partnership with his soul and yields to the divine will that sees that all is well. This makes him capable of perceiving universal connections and helping many people to develop. He becomes a role model for others who can be guided by him and his work.

Saturn in the 11th House

Saturn in the "Thinking House", where thoughts take form, creates formal and spiritual ideas about existence that are stable and as far as possible withstand the changes of time. In this fixed house they mature into personal laws and principles that provide strength, value and stability. The basic principles must be rock solid and be able to withstand any attack. Saturn in the eleventh house always indicates ethical stability that often appears strident, and stands firm in the face of all opposition, like a mountain. One is able and strong enough to be responsible for oneself, and usually has a sound sense of good manners, decency and values. The corresponding ideas are truly complex. All their ramifications are well thought out so that one is rarely stuck for an answer. This kind of person can also be stubborn and intolerant when it comes to defending their spiritual principles and asserting their own opinion.

In the eleventh house the focus is on ethics, as opposed to on morality in the fifth house. Morality is ostensibly more about external behaviour and regulates what one can and cannot do. The ethics of the eleventh house are concerned with a broad, spiritual picture that tries to explain the world, set standards and say something about how people should treat each other. Many people with Saturn in the eleventh house had a mother who showed a strong ethic in both her words and her actions. Children adopt these values without thinking, but later criticise them all the more strongly, especially during adolescence. This often leads to a basic mistrust of all "isms", of social systems or institutions, so that throughout life they retain a critical attitude towards, or a tendency to rebel against, forced truths. We only build on what we have personally experienced.

♄ **in the cardinal zone**: here a dynamic will is added to the concentration of thoughts. Depending on sign and aspects, this Saturn position indicates a forward-looking attitude. Saturn bestows a natural authority and has a certain intellectual power over other people; it is a role model for many. Depending on which ideas it believes in, it can create a picture of the future that gives other people's self-confidence a prop with which they can identify and feel safe. The ideal concept of man that is being worked on here is based on much intellectual work; all efforts go into achieving a convincing closed system. Everything must be real and true, tried and tested, and the form is refined until it can fully express the spirit, the idea. Someone with this Saturn position does not take the easy way out. Everything must be achieved empirically

11th House ♄

Bruno Huber
Founder of the Huber Method
29.11.1930, 12.55, Zürich
♄ cardinal zone 11th House

over time. The existing structures of the present can be seen clearly, as can the past. From this he learns how the present came to be and uses logical deduction to produce a clear idea that becomes his own personal truth and serves many people as a guiding principle.

There is often the wish to put long-cherished and now perfected ideas into practice. People with Saturn in the cardinal zone of the eleventh house are often founders of organisations, societies and schools intended to pass on their own ideas. Once this is done, there can be conflicts with people who think differently, leading to power struggles. He becomes a proponent of his own ideas and for reasons of self-respect must also be convinced that he is the only person who is right. Concepts and ideas easily crystallise under Saturn's influence, often making him uncompromising, hard and obstinate when it comes to defending his own authority, expertise and intellectual property. Where there is impending antagonism, he is afraid that rivals could acquire his own ideas, creative achievements and accomplishments and reacts touchily to intellectual plagiarism. Although these people possess leadership qualities, they are not really suited to collaborations, which is why they are good at delegating.

♄ **in the fixed zone** of the eleventh house has a particular tendency to crystallise, so that ideas do not keep up with the changing nature of reality. This often makes them form false ideas of the world that are energetically championed even when they are manifestly mistaken. Growth, love and understanding then become impossible. Such people become dogmatic know-alls and are often really irritating to those around them. They propagate a false ethic that only serves their own ego and their personal image of what it means to be a great person. The elitist thinking of the eleventh house creeps into every area. But in the fixed zone it is particularly strong so that it can lead to a cultish spirit or group egotism, which only serves to massage their own ego. They hide behind ideas, concepts, patterns, forms and masks, which makes them even more isolated. So convinced of their own ideas, they becomes implacable and demonise dissenters. Examples of this pattern include sectarianism and the persecution of those of a different faith.

♄ **at the low point**, the point of change and reorientation, brings the experience of loneliness and isolation. There is also the experience of so-called virtues becoming vices. Sacrifice and renunciation, good deeds and high moral standards cut no ice with other people, they just meet with rejection. The process of inertia turns virtues into selfish demands and possibly even into vices. Every harsh criticism and punishment by his fellow men is to no avail. He sits all alone behind walls erected in false self-defence. Nobody is there to help. He insists on his honour, dignity and generosity while remaining isolated in an ivory tower of his own creation. At the peak of the crisis, an inner conversion takes place in which he realises that he is nothing without friends and other people. He must then go back to the people, to experience brotherhood and to implement ideals in cooperative solidarity.

♄ **in the mutable zone** of the eleventh house, the stress area before the twelfth house cusp, also causes compensatory motives. The effect of the mutable twelfth house can already be felt at the low point and dissolves all previously acquired security. People with Saturn in the shadow of the twelfth house do all they can to achieve mental and spiritual security and sit on the fence for a long time before they commit themselves. They try to cling to friends, to strong people or to religious beliefs but are abandoned all the same. At bottom they are always unsatisfied and insecure. They study spiritual laws, think and reflect a lot about life and the meaning of truth, but they still cannot shake off their fear that they could possibly be mistaken. They have to learn that the only place they will find security is within themselves. Friendships or ideological interests are then only useful if they provide security.

The transformed Saturn in the eleventh house deals with the motive of true human kindness, the idea of brotherhood encompassing all mankind. In doing so, it imagines a perfect social order that it wants to help put into practice. As a political or spiritual leader, it sees its duty as being to bring worldly affairs into line with spiritual principles. It feels that its vocation is to see that human values and laws are not infringed. That is why spiritual principles determine the guidelines of its actions. What is achieved must benefit as many people as possible. Acknowledged truths arise from a grand vision, that can lead to the formation of a systematic theory with contents that, due to their organic and coherent nature, can be understood and used in life by many people.

12th House

With the twelfth house the circle of the zodiac is complete. This is the last of the astrological houses and in a sense includes everything that was experienced in the others. It corresponds to the water sign of Pisces and is motivated by the mutable cross. In a mysterious way, the twelfth house makes a connection with transcendence, with the being that exists deep within us and is constantly recreating our existence. The twelfth house has always been considered as the place of withdrawal, of the hidden latent strengths within us, as the house of isolation, anonymity and seclusion. The forces of externalisation come to rest; here we are quite alone, in the silence of our own room as it were, where we can experience the sensitivities of our own soul. Like the first house, the twelfth belongs to the I-side of the horoscope. While the first house indicates the self's powerful push out into life, the twelfth house requires it to withdraw to become mindful of the spiritual and emotional dimensions from which it once emerged.

Nearly everyone with an ego planet in the twelfth house tends to be introspective and have a vague longing for a "country that speaks their language", for people that really understand them or to belong to a greater whole. The twelfth house is an introverted space and, from the point of view of the desire for worldly success, the quietest corner of the horoscope. It is not an easy place for the ego to evolve, because there are natural destructive processes at work here that counteract its expansion. Like the eighth house, it is a house of change, of death and rebirth, but in a higher sense.

It is not so much a matter of letting go of material forms, as in the fixed eighth house, but of the expansion of consciousness into the realms of a transcendent whole. It is a long journey until the lighting up of universal consciousness, whose ability to transform itself easily leaves all static boundaries behind. This leads to the experience of the original unity of life, realising its true meaning in expanded consciousness. Hence the twelfth house is an area of crisis for the personality, which must constantly be developing and changing towards transcendence.

This area of the chart was formerly known as the Monastery, the Hospital, the Prison or the "House of Clandestine Enemies", explained by the fact that here destructive forces are present in man himself. The "clandestine enemies" are present within us, usually in the form of repressed, unresolved experiences that often pop up uninvited from the unconscious to depress and demoralise us. In the twelfth house, all energies are drawn back within us, usually with the result that worldly success is not taken so seriously. That is why many people work in the shadows; they do not want to be seen. This also explains why this house is called the "nameless helper in times of need", which quietly does good. Examples would be the spiritual healer or social worker who work for the socially disadvantaged, those in need of care, drug addicts; they help to heal and repair other people's pain. This helping and healing is the positive side of the house of Pisces. The negative side is the conspirator, the secret service who set traps, the schemer who undermines reputation and status and spreads rumours and panic.

Sun in the 12th House

The twelfth house has a counteractive, compensative effect on the Sun, the part of our ego that strives for self-actualisation and autonomy. This house makes us want to remain quietly in the background, whereas the Sun naturally acts externally. On the one hand we want our expertise to be acknowledged, or at least to have an effect on the environment; on the other hand we're worried about exposing ourselves, because we're afraid of not being taken seriously. This attitude is usually caused by a repressive upbringing. Perhaps we were told: "You are too young for that, you can't understand it yet".

There are many ways of repressing the Sun's self-confidence in childhood. It can be due to the shyness or timidity of the parents; perhaps the whole milieu in which the child grew up has hindered development of a healthy self-awareness. Most signs, especially mutable and fixed ones, have a sensitive reaction to repression. If our self-confidence is greatly limited, we experience over and over again periods of discouragement and self-contempt, which we must work our way out of by cultivating a deep, spiritually-based self-confidence. If we are unable to do that, we spend our whole life as a wallflower.

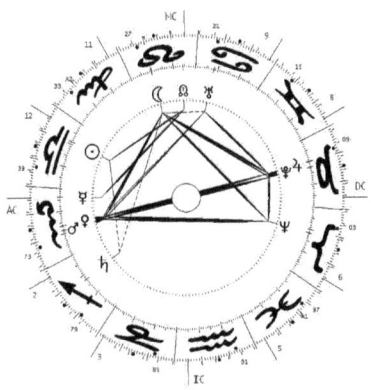

Mahatma Gandhi
2.10.1869, 07.45, Probandar/India
☉ in cardinal zone 12ᵗʰ House

☉ **in the cardinal zone** of the twelfth house allows the ego to be effective to some extent. Generally with a twelfth house Sun self-confidence is not strongly pronounced, but it must also definitely not be damaged, sad or depressed. Depending on sign and aspects, feelings of inferiority can be overcome in a caring profession, helping other people, where the need to transcend the personal is satisfied. Self-confidence even has a particular inner strength in the cardinal zone, according to the motto: "I am not completely useless, I am a special person, who does good from a tranquil place. I am at one with myself, a universal power flows through me, which changes and heals the people around me."

That is why such people enjoy the caring professions, where they can intervene sympathetically and clear-sightedly in situations where others have long since abandoned hope. When they are needed they transcend themselves. Once they have found a transpersonal task they can identify with, they can then easily transcend their ego in the spiritual sense of this house; they feel called upon to act by a higher order.

Their self-confidence then becomes dependent on an ideal, a good cause or a person. In the context of religious or social organisations, they work selflessly to spread ideas. They have a good influence on their flock because they manage to awaken sympathy and hope where they had ceased to exist. They can be priests or missionaries, in clinics as doctors or nurses and in all kinds of humanitarian organisations. Some make sacrifices, try to expose and solve social problems and, depending on sign or aspects, act as an example of Christian brotherly love.

☉ **in the fixed zone** of the twelfth house cannot make an appearance by itself. From this position it can do nothing to advertise itself, and instead represents itself by understatement. If they tried to show attitude, they would worry instinctively and people would laugh at them, so they prefer to keep quiet. But they can influence others from behind the scenes and be an *éminence grise* who provides motivation and corrections. This Sun can be more powerful behind the scenes than the person it influences is on the stage. However, if an *éminence grise* is left sitting in the corner without "a king on the throne" to influence, it becomes bored, depressive, pessimistic and alarmist. It has to look for a "king", an ideal or an institution that it can serve. Having this kind of secret power is a natural form of self-protection that one can exercise in this way. Occasionally this kind of person with the Sun in the twelfth house can achieve a degree of prominence through their behind-the-scenes activities.

If Sun in the twelfth house suffers too much pressure, perhaps from an opposition, a large quadrilateral or a debilitating Saturn trine, then its self-confidence is thwarted and it becomes a slave to ideas. The infinite, unlimited expanse of the twelfth house can also cause extreme types of behaviour, in both positive and negative senses. When the self-confidence has to be supported in this way, and becomes more and more out of touch with reality, the person is misunderstood and hides behind himself. If something goes wrong, he closes up completely and is quite unapproachable. He burdens the environment with his frustration and can wear other people out.

☉ **at the low point** has direct access to the inner core being. In the spiritual sense, the twelfth house is concerned with perceiving the higher self, which is formed by our own inner spirit and connects us to eternal Being. Here, one does not act, but meditates, reflects and observes. One is usually not interested in worldly success and is happy to stand back. One is introspective, detached from the world, a dreamer, often interested in the absurd, tending to wonder, contemplate and also criticise. This is a contemplative, cognitive area, and a kind of "testing ground" for change for the ego planets. The outward-thrusting forces of the ego undergo a conversion/reversal, accompanied by abandonment of external success, which for many people is a complete U-turn. The desire for success is paralysed and internalised and a person with this Sun position often sets himself strange, irrational goals. The person himself decides if it is a true spiritual quest or an escape from reality.

☉ **in the mutable zone** of the twelfth house, in the shadow of the AC, causes a heightened urge for self-manifestation. Gauquelin's research into planetary positions before the AC has already established a maximal increase in intensity (top athletes: Mars before the AC). Just as before other house cusps, the activity of Sun before the cardinal I-point is compensatory. Here the ego aspires to achieve great things: "I'll show them (or him, usually the father) who I am and what I can do."

Even if they fail at first, these people do not give up, they always hope for another, better opportunity. If it doesn't work out today, then it will another time. Depending on the Sun's sign, they are unusually sure that one day their chance will come. They prepare their great entrance in silence. The self manifestation power of the AC comes in surges, so that self-confidence fluctuates between conceit and half-hearted self-contempt. Many feel under constant pressure to show themselves and to compete with others. Others work in silence on improving and perfecting themselves, so that they are prepared when their chance comes along. Because they are compensative, they are often more interested in the impression they make on other people than in real achievements. The sign must be taken into account in order to understand the compensation correctly. A cardinal sign will definitely be more egocentric than a mutable one.

The transformed Sun in the twelfth house can achieve transcendence during its lifetime. In the twelfth house we are connected to a spiritual dimension in which we return to the origin of life. The otherwise outwardly-thrusting forces for self-expression are turned inwards and can only act in line with the inner life motivation. They want to serve and help and are controlled, either by the soul itself or by a spiritual being under divine direction. This type of Sun discovers self-healing forces in its centre of being and radiates them out into the environment. It has produced many true healers.

Saturn in the 12th House

The twelfth (Pisces) and eighth (Scorpio) water houses are places of change and the process of death and rebirth. In the twelfth house, we seek primal belonging, regeneration (religio) from the fountainhead, the "Return to the Father's House". As the security principle, Saturn has a much greater affinity with material things; the spiritual is too instable, too intangible. So Saturn clings desperately to old habits and structures, but without warning it can suddenly throw them all away. We often do not know when and why the change has occurred.

Saturn in the twelfth house has many faces, and is difficult to assess. How it copes with this boundary-dissolving house naturally depends on the sign and aspects. Saturn in the twelfth house frequently indicates a person who works self-critically on improving himself. Such people suffer setbacks without complaining and can cope with the worst, apparently taking it in their stride. But that is only the appearance. They conceal their true motives and cleverly implicate others in their plans without them noticing. They often have a sneaking ambition to work from the shadows in order to get ahead.

Most people with Saturn in the twelfth house find it hard to build security for themselves and set reliable boundaries that have some permanence. In the watery Pisces house, Saturn is on shaky ground, on mutable ground. Saturn's natural fear of the unlimited, infinite space of the twelfth house means it is constantly looking for a firm foothold. It runs after illusive securities, and again and again is taken in by stronger people, sometimes becoming the victim of false beliefs. Many lack a natural sense of delimitation, protective behaviour and rejection. Depending on sign and aspects, they are at the mercy of internal and external influences, which one would hardly expect from Saturn.

For many these symptoms are connected to the relationship with their mother. In this Saturn position the mother was nearly always a problem. She was probably an overanxious person who made a philosophy or religion from her own fear and inner need, awakening a sense of guilt in the child. There is a marked element of guilt and a guilt complex. Depending on sign and aspects, they are propelled by ethical or religious beliefs and are unchangeable. This type of mother could not be contradicted, as befits the twelfth house; she was "in harmony with the cosmos" and was raised to heaven.

In the case of men, the mother image is often transferred to the wife. Some put their wife on a pedestal like a holy statue. When the woman wants to break free and become emancipated, these men's world falls apart. Others keep a relationship going that has become unbearable, even if it has long since lost its spark.

Some cling to matter and look for security in possessions, with a strong attachment to objects – or they construct themselves a pseudo-philosophy that is intended to give them spiritual security. Some give another meaning to reality, in a way reinterpreting it, giving rise to a life-lie that can eventually become a prison. This includes those who sacrifice themselves, like the mother who lives only for her child.

♄ **in the cardinal zone** often makes one philanthropic, caring actively about the plight of the afflicted and the poor. Depending on sign or aspects, it can be a philosophy of sacrificing performance of personal duty, so these people often neglect themselves. The destructive processes of the twelfth house are intended to dissolve the crystallised core of the ego, which for some people can lead to total exhaustion or the loss of self. Here the ego is sent to that place where it naturally belongs. This Saturn ego cannot be expansive and dominate others, repressing them or committing to them. Instead it can only know that it is part of a whole. The ego is reduced to this minimal size in the twelfth house. This has to happen, because it should have an organic and naturally normal size before it can really transcend into a greater being. Saturn also appears here in the guise of the "Keeper of the Threshold". Further steps in the developmental process can only be taken with a refined awareness of reality. That is why Saturn has a disillusioning effect.

♄ **in the fixed zone** of the twelfth house usually indicates a repressive upbringing and there is always subliminal fear present. It serves the theme of change, for here the self must turn inwards and deal with its real nature. This is an area where the self can become what it really is. If one is not ready, sometimes fate forces things. Usually illnesses result from excessive outward exertion and offer the possibility of a polar reversal. People who have not yet consciously understood the problem of this Saturn position express themselves via a crass materialism in which the basic approach to life is revealed. This is not only about earning money, and also not about the fear of illness in an obsessive sense, but primarily about well-being and affluence. Everything concerning the personal body and its safety becomes the standard for all things, whether they want to admit it or not.

But as already mentioned, the twelfth is a house of crises concerned with ego conversion, which brings the far-reaching breakdown of egotistical motives. Hence Saturn in this zone often causes tough ordeals; it requires the relinquishing of external or material securities so that internal ones may be gained.

♄ **at the low point** indicates that the conversion has already finished; such a person is often characterised by an inner maturity. People who have already completed this low point reorientation are free from obsessions about health, money or personal prestige, and can be seen to be mature from the outside. The low point is the switching point where we stop being materialistic and break through to a spiritual approach. There is frequently a certain resignation, a pessimistic undertone. These people do not expect much from life, and have soon had to adapt to reality. Depending on sign and aspects, they are happy with a little success.

♄ **in the mutable zone**, in the shadow of the ascendant, can toughen up the ego with constant self-restraint and holding back its own development. The compensation of the AC shadow pulls all ego forces to this point, so there is a lot of inner resistance to any change and learning. This Saturn position (the nearer to the AC, the stronger the effect) is also called a "refusal to be born" (see chapter 7, "Planets at the AC", page 286). This is also part of the ego conversion. Self-image and life motivation must be changed and this depends on the extent to which the person concerned has already experienced the spiritual dimension. When approaching the I-point at the AC, it generally requires a lot of courage to cope with the crises indicated in the twelfth house. One is painfully aware of the deep inner need that personal standards, fears and attitudes to physical existence will have to change, and must become ready to learn.

Interpretation of compensative tendencies depends on how Saturn is integrated into the aspect structure and where the other planets lie. That can change the picture. Other positions can lead to a contrary judgement. In all compensations, it is also necessary to see whether stress planets are linked to the three spiritual planets (Uranus, Neptune, Pluto) by any aspect. If this is the case, the changes wrought by the transforming forces on the ego last a lifetime.

The transformed Saturn in the twelfth house will test itself again and again, to check whether its personality is refined and stable. There has usually already been some sort of pole reversal, usually caused by abandoning a wrong attitude to life and seeing earthly existence not as a punishment but as a learning process. Such a reversal depends neither on spiritual abilities nor on the level achieved, but usually on insight gained by working on one's own character. For people with Saturn in the twelfth house, it is good if they can sometimes stand back and think about life in private.

6. The Planets in the Zodiac Signs
using the example of the Moon

The Man in the Moon - or the Moon in Man
Bruno Huber

• Anima and Animus • Role Models • The New Interpretation •
• The Feelings • Mother • Saturn • Paradigm Shift •

The Moon as our Feeling Nature
Louise Huber

• Reflection • Dependencies • Learning Processes •
• The Here and Now • Subjective I-Experience •
• Theories and Methods • Transformation of the Moon Ego •
• The Refined Moon • The Child within Us •

The Moon in the Zodiac Signs
• Combinations and Analogies •
• The Three Crosses • Development Processes •
• Table of Planetary Rulers (exoteric and esoteric) •

• **The Moon in the Cardinal Signs** •
• Aries • Cancer • Scorpio • Capricorn •

• **The Moon in the Fixed Signs** •
• Taurus • Leo • Scorpio • Aquarius •

• **The Moon in the Mutable Signs** •
• Gemini • Virgo • Sagittarius • Pisces •

The Man in the Moon – or the Moon in Man

Bruno Huber

"I am a man – and a new man at that – and I am fed up with the Moon always being associated with women – as though they had the monopoly on emotions! I have feelings too and I like them."

This is a quote from a man who is tired of only being allowed to be clever, strong-willed and efficient, and who would like someone to lean on and a shoulder to cry on once in a while. He has put his finger on a problem that I have come across again and again as counsellor and therapist – for many years and more and more often. Conversely, I have also noticed that more and more women are looking for "soft", sensitive and empathetic men. It is obvious that the definition of what it means to be a man or a woman has undergone a significant change and is still changing! It therefore seems to me that the time has come to look for a new understanding that is in line with this development in our astrological interpretation, according to the principle that "you can't put new wine into old bottles". Our new wine is a new type of man, who is capable of forming the foundation for a New Age.

Anima and Animus

In all my years of searching for valid and logical definitions of astrological factors, particularly the planets, the Moon always gave me problems at first. While I was still guided by the existing literature, I was unable to find an accurate definition of it where emotional reactions, relationship problems and the concept of the adult were concerned. According to C.G. Jung (24), whose approach to psychology I followed for a long time, we are dealing here with the archetypes anima and animus. Problems of human coexistence, particularly within couples, eventually always turn out to be caused by our parents. The child experiences its first and therefore most influential role model of a man and a woman, father and mother, from the example of its parents (or primary carers). The way they interacted remains in the psyche of the child when it becomes an adult as the matrix for all future partnerships. When they come to form their own couples as adults, they always try to recreate this pattern. We are subject to the unconscious (gratification) urge of this matrix, whatever it may bring in terms of joy and pain, pleasure and problems.

Role Models

This shows us how important our parents are to us, particularly for our adult sexual lives. It is therefore very important to be able to determine the factors relating to the father and mother in each individual horoscope. The literature of classical astrology suggests that the position of the Sun tells us about the influence of the father. Even if variations are suggested (e.g. 10th house/ 4th house), the Sun seems to be a good indication of the child's experience of the father. However, when it comes to working with the Moon as the mother, we do not get very far and have trouble knowing where to start. For example, some talented astrologers do manage to give good advice in the case of relationship problems by using their gift for observation and a lot of intuition. With all due respect to such astrologers (of which there are some famous examples!), I think that astrology as a science (which should work with proven criteria that are reproducible by other people), fails here.

This will be a deficiency as long as we stick to the traditional pairings of Sun–Moon as father–mother or man–woman. Psychology is not terribly helpful here either, as the Jungian anima-animus polarity is widely used. Jung actually formulated in psychological terms what astrology had advocated during the entire patriarchal age: that the Sun is the masculine principle and the Moon the feminine one. The concept is outdated as it is too narrow. It was a pupil of Jung called Erich Neumann (31) who first showed this, and he was sharply rebuked by the master for this, although constructive criticism does not constitute rejection in itself. Neumann extended Jung's duality to a trinity. He took the father and mother to their logical conclusion, based on their functional roles: after all the child is the parental partnership's *raison d'être*. He made the child an independent principle in its own right, restoring the child to its rightful place as part of an eternal trinity. It is now free to be itself instead of just being a copy of its parents, as before.

Incidentally, this concept is not new. This theory and actual examples of it existed in pre-patriarchal times. For example, the "revolutionary" pharaoh Akhenaton had publicly represented the trinity of the family in the 14th century BC, by being driven about the city in a carriage with his wife and children and playing with the children, for all to see. This was shocking behaviour at the time. Children were never supposed to behave as children in public; they were just immature creatures at a developmental stage on their way to adulthood, when they had to follow in their parents' footsteps.

Another example specific to astrology is the way the Moon was defined in those times. In the matriarchal culture of the Middle East, i.e. in Babylon or Egypt, the term "receptivity" often cropped up, but never the meaning of fertility. The latter is not really found relating to the Moon until the (very patriarchal) height of the Greek culture. For the Babylonians, fertility was always associated with Saturn, which was the original mother, the fruitful earth, the city as the refuge of the people, etc. It is obvious that receptivity and fertility are two different things. People can be receptive (e.g. for love), but only women can really be fertile. And a receptive woman is not necessarily fertile.

It was these concepts of receptivity and the child that gave me the first suitable basic approaches for a reinterpretation of the Moon. It was Neumann (33) who first enlightened me, for his definition of the child was so appropriate for all possible Moon positions in every horoscope. Transferring this into logic made great sense from an organic point of view. What is a child's consciousness really like, once adult projections are taken away?

The new-born is not yet able to think for itself, and only has the potential of an intellect that is very willing to learn. However, it does have something that it can use immediately, namely a wide-awake sensory experience: sensitivity (excitability) and receptivity, hence impressionability. Right from birth, it is overwhelmed by the sensory impressions of touch, smell, colour and sound that flow into it from outside, and by the sensations coming from its internal physical processes of eating, digesting and excreting. It is already able to enjoy what is pleasant and be afraid of what is unpleasant.

It expresses happiness or unhappiness with its surroundings in unmistakeable ways, and learns very fast. It quickly learns how to manipulate those around it so that it can make itself as comfortable as possible. This is the same state of awareness represented by the position of the Moon in the adult. It is infinitely more differentiated there though.

The New Interpretation

In our Moon, we are all subjective beings who perceive ourselves according to how we are affected by our environment and by our own body. So, as the Moon, I make subjective judgements as to what is pleasant and unpleasant, what I like and dislike. These judgements are based on perceptions and I become aware of them as attraction and aversion, love and hate, joy and sadness, pleasure and pain. This could be defined as follows: the Moon's causative abilities are sensitivity, receptivity and the ability to learn through inquisitive receptivity. An adult's abilities have all been acquired in this way, i.e. by making subjective judgements of our own experiences, and we call these subjective judgements feelings.

The Feelings

These very personal feelings are in a certain sense our whole world. For they control our interaction with our environment, and therefore our entire social experience. Above all, they allow me to select (sense) out of all the people I meet those people who will bring me the fewest problems and the most joy, pleasure, quality of life, understanding and love. So as a small child I first became aware of myself through sensations of pleasantness and unpleasantness, and as an adult I am at home in this emotional world. However, my self-esteem is also completely dependent on approval from those around me. That is the reason for the much-maligned, but unavoidable mood swings.

The environment plays a lifelong role in the evolution of the feeling self, which in childhood and adolescence means the parents (or whoever takes this role). The relationship we have with them determines the course of our emotional development and therefore our later abilities to relate to and socialise with others, in both the qualitative and quantitative sense. So when we try to interpret the Moon position in the horoscope of an adult, we can find many traces of the influence of their parents. As the mother (or surrogate) normally has the greatest and most direct influence from birth and in the first years of life, it is understandable that the definition of the Moon can also include the mother, but not necessarily.

Mother

The old meaning "The Moon represents the Mother" is not really wrong. There are elements of the experience of maternal influence in the child's impressionable psyche. This influence varies in strength from person to person, depending on the intensity of enjoyable experiences and on any problems that the mother was experiencing at the time.

The Moon is therefore not the physical mother herself, but just a reflection of her, the reflection that the child eagerly adopts as a structure (matrix). In the same sense, the childlike, neutral Moon must also be able to show the paternal "imprint", if the father has made his presence felt strongly enough. It is easy to check this in the horoscope if the Moon has a direct aspect to the Sun. This is clearest in the case of a full or new Moon, which always indicates a stronger, more direct paternal influence. The paternal bond and dependency they show is just as strong as the maternal bond is in the better known Moon/Saturn conjunctions and oppositions.

Saturn

The child experiences itself in the Moon. It experiences the father in the position of the Sun and the mother in the position of Saturn!

The main role of the mother is to provide nourishment and protection, and to teach the child about the realities of life. These definitions have a definite affinity with those always associated with Saturn, if we disregard that of the "Evildoer". One can always counter "What about maternal affection, warmth and tenderness", which is a rather emotional argument. It comes from an old-fashioned, exaggeratedly romantic maternal image of Mother of God-like devotion and self-sacrifice that was supposed to make women's subordinate and one-sided role more palatable. Where this inclination was a characteristic trait of a mother, which is by no means always the case, it goes back to the personal Moon need of this mother, for example for affection. This allows the child to also experience the mother's Moon, not just her objective and of course indispensable Saturnine maternal role.

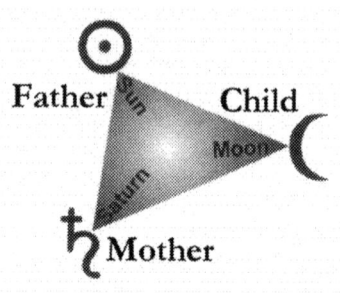

Paradigm Shift

The earth's early civilisations were matriarchal. These were superseded by two to three thousand years of patriarchal civilisations, depending on the cultural area in question. Both were necessary stages in human development, but they are very one-sided and therefore caused great suffering for the subordinate gender. They were also characterised by intolerant, dualistic thinking, in which human actions solely driven by order and security (Saturn) or success and power (Sun) were in a position to oppress mankind (Moon) at any time. There is now a paradigm shift taking place. A third factor, the person or the child, is more and more taking its place alongside the polarity of father and mother. This could be in the form of relationships, love, reason, information or the willingness to negotiate.

There is now talk of a paradigm shift being necessary for the healthy development of mankind. From an astrological point of view, the paradigms were Saturn-based and Sun-based. We must overcome the one-sidedness of the Saturn-Sun duality and the misguided Sun-Moon polarity. The way forward definitely lies with the development of an awareness that involves the correct interpretation of the Moon as a third, perhaps childlike-naïf but spontaneous, inquisitive, organic and integrative way of experiencing and assimilating. "Unless you become like little children…"

The Moon as our Feeling Nature

Louise Huber

Our feelings are not stable; they are like water and are subject to the laws of ebb and flow, day and night, light and dark. In astrological symbolism, the element of water, the Moon and the mutable cross are used to define the feeling self. The mutable, phase-rhythmic principle corresponds to the mutable quality of the feelings and also of the phases of the Moon, which are also analogous with the changeability and instability of our feelings. Seen from earth, the Moon is constantly changing. When the Moon is full, it shows us a bright, round face; later only half a face and before the new Moon it almost disappears. This is in keeping with the phasic character of the Moon ego, our feeling nature.

Reflection

Another characteristic that the Moon has in common with the feeling self is its ability to reflect. As the earth's satellite, the Moon has no light of its own, it reflects the Sun's light and is only visible when the Sun shines on it. Our feeling self also needs the environment to be aware of itself; it experiences itself almost exclusively as a reflection of the outside world. Everything that affects our psyche is reflected back in a way that reveals our innermost nature. This reflecting process enables an exchange between outside and inside. We need external stimuli; sometime just a single look is enough to activate our feeling self and make it react appropriately. We are always keen to receive such stimuli, hence our need for affiliation. Man is a social being, who cannot be alone for long, he is always looking for other people who belong to him, who care for him and protect him. When one person says to another: "I love you", this is like the phase of the full moon, creating a feeling of complete validation and acceptance. However, if there is nobody to love us, we are sad, confused and alone. This emotional state can be compared to the new Moon. If we are accused of a crime, and prosecuted, the fear gives us emotional stress. Suffering and pain are also Moon ego experiences that are usually considered to be negative. Because the reflection of the feeling self is always polar in nature, opposites are experienced alternately, like the alternating full and new Moons. The Moon ego activates love and rejection in turn. They take it in turns because reflection is ruled by the law of opposites; we are constantly caught in the polarisation between love and hate, reward and punishment, joy and suffering.

Dependencies

Of course, everyone would like the elation of love to last for as long as possible, so we delude ourselves, make demands and have expectations that cannot be fulfilled or come to nothing. We are then disappointed and blame circumstances or other people. This gives rise to conscious or unconscious defence mechanisms and dependencies on those we love, or also on ideas, situations or stimulants. The Moon as a reflecting principle often tricks us; it has trouble seeing things as they really are. Reflections can distort many things, giving them a deceptive and unresolved appearance. One moment something is great and fantastic, and the next it is disgusting and repulsive. "Up one minute, down the next" describes the typical mood swings of the Moon ego. But, like the phases of the Moon, we know that on this level everything is transient and subject to change, which is why deceptions and illusions cannot last forever either. So it is wise not to cling to them, but to gain distance, neutrality and objectivity by letting go of them.

When we have understood that, like the phases of the Moon, nothing lasts forever on the emotional level, we will not allow feelings of for example sorrow or vindictiveness to control us or to be pulled this way and that.

Learning Processes

Like constantly flowing water, the feeling self is the source of a never-ending flow of wishes and moods which are always bringing us new experiences, and therefore creating an ongoing learning process. It is said that love is the greatest teacher. Our social interactions and constantly changing circumstances are always setting us puzzles that we want to solve. All learning processes are influenced by the contact principle, and it is up to us to recognise this and to understand its rhythmic nature. By being more aware when we love, we avoid extreme polarisations. By trying to react with sensitivity, flexibility and heightened perception in social situations, we nourish our relationships with partner, family and nature. Awareness liberates us from the eternal cycle of emotional highs and lows.

The Here and Now

If we are consciously Moon-like, without fixed ideas and expectations, we live completely in the here and now, react spontaneously like children to the life around us and are quite happy with our lot. We learn to be more relaxed and playful in social interactions and do not take our need for love so seriously. At the moment, the Moon as a purely social tool is becoming better understood. The magnifying effect and subjective nature of experience can now be understood, relativised and neutralised. We already know a lot about human relations, communication, social connections and the human psyche in general. Psychology enables us to understand the laws of polarity of projection mechanisms, and also the polarity of anima and animus within ourselves, the attraction of the sexes, etc.

Subjective I-Experience

We also know that the feeling self is the most subjective part of our personalities, mainly because on this level we can only experience our own ego through contacts and relationships. So when it comes to evaluating the Moon's position in the horoscope, we assume that we nearly always react egocentrically, which is completely natural. In many cases we have no ability to differentiate, firstly because we can only understand things by relating them to ourselves, and secondly as our feelings are constantly changing. It is no wonder that our intellects have trouble making sense of it all. When we look at water, something is always moving. Even the slightest puff of wind can ruffle the glassy surface. If the water is frozen, we can't see anything any more as ice reflects nothing. Similarly, if our feelings are frozen, we are frustrated. If we can no longer feel moved or stimulated because we are numbed and turned to ice by disappointment or fright etc., we are only half alive, and are incapable of either feeling enjoyment or learning. That is why we should ensure that we remain emotionally responsive. We can take responsibility for our child-like feeling self by making sure that it receives enough nourishment (tender loving care), praise and approval, warmth and protection. So whether we are happy or sad actually depends on our mental hygiene, personal responsibility and self-esteem.

Theories and Methods

Many theories and methods have already been developed as to how to handle our feelings. Psychological testing methods are not satisfactory as they try to pigeonhole people. Labelling people makes them feel pinned down and inhibited. But when it comes to feelings and psyche, everything is in a constant state of flux. The answer is flexibility, letting things flow and dispensing with conditions, so that we can approach the world of our emotions in a neutral and playful way. For what is right today can be wrong again tomorrow. There is hardly anything dependable for us to work with.

This law can be used for all relationships, especially intimate ones, for this is exactly the nature of a romantic relationship. When regulations and stability creep in, spontaneous love is instantly lost – the flow stops. The vital flux can then re-emerge in a new spontaneous encounter that as such lacks routine, form and structure, hence the need for another encounter now and then. But stubbornly sticking to the idea that relationships must last forever is not in line with the principle of the Moon. Someone who does this usually has Saturn with an aspect to the Moon, or their Moon in a fixed sign.

It should be noted that in the new age that is dawning, there is a process of human emotional change and development of awareness underway that involves each and every one of us. The paradigm shift has changed many traditional value systems, and created new norms for human relationships. The ongoing development, nurturing and integration of our emotional nature is therefore an important aspect of our Moon description.

Transformation of the Moon Ego

Transformation on the Moon level is far more difficult than on the Sun level. People in an emotional crisis always go through a period of solitude, which is what the Moon finds hardest to bear. For the Moon ego, being alone and unloved is a very frustrating experience. Usually it cannot come through such crises alone, it needs other people's help. A Sun can deal with a crisis much more easily, because it is independent and has the ability to differentiate. A Saturn that is in tune with reality can repress and somatise crises into the body.

Serious emotional crises do not end without help, which is why many people visit psychiatrists, psychologists or astrologers. In earlier times, people with emotional problems turned to the priest for the spiritual guidance they needed. Today, astrological-psychological counselling can be very helpful, as it knows the laws of development and also considers the esoteric aspects. When we find out that nearly all therapeutic treatments are based on the principle of the Moon, astrological knowledge of the Moon can be very informative, because it enables us to know why someone is going through a crisis, what he must learn from it and how he can be helped.

The Refined Moon

According to the esoteric philosophy of Alice A. Bailey (8), the Moon crisis corresponds to the second initiation, in which the emotional body is refined, purified and stabilised. Afterwards, it serves the soul as a pure, untarnished reflector for unconditional and universal human love. We have already dealt with this topic in relation to the three spiritual planets in chapter 3. We remind you that from an esoteric point of view, the Moon level is the astral level, which is full of archetypal patterns of behaviour. These are available to everyone, and can be used consciously or unconsciously. If people are consciously guided by the principles of the Moon, they can develop a kind of instinct that helps them to deal with anything life can throw at them. You can even call it an unconscious security instinct. In other words, it is a level in which all our experiences accumulate and then later influence our lives as emotional instinct and warn us of dangers. If these experiences are stored correctly, they can become a trustworthy and successful inner guide. This process also activates healing forces within us.

The Child Within Us

The refined Moon is one of such self-healing forces. It is something inside us that guides and leads us. If the Moon is converted by transformation, it automatically functions correctly. The Moon then resembles a mirror-like lake in which the soul is reflected, in the words of Alice Bailey. We then realise that the astral level is an illusion and that nearly all subjectivity and projections are delusions. With this knowledge, they gradually disappear; our emotional nature is purified and calmed. Our emotional nature has come home, and leads us straight to where we can find what is right for us, when everything falls into place. With a purified and refined Moon ego, we are drawn towards those who love us and accept our love. With a transformed Moon, we are a pure mirror for the soul, are full of love and find good things everywhere. The promise is clear: "Unless you change and become like little children, you will never enter the kingdom of Heaven." Someone who has reached a stage in his life where he is quite disillusioned after being refined by suffering and purified by water, knows this kind of feeling and the power of love. The kind of love we are talking about here is unconditional love, which is only positive, only wants to do good and has no negative material ulterior motive.

The Moon in the Zodiac Signs

Although the feeling nature is hard to grasp, there are some interpretation rules that help to define its needs and motivations. The combination of sign and house involved plays an important role. When we describe the Moon's position in the signs, we must also consider in which area of the horoscope (top, bottom, right, left) it is situated. This basic division already tells us a lot about the social behaviour of the person concerned. In chapter 5, we saw that the Moon prefers to be on the level of the horizon, where it can make contact instantly. That doesn't mean that all contact is good, just that the person has learnt how to make contact. The sign is also important. With Moon in Aries in the seventh house, the person will reach out emotionally to the You and relate intensely, whereas in Virgo in the seventh house, feelings adapt to the You and want to work with others because of the earth element of Virgo. Finding the correct combination of sign and house always enables us to establish a person's emotional characteristics.

Analogy Table of the Threes			
Planet:	Sun	Saturn	Moon
Cross:	Cardinal	Fixed	Mutable
Motivation:	Will + Power	Security	Love + Contact
Time:	Future	Past	Present
Ego component:	Thinking	Physical	Feeling
Aspect Figure:	Linear figure	Quadrilateral	Triangle
Colour:	Red	Blue	Green
Quality:	Performance	Substance	Awareness
Gender:	Masculine	Feminine	Neuter

Combinations and Analogies

A wise teacher once said: "In astrology we must be able to think in terms of analogies." This means finding affinities on each level and combining the different elements involved. With this perspective you'll understand that the description of the Moon position in the signs allows certain analogies to be made, which are also valid for the Sun, for Saturn and to an extent also for the other planets. With a good knowledge of astrology, you can also use the zodiac descriptions of the Moon to deduce the influences of the signs on the tool planets (Venus, Jupiter, Mercury, Mars) and on the spiritual planets (Uranus, Neptune, Pluto). Unfortunately, we don't have the space to do this here.

The Three Crosses

It is helpful to divide the signs and houses into the three crosses, cardinal, fixed and mutable. Not only do they represent the "three pillars of heaven", but they are also the moving and motivating principles that create conditions in our emotional bodies which determine how we will develop. These motivations are particularly important when it comes to describing the planets and developmental transformation processes. Accurate reading and understanding of the different elements in the horoscope is also based on the cross qualities.

In the zodiac, a cardinal sign always comes first, followed by a fixed sign and then a mutable sign (16). All three crosses are interdependent and provide an organic flow of energy in the creative process. An idea emerges in the cardinal cross, is given structure in the fixed cross, and is criticised and improved in the mutable cross. These three primary principles are the basic motivations contained in all elements, and in the case of the planets represent their motivational quality. The cross qualities are essential for every astrological reading. They also correspond to the three zones of a house, as described in chapter 5. In the analysis of the feeling nature, they give clues about the structure of the feeling self, about basic needs that always need to be met and cannot be changed. The answer to the question "How is my Moon motivated?" offers a key to both our own feelings and those of other people. If the Moon is in the cardinal cross, it can get what it needs, in the fixed cross it holds onto what it already has, and in the mutable cross it needs variety. The same is also true for the other planets.

We have already seen that the Moon needs contact and love, that it is not capable of being self-sufficient, for nature tells us this. Without the Sun's light it is invisible. Considering the cross quality, it is immediately apparent that the Moon is more at home in the mutable signs (Gemini, Virgo, Sagittarius, Pisces), because they correspond to its varying needs. Spontaneity, flexibility, adaptability and openness to what is happening on the contact level and the ability to tune into it, are all enhanced by the mutable principle. But not everyone has a mutable Moon, so it is important to learn about the other cross qualities.

Development Processes

The planets, and particularly the Moon description, indicate the developmental journey that a person should undergo in a particular sign. In every sign, there is a crisis or developmental mechanism, which is described in *Reflections and Meditations on the Signs of the Zodiac* (20). It is a three-step, three-stage process that is easy to follow. To go over

Table of Planetary Rulers (Exoteric and Esoteric)
Transformation of the Planetary Rulers

Sign	(Opposite Sign)	Exoteric Ruler	Esoteric Ruler
Aries	(Libra)	Mars	Mercury
Taurus	(Scorpio)	Venus	Vulcan
Gemini	(Sagittarius)	Mercury	Venus
Cancer	(Capricorn)	Moon	Neptune
Leo	(Aquarius)	Sun	Sun
Virgo	(Pisces)	Mercury	Moon
Libra	(Aries)	Venus	Uranus
Scorpio	(Taurus)	Mars	Pluto
Sagittarius	(Gemini)	Jupiter	Earth
Capricorn	(Cancer)	Saturn	Saturn
Aquarius	(Leo)	Saturn/Uranus	Jupiter
Pisces	(Virgo)	Jupiter/Neptune	Pluto

the basics again: the traditional or exoteric planetary rulers of a sign function as driving forces on the material or physical level, the esoteric planetary rulers function on the conscious level (according to Alice Bailey (8) – see table above).

In the developmental journey of our feeling nature, or of other planetary qualities in a sign, the aim is now to make the transformation from exoteric to esoteric sign ruler. The change happens when the whole sign axis is polarised: the confrontation with the qualities of the opposite sign usually causes a crisis leading to an intensive learning process. The developmental goal is expressed by an esoteric seed thought, which we give at the end of the description of each sign. The above table shows an overview of the development process.

In the following sections, we interpret the Moon position in the horoscope grouped according to the three cross qualities (cardinal, fixed, mutable). As mentioned above, the main issues are the development and transformation processes that the Moon in each sign has to go through. For aware people, it is useful to know which laws of development the Moon in each sign is governed by, which refinements, changes and learning processes are necessary in order to develop optimally. We make a distinction here between the material and the transformed levels.

The Moon in the Cardinal Signs

(Also relevant to other planets, as appropriate)

Aries, Cancer, Libra, Capricorn

The cardinal cross symbolises the impulse principle. Its motivation is will and power. If the Moon lies in one of these signs, the feeling self finds expression in striving for power, being proactive, performing, achieving goals and conquering. It is a strong Moon with powerful feelings; in the fire sign it overcomes obstacles, in the water sign it puts itself out for loved ones, in the air sign it resolves conflicts and in the earth sign it is stable, reliable and focused.

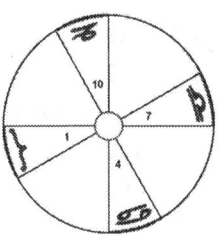

Conquest

Someone with a cardinal Moon is courageous and does not wait for the Sun to shine on it, it goes straight for the target, and has a conquering energy with which it clears obstacles out of the way. It does not waste time asking if anyone minds, it just takes what it needs. The cardinal cross is like the masculine principle, which actively and boldly breaks through barriers and overcomes resistance. A Moon with cardinal motivation will assert its will and try to gratify its feelings. This Moon is able to assert itself, and resolutely takes what it believes it is entitled to. It always wants to be on the winning side and cannot tolerate failure.

Egoic Will

The egoic will and the Moon as subjective little ego combined with the cardinal principle frequently cause social and romantic problems; they give love in order to receive it, they protect the weak so that they look like heroes. This motive can cause opposition on the contact level and be perceived as egotistical. But they also have their place in the evolutionary process, and should not be considered negative. For example, when a person with a cardinal Moon meets someone with a sensitive Moon, perhaps at the low point, he can find it difficult to trust him. Such people need a dynamic Moon in those they meet to get things going.

Dynamic Moon

Complementarity and balancing are cosmic selection mechanisms. They are natural laws that automatically bring people together who have something to offer each other. Although the cardinal cross does not provide the feeling self with any great sensitivity, the dynamic of this cross brings about movement on the feeling level. A cardinal Moon can dissolve any congestion or blockage with the force of its will. It is a courageous Moon that resolutely removes obstacles and can also help other people out of tricky situations.

Aries ♈ ☽

The sign of Aries combines the cardinal cross with the fire element. As an I sign, Aries is the prototype of the cardinal principle, which is why an Aries Moon is so courageous, dynamic and lively. Such people have fiery emotions, are quick to anger and react enthusiastically to any challenge. They are always ready for new, exciting experiences, and love adventures. They make a very personal commitment in emotional matters; when they love someone they are loyal and can be relied upon. They are daring and successful. Even if they do sometimes overestimate their own abilities and overshoot the mark, they are not easily discouraged. They are naturally predisposed to dominate. Setbacks motivate them to even greater efforts and they want to get rid of obstacles that lie in their way with a single stroke. They are fun-loving, lively people, who always approach life in a new and fresh way and are surprised when other people do not feel the same.

They have the feeling that everything they do is unique. People with an Aries Moon have a lot of self-belief and are convinced that they are the best and that they have done everything all by themselves from start to finish. They want to control everything and it is hard for them to share their triumphs or to collaborate with others. Many enjoy competition and rivalry and like to measure their strengths against other people's. They feel compelled to draw attention to themselves, to set the tone or to take charge. They are proud of their own achievements and are disappointed when other people do not take them as seriously as they do themselves. If someone does not think they are fantastic, they forcefully try to convince them of their uniqueness and greatness, they boast about themselves and do not let them be until their opposition or doubts have been overcome. They want to win and prevail over others.

Material Level

On the material level, Mars rules and animates the fighting nature of people with an Aries Moon. Opposition only encourages their high spirits and dynamism and makes them redouble their efforts. They often use force to get rid of resistance. They cannot accept limitations and cannot stand rejection, which makes them defensive and liable to overreact. They run head-first into danger without thinking about the consequences. Those around them hold their breath at their recklessness and ingenuity, and they shock gentle and sensitive people with their wild ways. They are unashamedly competitive. Thinking that they are the best, the most successful and the only ones who can get things done makes them unpopular. They assert their wishes with no consideration for the feelings of others, often pushing them aside and trampling them underfoot. If their wishes are not satisfied immediately, they easily get depressed and blame those around them or their partner.

Transformation

The Aries Moon must also go through a process of maturation. This three-stage journey, as in all the signs, entails the transformation from exoteric to esoteric ruler (from Mars to Mercury), and takes place on the polar axis. It is also important to know that failure and rejection enable the cardinal cross to experience the conversion crisis that leads to maturity. The transformation from the blind material level to conscious mental control takes place by means of this crisis mechanism.

The developmental journey in Aries goes through the opposite sign of Libra, where rejection makes the Moon develop sensitivity and learn to consider the requests and needs of its partner as well as its own. Failure is the lesson that teaches Aries to overcome selfishness. But this Moon finds the lesson hard to learn, especially because it does not understand why it is now on the losing side, despite doing everything possible and giving all, which always worked in the past. Its commitment was sincere, it devoted itself completely to a person or a thing, and now it is being shown the door. This is incomprehensible and destroys something it put every effort into. It is hard to accept that it is no longer on the winning side and that its efforts and commitment are worth nothing. This is a defeat like Napoleon's at Waterloo.

The transformed Moon-ego in Aries is eventually confronted with itself on the encounter axis, and the theme of the "I-You axis" should be integrated into this conversion crisis. Although the You is initially experienced as something completely different, and frequently alien and threatening, during the conflict with the opposite sign of Libra, a process of familiarisation occurs that activates Mercury, the esoteric ruler. Mercury, as the planet of the intellect, gives the Aries

Moon the control it needs over its drives (Mars), and it learns to think first before it acts. In other words: it must become sensitive to the You and to other people's feelings and reduce its emotional intensity. In curbing the dynamism of its feelings, it becomes cultivated and refined enough to be accepted by the You. This enables a real and potentially very creative exchange to take place between the I and the You. Its will and focus have a creative effect on the motives of the emotional nature, and they stimulate and encourage love. It helps to bear in mind the esoteric seed thought for Aries (20):

"I come forth and from the plane of mind, I rule."

Cancer ♋ ☽

Here the cardinal principle is combined with the element of water. Water is the symbol for our feelings, so a Cancer Moon naturally has strong feelings of sympathy and antipathy. Mood swings are the order of the day. It can be interested in someone one day, only to forget them the next. It overreacts to all social stimuli (both negative and positive), and is gripped and carried away by them. When a grain of sand falls into water, it causes expanding ripples. This leads to an unstable feeling self, which appears moody and inconsistent. Overreactions often make the emotions run wild and cause exaggerated high-intensity feelings, which are quick to evaporate. The Cancer Moon flows towards love; if love is lacking it suffers deep inside and becomes depressed.

As a cardinal sign, the Cancer Moon also has will impulses that are mainly oriented towards the fulfilment of its own desires. It is always interested in being loved, connected to other people, belonging to them and being present at all occasions. As the Moon has the deepest desire for other people's attention and appreciation, the Cancer Moon is ready to do anything to obtain this appreciation. It develops ideas, fantasies and representations of the social life that it wants to become reality. It is often never satisfied on the emotional level; it can never get enough. It manipulates the environment so that others consider its feelings, which it takes very seriously. If it does not receive attention or appreciation, it suffers and is deeply offended. Like the crab, it creeps into its hole, hides behind its pincers and accuses the whole world of refusing to do as it wants. It sinks into self-pity and blames other people for its woes.

Material Level

On the material level, the Moon is a double ruler, which gives a childlike attitude with infantile behaviour. Such people are dependent on the influences of the environment, over-adapt, and are troubled by an unconscious symbiotic need for closeness, a nest, food and tender loving care. Most of them do not really know what they want on this level, and are tossed around by the emotions of the environment. They depend on their family, mother or partner and refuse to grow up. Security is important to them, so they strive for stability and would prefer to live always in the same house and same town. If the childlike Moon ego does not get what it thinks it is entitled to, it is thrown back on itself and must take responsibility for itself too. That means it must learn to fulfil its own desires and find security within itself.

Transformation

The transformation follows the crisis in the opposite sign of Capricorn. The expectation of being loved and cared for forever by mother or by other people cannot be fulfilled. Many Cancer Moons have to mature in a period of solitude after being abandoned; others are thrown out of the nest so that they have to find their own wings. The Cancer Moon initially reacts with self-pity; it feels betrayed, misunderstood, rejected and abandoned and for a while, retreats hurt into its shell. When it loses the protection and belonging of the nest and does not receive the warmth it needs, its nesting instinct is thwarted and it suffers unspeakably, blaming the circumstances. If it wants to punish the world by withdrawing from it and no longer being nice to people, this triggers a process of purification and maturing.

All water signs are concerned with purification, the sluices open and the tears flow. It is not for nothing that the old books say that "Cancer is quick to cry". After having a good cry, it usually feels purified and behaves as though nothing was wrong. If one has a Cancer Moon partner, one should not run after them and comfort them, but let them be. That is clear at the opposite sign of Capricorn, who climbs alone up the mountain. The transformation happens by integrating Capricorn, which symbolises retreat and closure. One should therefore let the Cancer Moon sulk, withdraw into itself and purify itself until it is ready to emerge again and be free. Then it will reach the level of awareness where Neptune becomes its esoteric ruler.

The transformed Cancer Moon shows on this level a deep love for all living things. This emerges through the transformation from the egocentric Moon ruler (which experiences everything subjectively) to the universal human kindness of Neptune (which cares for others unconditionally). The transformed Cancer Moon is open to the feelings of others and always knows how to give sympathy and comfort. Possessing a cultivated and extremely sensitive emotional nature, it assumes a maternal role, taking others under its wing and feeding, comforting and looking after them. A Cancer Moon is always there when it is needed and ready to help others, keep the family together, respect traditions and do social work. Neptune, the esoteric ruler, enables it to operate where suffering and need prevail and to sacrifice itself when necessary. It often forgets its own interests and neglects itself in the process. If this becomes a permanent state of affairs, it must find a balance and learn to look after itself as well, feed and strengthen itself, get in touch with its own wishes and fulfil them for the sake of its own psychological well-being. Then it can emerge strengthened from its shell and bathe others in its inner light, warmth and care. The esoteric seed thought for Cancer is helpful here:

"I build a lighted house and therein dwell."

Libra ♎ ☾

The cardinal principle is combined with the air temperament in Libra. This is a good combination for the Moon's sociability. It is ideally suited for love and getting on easily with other people. It gives others the feeling that they are loved and understood. The Libra Moon is deeply happy when it lives in love and harmony with other people. It is good at playing the role of the lover, as long as it thinks that it gets back as much as it gives. As soon as this is not the case, it withdraws. It does not allow itself to be used because Libra is primarily motivated by the principle of balance. The cardinal will impulses also ensure that any unbalanced situations are made fair again. Although it is prepared to do anything for the one it loves, it always expects (consciously or unconsciously) favours to be returned. The sign of Libra is always searching for balance and if a Libra Moon does not get the same respect and love in return, it looks for love and approval elsewhere.

The ability to devote itself completely to the You allows the Libra Moon to react sincerely in social situations. Over time, it develops a real talent for enhancing the life of its partner, but its emotional nature always hopes for love in return. This motivates many of its actions. It is imaginative in its dealings with the You, but in reality is hungry for love. It often has idealised and romantic notions about the You, or the partner. It is hard to resist the charms of a Libra Moon, which easily bends loved ones to its will. It is able to project ideas onto the partner and put gentle pressure on them to make them do as it wants. People with a Libra Moon are very choosy; consciously or unconsciously they demand a certain type of behaviour from their partner in order to receive certain things, and try many sly tricks to bring them round to their way of thinking. We should not forget that cardinal will impulses are active in this sign, and that they are directed towards the You.

Material Level

On the material level, Venus rules. The Moon ego wants harmony at any price, cannot stand anything ugly and always wants the best and most beautiful things for itself. It creates a "semblance of harmony" which is very fragile. The Libra Moon does all it can to avoid anything that brings conflict and threatens to disturb its happiness. It cleverly tries to maintain the appearance of harmony, which becomes hollow and empty, because it only consists of formal conditions but lacks love. On this level, the Moon looks for pleasure in material things, in luxury, elegant clothes and takes what it can get from the You. It is a milder form of business acumen, in which one is always ready to pay for one's own comfort. Libra is ruled by the law of balance "You reap what you sow". However, relationships are governed by other rules, and this misses the point. True love is characterised by a spontaneous, unconditional openness, which does not "trade" with feelings and aims to touch the soul. If this is lacking, in time the partner loses interest in the superficial and boring Libra Moon, which leads to the crisis of rejection, of no longer being loved.

Transformation

The crisis takes place at the opposite sign of Aries. The Libra Moon experiences its "Waterloo" in the polarisation of the I versus the You, and defeat by rejection, usually in connection with partnerships. Conflicts have become unavoidable; the partner's feelings have changed and the fight between I and You begins. Perhaps the partner has noticed that they have already given enough and that what they have received in return no longer corresponds to what they have put in. Promises, assurances or flattery cannot help, neither can beauty, elegance nor the willingness to compromise. In the defeat phase, one runs into a brick wall, the partner has had enough of being manipulated and is no longer interested in assurances – one is rejected, abandoned. In this crisis, the Libra Moon feels completely powerless and desperate. It has the feeling that everyone is against it, is attacking it and blaming it. Separation is inevitable – it is left alone and thrown back on itself. On the other side of the axis lies the I sign of Aries, which forces the Libra Moon into its own centre. This is the only way that the transformation from Venus to Uranus, the esoteric ruler, can take place.

The transformed Moon ego in Libra emerges reborn from this crisis. It will believe in love again, but is now more mature, intelligent and honest. Now it can act wisely and no longer put pressure on the You, the partner. In social situations, this Moon finds it easy to put itself in others' shoes, offer new solutions for problems, show how agreements can be reached, make intelligent judgements and advise others. The creative intelligence of Uranus is used now, just as in mythology, where Libra can even make correct judgements blindfold. So when the Libra Moon has attained the refinement of maturity, it consciously knows what to do and say and can face life's problems with confidence. It now has an uncanny intuition for correct standards and judgements, for the right, fitting and fair word. That is the exaltation of Libra, it is the transformed Moon, which functions brilliantly in partnerships and knows that others have just the same rights as itself. A creative balance in the relationship with the You is thus established, the integration of the shadow. The esoteric seed thought for Libra is also useful here:

"I choose the way which leads between the two great lines of force."

Capricorn ♑ ☽

Here the cardinal principle is combined with the element of earth. The earth makes the Moon sensory, it is the Jupiter temperament. It used to be said that the Capricorn Moon was cold because Capricorn was ruled by Saturn. The earthiness makes this Moon very sensual and the cardinal principle gives it will and power, so that it is a Moon that is able to get what it wants. Love usually serves some objective purpose; the Capricorn Moon nearly always has a goal to attain. It is not a spontaneous Moon, and it does not turn to others without good reason. Its feeling self requires security, and it takes a while for it to be sure that others are decent and will not betray it. It takes formal criteria like status, career, occupation and income into consideration here. As we have already mentioned, a Capricorn Moon nearly always needs an objective reason to make contact with others. It is hard for it to understand the idea of loving for its own sake. As an individual sign, Capricorn knows emotionally what it is worth and values itself highly. This is an individualised Moon, which does not allow itself to be used for others' ends, but wants to choose and decide for itself. It has a realistic attitude and an objective view of emotional and romantic matters. It looks for benefit, for concrete evidence of commitment and possible help for its career in almost all relationships. If everything turns out to be safe and reliable, it can also start to open up emotionally, and only then will it shows its feelings. In the right frame of mind and situation, it has a fantastic mastery of the whole range of emotions and can fascinate those around with its charm and emotional richness, which astonishes everyone. But it often takes a long time to reach this stage.

A Capricorn Moon usually seems proud and arrogant to people who do not know it. If it wants something from them, they can reject it abruptly. It exercises a natural power over its environment. The Capricorn Moon can easily get what it wants; it can function with its feeling self. After all, it is Capricorn that guides the cardinal principle up to the point of individuation in the horoscope. A Capricorn Moon also climbs relentlessly upwards so that it can dominate and achieve the goals it has set. If a Capricorn wants a certain man or woman, it will get them. It knows exactly what to do and when, prepares itself and proceeds methodically. It knows how much effort to put in and how long for. It is an unerring Moon for whom the fulfilment of its own desires is very important. In times of stress, the Capricorn Moon tends to take its job too seriously, neglecting romance for the sake of work and the achievement of goals. It demands a lot from itself and from other people, and works extremely hard due to ambitious goals and high standards. Only when goals have been achieved and duties are done can such people relax and enjoy life.

Material Level

On the material level, people with a Capricorn Moon are particularly interested in obtaining success, recognition and personal power. They choose a partner for practical reasons, looking for a person who will support their goals and be useful for them. Many marry for money so that they will be provided for and enjoy a certain status. Others put off marriage and starting a family until they find the right partner who can offer them a secure lifestyle. Many are selfish in their demands on their environment, for on this level Saturn is very strong, hard and uncompromising, and does everything it can to avoid falling from the top of its mountain. The crisis causes an inner reversal; it has to come down from its peak, to the sign of Cancer, to its original source. Its ambition has distanced it too much from love. At the height of its power, it believed that it did not need other people. In this autonomous state it is alone and a really lonely person.

Transformation

The transformation crisis of the Capricorn Moon begins when success is hard to come by and it has to deal with rejection and failure. These come both from outside sources and from serious mistakes that it has made itself, the consequences of which it has to live with. The quality of its work drops, it loses power, status, friends and sometimes its job. The fall from the pinnacle is unavoidable in this transformation crisis. For the Capricorn Moon in particular, it is unthinkable that people and situations can get out of control. For a long time it cannot accept this and it tries to keep the old forms going. In spite of this, what it was trying to avoid happens. Often what it had worked so hard for is taken away and it is blamed by those around it. This breakdown dissolves its resistance and calls for integration with the opposite sign of Cancer. In other words, it must become humble again and take emotional values seriously. When it climbs back down into the nest and admits that it needs love, warmth and tenderness like everyone else, it will be able to live in the collective again. In the process, it has to stop thinking about profit and allow itself to love spontaneously.

A Transformed Capricorn Moon will then climb back up to the heights of individuality, treat others with great understanding, be an example to them and help them in times of need. It tries its best to be fair and to keep its word. It likes to take on duties and responsibilities for the community, and fulfils them faithfully and conscientiously. It skilfully negotiates obstacles, steering clear of them as much as possible, and waits for the right opportunity to get rid of them. It usually radiates strength and security in emotional matters; even when it seems cool and objective, it offers others guidance, support and stability. Once a transformed Moon ego in Capricorn has committed itself, it takes its marital and parental duties very seriously. Such a person possesses good leadership qualities and a developed sense of responsibility, not least because he is afraid of doing something wrong and hurting other people. He climbs down from the height he has reached and shows other people the way up.

The esoteric seed thought for Capricorn expresses this clearly:

"Lost am I in light supernal, yet on that light I turn my back."

The Moon in the Fixed Signs

Taurus, Leo, Scorpio, Aquarius

The fixed cross is formed by the signs Taurus, Leo, Scorpio and Aquarius. Its basic principle is that of a shaping force with two basic motivations: security and persistence. In this cross, the feeling self is structured and its spontaneity and flexibility reduced, so that it is expressed in a steady and stable form. This 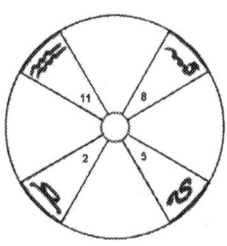 cross also has its place in the whole. The fixed cross gives shape and structure to the impulses of the cardinal cross, which enables the ideas of the cardinal cross to be expressed and maintains them for as long as possible. This quality also enables the feeling self to attain a certain stability, but still allows it to express desires and emotions.

Security

A fixed Moon looks for security, for a constant flow of emotion that flows inexorably towards a distant goal, as in the bed of a river. It would like to hold onto what it loves, and not lose it again. Repetition is no problem for it. On the contrary, if everything stays the same, it feels comfortable and secure. That is why it avoids change and would like to enjoy what it has obtained until the bitter end. In the process it constructs security measures to prevent possible loss, thus creating an inner contradiction to the nature of the Moon, which would like to react spontaneously, but the fixed cross forbids that because it could be dangerous. Basically, the Moon is the curiosity within us that makes us long to experience new things deep inside. Even in the fixed signs, it attracts us to what is new. But because here the energies flow more slowly, wishes are often paralysed and longings unsatisfied. Many feelings peter out before they can be gratified. This leads to frustration, because the fixed principle is the opposite of the Moon's quality.

Dependency

Another peculiarity of the fixed cross is a dependence on formal conditions, representations and demands. When contacts of an emotional nature don't go according to a certain format, the Moon doesn't react. If it also lies in the fixed zone of a house, it sets conditions and tests others until its fears are either confirmed or disappear. This position is also called "Sandwich Moon", because it is wedged in, and experiences restrictions and fears. A fixed Moon keeps the doors closed until convinced that it can do otherwise. It feels secure in enclosed spaces and wants to coexist with the people who live there in a protected bubble, rejecting everything that disturbs this security.

Habits

The fixed cross clings to familiar states, whether good or bad. The processes are quantitative, which means that such people always need the same disappointments and experiences, the same strokes of fate until they change their behaviour. Transformations and changes usually only happen by dint of repetition and exhaustion. The crises of the fixed cross are all types of loss, i.e. exactly what someone with the Moon or strong fixed component (sign or house) is always trying to avoid. These are jealous Moon positions, which carefully make sure that they don't miss out on anything. They blame other people if they don't get what they think they're entitled to, and if denied, they look for revenge. Because they base self-esteem on how much they own, money, substance, people or freedom from guilt mean a lot for personal security. So they fight for these to the bitter end. In spite of this, in the fixed cross the loss of security is the most important experience for transformation or further development. Only when the Moon loses its fears and opens up confidently to love can it live in peace.

Soul Mate

A widespread concept of the fixed cross is the belief in the soul mate. People with the Moon (or Sun) in a fixed sign are nearly always looking for their other half, their soul mate. Every time they fall in love, they're convinced they've finally found the right person. The need for oneness with the one they love comes from deep unconscious layers, from the area of human archetypes. To understand this longing, it helps to go back to Adam and Eve. Legend has it that they lived in paradise in a unity of consciousness, a state of total symbiosis. They did not even know that there were two genders. When they were tempted by the serpent to eat from the tree of knowledge, the symbiotic relationship was broken. Suddenly they realised they were naked and perceived themselves as separate people, recognising the You's otherness. The result was that they were driven out of paradise, and had to learn to live with polarity. However, the knowledge and a deep longing for wholeness remained.

So the search for the soul mate began at the starting point, i.e. in paradise. Man therefore has a lifelong yearning to return to this state of oneness that existed in paradise, and hopes that he can recreate it in love by merging with the You. That is the drama of love, the basic need of every person and also a great emotional illusion. People with the Moon or many planets in fixed signs or houses experience the strongest disillusionment and disappointments in love.

Taurus ♉ ☽

A Taurus Moon is considered to be conservative, close to nature, sensual and loyal. With the earth element, Taurus is the prototype of the fixed cross, so spontaneous feelings are inhibited. However, Taurus has a good instinct for genuine values, is economical with its feelings and only commits to people who are worth its while. People with a Taurus Moon have stamina and tenacity. In all relationships they build a solid foundation of security. In a closed context with people they trust, they are emotionally free and open, while in a strange environment they are reserved. If everything is in order, and seems to be safely in line with an agreement, they even develop strong sensual feelings of affection, beauty and the art of love. With Venus as ruler, the Taurus Moon has a strong desire for harmony, pleasure and closeness to nature, plus a talent for the artistic design of their surroundings.

People with a Taurus Moon long for unchanging security and feel much safer when they have their own home. They can look after themselves very well. Their self-love and natural lifestyle mean that they will never overexert themselves and their energies will never be prematurely exhausted. A Taurus Moon often believes that it has to set itself boundaries so that nothing bad happens to it. It holds back until sure that its feelings are returned. If such a person wants to push for something or make changes happen quickly, it can react with extraordinarily stubbornness. If provoked, it quickly becomes defensive and angry. They feel restless and depressed if their relationship is jeopardised. They suffer from jealousy, imagine the worst and make themselves afraid of loss. Such feelings easily lead to compensative behaviour, emotional stress and paranoid imaginings. If they become emotionally blocked, their feelings stagnate and are expressed as frustration or aggression.

To understand better the Taurus Moon, it helps to consider the law of economy based on supply and demand. If there is no demand, it cannot love; it cannot easily arouse demand by itself. A cardinal Moon can do this because it possesses a conquering energy. The Taurus Moon usually needs to be sought after and needed, otherwise it does not give of itself. If nobody is there who would like to have it or to love it, it quickly gets frustrated. The disappointment is particularly strong if it is in an unequal relationship where the other takes more and saps its energy. A Taurus Moon finds it hard to take such a constant loss of energy over the long term. Although it resists, it is difficult for it to break free and it often holds on for too long. These repressions can cause psychosomatic illnesses.

Material Level

Venus is the traditional ruler on this level; it makes the person comfort-loving, slow and phlegmatic. They cling to useless things, and don't want to move or to work on personal development. They are usually convinced that everything is already just fine as it is. With an undifferentiated awareness and physical inactivity, material pleasures rule the sensual life; comfort, satiety, greed and self interest are the result. They always think of themselves first and of satisfying 'my' feelings and 'my' hunger for possession, food, love and comfort before giving anything to other people. On this level, they unashamedly enjoy the good things of life, and worry little about the needs of others. The inertia of matter can be a burden for a whole life-time and mean stagnation for a long while. Any idea of change and further development is energetically rebuffed and blocked until the necessary crisis takes place. The toughness of the shell that has been constructed determines how drastic the stroke of fate must be to break through it.

Transformation

In the transformation from exoteric to esoteric ruler, the Taurus Moon has the possibility of freeing itself from emotional rigidity with the sign of Scorpio (polar opposite principle). Helped by Scorpio's strength, it undergoes a fundamental change in motivation through a death and rebirth process, from which it emerges refined and purified. The main criterion for change is being confronted with the transience of existence. It often has to accept the loss of love and realise that this only gave an illusion of security anyway. In psychological terms, it will overcome egoism and learn to heed the needs of others. Any speculation about love being the answer to everything, or personal enrichment or absolute security disappear and fade away in the transformation crisis. Fear of loss is overcome when looking separation or death in the eye, with the realisation that everything terrestrial is transient.

The Transformed Taurus Moon is rooted in the maternal source of being, it loves and cares for nature and lets others share its powerful inner protection. According to Alice A. Bailey (8), the esoteric ruler is Vulcan, guardian of the 1st Ray "Will and Power", which the Taurus Moon is exposed to at the high point of its crisis. In this powerful and far-reaching experience the Moon is suddenly taken back to its original home and experiences the primal essence of its being. It is surprised to find that this oneness feels just like symbiosis with the You, which makes Maya, the illusion, disappear; it knows where it belongs, where its original home is. Such people are towers of strength on the emotional level. They can be relied upon, are always there when needed, offer the right kind of help spontaneously, and don't wait around wondering what to do for long; they just do things right and sort them out. Their practical bent makes them helpful and useful wherever they are. They do not let themselves be influenced and tempted to desert their responsibilities. The same law of inertia that causes a standstill on the material level can indicate incorruptible motives or continuous awareness on the spiritual level. Once it has selected a goal it cannot be dissuaded from it. The esoteric seed thought for Taurus clearly expresses this attitude:

"I see and when the Eye is opened, all is light."

Leo ♌ ☽

Here the fixed principle is combined with the fire element, which symbolises passionate feelings. The Leo Moon clings to relationships with a constant intensity. It is considered to be generous and fun-loving, and radiates a charisma and zest for life that captivates others. When these people laugh, everyone laughs with them, it is hard not to join in. The Leo Moon needs feedback from its surroundings, and structures the environment so that there is always an exchange of energies providing enough response.

The king sitting on the throne is Leo's symbol. Things are measured in quantities here: the bigger his nation, the greater his influence. The more applause he receives, the more secure and powerful he feels. As ruler of this sign, the Sun bestows a fiery strength and lets the Leo Moon cleverly use solar energy to satisfy its feelings. It goes to great lengths to impress others with its emotional intensity in order to be loved and admired (showing off). This fiery sense of self usually makes such people sure of themselves and gives them a developed self-esteem, which often leads them to make special demands on those around them. For example, for them it goes without saying that they should always have the most beautiful woman, the strongest man, the biggest slice, the first place or the best menu.

The Leo Moon is proud by nature, and prefers to give advice rather than to receive it. Many find it hard to ask for support and help from others. They want to control everything themselves and do not like to show that they may need help. This often makes them keep up a front that bears no relation to reality. Their own self-respect stops them from exposing themselves. If others see through them or unmask them, it's as though the Leo Moon has lost its identity, and is afraid that people will be able to see its inner insecurity. So it prefers to remain closed and to keep watch at the gate to its Moon ego.

Setting the boundary of its own kingdom is another important trait. No outsider may enter its sphere of competence. Whoever tries this is rejected or even eliminated. The boundary-setting of the fixed cross is like the territorial behaviour of animals. It protects its intimate sphere with clever defensive manoeuvres; the Leo Moon does not easily give others access to its soul. Only the chosen few are allowed to enter, and this privilege must be highly treasured, valued or paid for.

Material Level

On the material level, the Sun rules in an undifferentiated way. But as the Sun is also the esoteric ruler of this sign, the sensitivity of the heart must be developed on a conscious level. At the material, blind stage, people with a Leo Moon want to dominate their environment and call the shots. They think the world revolves around them, that their demands have priority and that others must fall in line behind them. In love they are passionate and intense, possessive and demanding. People close to them are there to satisfy their needs and must be available at all times. They are happiest when receiving unquestioning admiration. They misuse their own love power to obtain this. Possessive love, in which the other is used to satisfy personal desires, is typical of this level of development.

For the Leo Moon it is the most precious thing in the world to fall in love and to merge with one special person. But the partner has to feel exactly the same way. Otherwise he is deeply offended and his vanity is wounded. This also makes the Leo Moon a jealous Moon. It goes against his nature and wounds him deeply if rivals or "other gods" appear. He is convinced that he is the best. He wants to lay his noble heart, his passionate love, his eroticism and the best of himself at the feet of the one he loves, and it must be appreciated!

Transformation

The transformation is triggered by the loss of love, when the Leo Moon is left or doubted by people he loves. The crisis starts when he has to share or play second fiddle. In the polar tension to Aquarius, he finds that he is just part of the whole and as such is replaceable. He learns, albeit against his will, that every part of the whole is equally important, that we are all one and that the world does not revolve around him.

It is a painful lesson for someone with a Leo Moon to have to share their partner with someone else. It is hard for him to take and breaks him apart; he shuts himself away to protect himself. The fixed principle builds walls and accuses those who did this to him. He punishes with contempt those around him who no longer love him as the best and greatest person, and do not immediately jump to their feet when he appears. In this crisis, a Leo Moon is deeply hurt inside and sees no other possibility than to isolate himself and cut himself off from any contact until he really starts to stew (as befits a fire sign!) and the fiery conversion also takes possession of his soul.

The Transformed Leo Moon has his heart in the right place; he has been refined and is now mature enough to love sincerely from the heart. Now he can radiate love energy and love other people. Such people put themselves out for those weaker than themselves, giving them courage and confidence and helping them out of trouble. They possess healing powers thanks to solar energy, which can really give solace and strength to others. Along with their fiery heart, someone with a Leo Moon can also develop the sensitivity to look into the heart of his brother so that he can love him once more. This is the Sun principle that brings life and symbolises the optimism, *joie de vivre* and liberating laughter of the refined Leo Moon.

This natural humour, joy and eroticism is Leo's real emotional warmth. He has the ability to motivate those around him in the right direction, without thinking of what he is getting in return. He is a welcome guest wherever he goes, because he spreads cheerfulness and joy. The Leo Moon always brings something special and beneficial to the group, for after all it is life energy that we all need to survive and can never get enough of. It has a stimulating and constructive effect on our emotional world. The esoteric seed thought for Leo expresses the unity of the inside and the outside:

"I am That and That am I"

Scorpio ♏ ☽

The sign of Scorpio combines the fixed cross with the element of water. The cross needs security and stability, but mainly on the emotional level because of the water temperament. Scorpio is the sign of extremes, so the Moon as the feeling self undergoes major changes in this sign. Nevertheless, it is always busy looking for a stable position to avoid being lost in the whirlpool of emotions. In relationships, it runs the gamut of emotions between sympathy and antipathy, attraction and rejection, love and hate. He often vacillates between good and evil and is unable to separate them clearly. This tension enables him to find creative ways out of difficult situations without them getting him down, and saving his own skin. Love allows him to develop unimagined powers, and he transcends himself and makes sacrifices and goes without. He acts bravely for those he loves or for whom he is responsible. He deprives himself of home comforts if it is a question of sticking together and surviving.

He critically looks for shortcomings in his own character and in other people's. He can go too far though and frequently hurts others in the process, making them resent him. By constantly checking himself and other people, he learns to recognise his mistaken thoughts, wishes, words and deeds as such immediately, and avoids them where possible. He does not spare himself either, and is prepared to work hard on himself. This is a process of purification, which can become self-destructive in extreme cases. The death and rebirth process that is typical of Scorpio gives the Moon no peace; it is subject to the law of refinement and transformation. Life and death are the two extremes that are always putting him in either/or situations. This is particularly evident in partnerships and romantic relationships. He vacillates between holding on "till death do us part" and refusing to commit to love. People with the Moon in Scorpio are either passionately searching for a partner or avoiding commitment like the plague so they do not get hurt.

Many are very afraid of change and problems, and prefer to remain alone because they believe that they could not cope with a relationship that finishes. This is why they cling to otherwise untenable partnerships. Even when relationships no longer work and bring him nothing, he finds it hard to break free. This is related to the sexuality with which Scorpio is usually associated. In relationships it can be a strong motivating force, often leading to a whole range of sexual dependencies.

Material Level

On the material level, people with the Moon in Scorpio suffer from a deep-seated fear of being abandoned. This is why they try so hard to find lasting relationships, and separations are out of the question. They even refuse to let their partner go if they want to split up, and make dramatic scenes. It is hard to live with such people, but even harder to leave them. They are possessive and jealous and can neither forgive nor forget. Separations can even be life-threatening, with acrimonious battles over possessions, alimony, children, etc. Once he loves something, the Scorpio Moon wants to keep it forever. The fear of losing his partner or love makes him capable of giving everything for it. He makes provisions, conscientiously does his duty, tries to make himself indispensable and to incorporate structures into the relationship from which the partner cannot extricate themselves. Scorpio Moons like to set traps to test other people and to make them submissive. They either awaken hopes or feelings of guilt in the partner or threaten to expose them.

The law of give and take, and the law of economics, works on the whole Taurus/Scorpio axis. Many have a psychological hold over their partner, both via the "carrot and stick" method and with promises and blackmail. They make their partner, children, siblings and even friends, dependent on them, taking every opportunity to increase their dependency. They control their partner, want to be informed of their movements or to be asked for their permission. When they do allow their partner or children to go out on their own, they spy on them and inhibit them with fear and guilt. They radiate menace, often even without speaking, so that the partner doesn't dare to not do what they want.

The Transformation

The transformation of a Scorpio Moon is a life-long process, but he can also refuse and reject any change. The transformation goes from the exoteric ruler Mars to the esoteric ruler Pluto. Pluto can lead its willpower in two directions: either the refinement and purification is carried out consciously, sometimes excessively and self-destructively, or all his willpower is used to put off the death or change and to defend his own standpoint to the bitter end. But the Scorpio Moon will take the step to end the eternal sorrow of love when he is ready. By overcoming the fear of the annihilation of the ego, he lets himself fall into the abyss and is caught by a universal power which is not of this world. But he must be ready to leave everything behind him in order to move on. At the height of the crisis, he must want the change, otherwise he will fall by the wayside and become more and more materialistic.

After the process of refinement and conversion, the transformed Scorpio Moon can be much more relaxed now that he is freed from brutish severity. He can free his mind and his whole personality from fear and move into the light. It is currently the Scorpio Moon's duty to purify the mind of all mankind from negative fears and the destructive use of force and aggression. He has the magical power to determine whether Pluto is used for self-destructive purposes or to build a better world. His forte is the magical process of mental purification, which can influence people's minds in a positive way when used with awareness. Just as before the transformation his intelligence was used to structure relationships to make them last, now he can bring light to the darkest corners of the human mind, either as healer, therapist or transformer of spiritual conversion energies. It is important for the Scorpio Moon to know that a new life is possible after death, and that he must resolutely move towards it.

The esoteric seed thought for Scorpio expresses this rebirth:

"Warrior I am and from the battle I emerge triumphant."

Aquarius

In Aquarius the fixed principle meets the air temperament. Air incorporates rationality into the emotional nature and wants the security motivation to be realised there. People with the Moon in Aquarius rationalise their feelings and are very good at simulating emotions, giving this Moon a certain dramatic ability. They are sparing and economical with their own feelings and keep them locked away until they are sure that they will not be wasted on the undeserving.

Aquarius is an individual sign, and people with this Moon position have their own ideas about love and contact. They do not usually conform to the traditional ideas of male and female behaviour, preferring to put the person at the centre of events, so that everyone can do as they want. They take responsibilities seriously, are sociable and friendly and fair to their peers, but are ruthless with their inferiors. They differentiate between levels and look for friends who are like themselves. When they love someone, they are faithful companions, whose loyalty and solicitude can always be counted on. They usually have a developed ethical sense or at least an idea of how to get on well with others.

Aquarius Moons also know how to love themselves, they cherish their individuality, freedom and independence. It is hard to make them do something that they do not want to do. They are rebels at heart against anything that restricts or controls them. Aquarius will just not do what is normal and usual, at least not of its own free will. It is often difficult to know when an Aquarius Moon will open up and when it will clam up. It usually happens abruptly. She can also cut herself off from friends without them knowing the reason why. She just drops them, either because she doesn't need them any more, or because they no longer fit into her view of the world. She makes great demands on those around her. She is emotionally independent, and does not find it easy to commit others. There is a special selection mechanism that provides security.

The Aquarius Moon is keen not to let emotions unbalance her, and builds a protective wall for her own security. This is why this is sometimes called the "Greenhouse Moon". She surrounds herself with an invisible wall to keep the You at a distance so that she is not affected by undesirable influences. This ability to pick and choose enables her to keep her emotions pure and clean. This is a cultivated and mature Moon that can look after itself and care intelligently for its physical, emotional and spiritual welfare.

Material Level

On the material level, the Aquarius Moon's intellectualism and imaginativeness are responsible for an inability to express real emotion. The emotions are contrived and technophile, often prudish and cold. The suppression and repression of feelings can even become a way of coping with life. This leads to a callousness that denies all that is lively and judges people according to how functional they are, i.e. by their status, rank and usefulness. This shows itself in a certain unjustified arrogance and snobbish attitude, and in extreme cases leads to the creation of bogeymen. They sometimes deal ruthlessly and cruelly with people who think differently to themselves. These are people who need every regulation to be fulfilled, specific objectives to be achieved and technical, objective tasks to be completed before they can find time for love.

The hardened Aquarius Moon often develops a cold sarcasm towards other people's sentimentality. Emotional problems are not taken seriously for they disturb the smooth functioning of everyday life and are therefore blocked. In extreme cases, people can be reduced to a functional machine, to just a number. Pride and arrogance in emotional matters are partly to blame for this. The clueless Aquarius Moon believes herself to be very sophisticated because she has no feelings. She is conceited, thinks she is better than everyone else and punishes others with contempt if they fall passionately in love. The Aquarius Moon can easily get sidetracked by utopian visions of the future, from which only a deep inner conversion can save her and enable her to participate in normal life again.

Transformation

When people with an Aquarius Moon climb into their ivory tower and have put enough distance between themselves and reality, the time for change is nigh. They feel lonely, isolated and detached from human life up there in the clouds. Everything seems so meaningless; there is nobody to share thoughts and feelings with. In this barren loneliness, the Aquarius Moon starts out to rediscover the love she has lost. The search begins for people who think as she does, who will love her as she is, unconditionally. When she experiences genuine communication as love, she is capable of being a great friend. She is not looking for friends to take advantage of, but is there when needed; for her friendship and fairness go together. If someone feels lonely, Aquarius Moon can be there at once, to give strength and support. Because she herself knows what it is like to be lonely, she can understand others' needs and raise their spirits again.

When the Aquarius Moon has left the ivory tower she has built in her mind, she will be ready to cooperate. She is prepared to abandon her idealism, visions, dogma and crystallised ways of thinking, because these are what has distanced her from other people. She recognises that without love we would just be intelligent robots, which is why everyone needs to experience true love. She is interested in the universal human kindness that is benevolent and without ulterior motive, which embraces everything and excludes nothing. She will be able to form meaningful relationships with others again. The esoteric ruler is Jupiter, and the transformation goes from Saturn/Uranus to Jupiter. Her worldview is then real, true and correctly proportioned, and was constructed by her to enable her to serve as many people as possible. She radiates fairness and trustfulness. She no longer judges people, but helps them to develop as individuals. This produces a deeply humane quality, which is the trust between people that leads to the "harmony of the original", which will be developed at the end of the Age of Aquarius.

The esoteric seed thought for Aquarius is:

"Water of life am I, poured forth for thirsty men."

The Moon in the Mutable Signs

Gemini, Virgo, Sagittarius, Pisces

The Moon has a natural affinity with the mutable principle. It has the same motivation as the mutable signs, i.e. love and contact. People with this Moon position are therefore particularly interested in human relationships, i.e. everything connected with coexistence, humanitarian, social and interpersonal relationships, love, contact and culture and art. They can interact spontaneously with their environment and respond to the needs of others with sensitivity. The mutable Moon is a "Moon of the here and now", it can immediately tune in to new contacts and reacts instantly and instinctively to changing circumstances. A person with the Moon in a mutable sign takes in everything that is happening around him, is not biased or demanding and has no power political goals. He has a certain freedom and can relate to people and things as he wishes. He can just drop everything if someone calls, and is able to live completely in the "here and now".

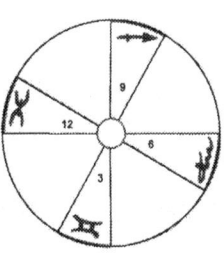

Devotion

A person with a mutable Moon needs a lot of devotion, understanding and love in his relationships. As the planet of contact and love, this Moon is always looking for perfect love. If he cannot feel comfortable in romantic and social situations, he at least tries to make the other person devoted to him. If he can feel the constant flow of emotions and enjoy the eternal changeability of life and socialising, he feels good. He just cannot understand people who do not make love the most important thing in their lives and whose duties cause them to miss out on opportunities for love.

Coldness and Crisis

Coldness impairs the ability to love, and people with a mutable Moon find it particularly hard to deal with. Their whole character is questioned when they are caught up in meaningless duties, services, constraints and following other people's orders. They lose their vitality and *joie de vivre* when all their time is taken up with mundane tasks. A person with a mutable Moon does not have patience with survival necessities for long. If there are no breaks or changes planned, his soul becomes sick and he becomes susceptible to psychosomatic illnesses.

The mutable Moon position has intense reactions to constraints and the withdrawal of love. For example, a woman whose partner has a cardinal Moon and is mainly interested in his work has little time for real communication. A mutable Moon suffers from the meaninglessness of such a relationship. These people can often see no way out of the deadlock. They go around desperately rattling closed doors, shouting for help and are incapable of setting themselves free. They panic and undergo an emotional crisis that can lead to all kinds of possible reactions. They are willing to put their lives on the line to gain the freedom they desire. They become typical runaways and drop-outs and do not care about the risks and dangers involved.

Differentness

The mutable principle is quite different to the fixed and cardinal crosses and therefore hard to understand. In the olden days, it was called the "weak cross", because these people appeared to have a weak character. This includes those people who are rejected by society: travellers, penniless artists, thieves, thugs, tramps and prostitutes. The cardinal and fixed crosses were always well thought of. In our modern society, they represent qualities worth striving for: the desire to succeed, potential, economic advancement, competitive spirit, career, hierarchical and political thinking. People with a mutable Moon do not feel comfortable in this kind of world, and their sensitive feeling nature rebels.

However, their existence is important. If love between people were neglected, and no-one cared about art and culture, then we would become intellectuals ruled by our heads without emotional warmth, and what would the future hold? The principle of love must be cherished and maintained, which is why the mutable cross has an important place in the modern world. It brings love, balance, joy, relaxation and amusement into our lives. In evolution, all three principles must be developed equally, each cross needs the others to make the whole. The polarity is broadened through the addition of the third axis, represented by the mutable cross, providing a deeper quality of relationship.

Social Awareness

In this century, many things have changed in favour of the mutable cross. Love between people is considered more important, social awareness has developed in recent years and psychological and esoteric thinking is spreading rapidly. Psychological research has led to a better understanding of human relationships in general; problems with one's partner, marriage and raising children can be handled and solved with more awareness. The mutable principle corresponds to everything relating to the human sciences, with education, psychology, counselling, and the healing and artistic professions. When it comes to human relationships, the mutable Moon breathes a sigh of relief, as here it is in its element. People with a mutable Moon are therefore happiest when they work in professions where they are needed, where they can work with others in a real contact situation. If they enjoy their work, if it is meaningful and improves human welfare, it brings out their best emotional qualities.

Love and Meaning

In a romantic relationship, people with a mutable Moon position have a lot to give. They open themselves up to the other's soul and identify with it. They do not push themselves forward and can wait their turn. They deal sensitively with the needs of others before expecting their own needs to be met. Their life is only meaningful and worth living if love, sensitivity, mutual respect and helpfulness have their place in it. It only has meaning if love is present, which is why a mutable Moon is capable of giving so much love and devotion. However, it does need the same amount in return. Because love is so important, its main objective, its innermost need, is to live with others in fair exchange.

Awareness

Now we have come a little closer to understanding the nature of the mutable principle. Another aspect of the mutable cross is the connection with awareness. This only occurs where curiosity, learning aptitude and change are possible, leading to ongoing development and growth. In our contact with the world, cognitive processes are constantly taking place to form our awareness. This involves asking why and looking for the meaning behind things and events. So it ultimately comes down to the search for meaning and the exposure of absurdity. This is directly linked to a cognitive mechanism in which new ideas and ideologies are born, religions and philosophies are compared and ways of thinking are evaluated and examined. This is why the mutable cross is also known as the cross of learning and cognition.

Development Crisis

We initially experience social situations via the houses, which contain the behaviour patterns which enable us to make contact and to learn. But in times of crisis, we must go back to the sign because this goes deeper. Of course, we can also get into difficulties with external structures, or conditioning. The house themes are most effective in a partnership, and a partner relationship also begins with them (14). But change and interior awakening go back to the sign. The difference between sign and house gives us an idea of what we need to do, it is related to evolution. It is a developmental principle, a learning process, which helps the inner self to unfold.

Vocation and Transformation

If a mutable Moon is still completely selfish, even childlike, immature and dependent on the environment, it cannot cope with life, and can find it hard to survive and suffer from addictions. He either needs a strong partner, a lot of love, or a meaningful activity so that he can stay balanced. The transformation of the mutable cross involves accepting limits and responsibilities. That means that one must focus on one single objective, one single person, and overcome the temptation to diversify. This requires the right choice of job or partner. If his partner does not have a mutable Moon, he can gain emotional satisfaction in a meaningful, serving profession. People with this Moon quality give meaning to their existence by being there for other people, which is why they prefer professions where they can experience and study relationships. They can work as doctors, healers, psychologists, priests, teachers, philosophers, artists and also salesmen and agents. If their choice of career comes from an inner vocation, they will have a meaningful life.

Gemini ♊ ☽

Gemini is an air sign in the mutable cross, ruled by Mercury. This combination gives an intellectual touch to the feelings, i.e. the mind influences the emotions. In people with a Gemini Moon, this can show itself as a healthy common sense, but also as a lack of emotion or as superficial, playful emotions. Its spontaneity, adaptability, intelligence and flexibility enable it to handle all aspects of a relationship with ease. It is curious about everything happening around it, is well informed about many things, and is always willing to pass on its knowledge. Alert, quick-witted, volatile and restless, it reacts to many things simultaneously. A fixed Moon will find the Gemini Moon's ability to respond in the moment unbelievable and amazing; it will have reacted long before the fixed Moon has had time to get itself together and check all its defences. It is well-known that the Gemini Moon finds great satisfaction in doing several things at the same time. She is well-suited to the mediative professions in which quick reactions are required. She is a born salesman and good at selling or providing services. She usually knows where to get hold of things and is well informed about the existing market situation. Also, she already has in mind someone to whom the goods bought can be further sold. She moves quickly and does not need to think for long when she wants something. The Gemini Moon is also suited to work as a travel agent, in the information and telephone services, as a teacher and in the commercial professions. From one moment to the next, they can make decisions and turn situations to their own advantage. They usually have a remarkable aptitude for languages, can learn foreign languages easily and also speak the language of the people, so that they make great teachers. They intuitively know how to convince people of things, have didactic talents and fascinate others with their words.

Because the Gemini Moon can tune in very quickly when it meets new people, it is not very loyal, being easily tempted by the diversity of possibilities. The mutable element is the elixir of life, in which she thrives and where her energies can flow. The sheer quantity of contacts and activities can lead to dissipation, which makes her restless and nervous. It is all too easy for her to promise things she cannot deliver, which leads to excuses that do not add up and are easy to see through.

Material Level

On the material level, and depending on house position, a Gemini Moon is a "jack of all trades". It is a collective Moon that falls in line with the standard behaviour of its environment. On the emotional level, she is guided by colleagues and relations and imitates them without realising it, becomes like them and has no real opinions of her own. She has no knowledge of strong, genuine feelings; for her emotions are nothing more than an exchange of information, and for some people, a night of love means no more than a handshake. Truth is relative for one who unquestioningly adopts whatever is in fashion at the moment. Because "everyone" does it, it is also right for her.

Levelling down is her problem here. Personal responsibility is delegated to other people, particularly to colleagues, fellow club members, relatives, brothers and sisters, the authorities. Their opinion is crucial for her, as is what she reads in the newspaper or what TV presenters say. The Gemini Moon always wants to know what others are thinking and feeling so that she doesn't miss anything. There is a special talent for getting hold of information that others cannot access. With her intelligence and curiosity she persuades people to tell her what she wants. She finds it very hard to keep a secret.

In relationships, the Gemini Moon often experiences a kind of inflation where love is only experienced superficially and not in depth. She is often unable to choose just one out of a number of relationships, and loses someone who loves her in the process. Gemini Moons keep all their plates in the air for a long time though, skilfully and intelligently manoeuvring back and forth between several different contacts and relationships. They enjoy having their cake and eating it too. In such situations, they like to use wordplay and ambiguities.  Humour is a proven way of dealing with problems, so long as they do not obsessively play the clown and contradict themselves. In an emotional crisis, they usually throw themselves into non-stop activity, make long phone calls or read three books at once.

Transformation

The crisis takes place on the opposite end of the polar axis, with Sagittarius. Sagittarius wants to find truth, value and meaning. That is the complete opposite of the relativising and impersonal emotional nature of the Gemini Moon. She dissipates herself until all contacts bring nothing but trouble and she cannot handle them any longer. When at the end of her tether, and getting out of her depth, she has to make the decision to turn inwards. This turning inwards is always possible when one hits rock bottom. This existential crisis on the Gemini/Sagittarius axis corresponds to the well-known lament in Goethe's *Faust*: "Here I stand, a poor fool, and am just as clever as before." Only then does the Gemini Moon set out to seek the truth in Sagittarius and to find a philosophy that will give meaning to life.

The Transformed Gemini Moon is able to focus feelings and interest onto a single objective and acquire all the knowledge needed to accomplish it. In all mutable signs, the transformation calls for a reduction in personal freedom and the use of willpower. But first she will have to learn that nothing else can take her any further. Usually it is the experience of true love that lets her find this out for herself. Such a deep emotional experience can save her from superficiality for a while.

To maintain this state, the Gemini Moon needs a spiritual goal: she must want to develop her higher self. For this, she requires a sophisticated concept, a well-rounded philosophy of life, a convincing truth, which she must find by herself. The esoteric ruler of Gemini is Venus, and the transformation goes from Mercury via Sagittarius to Venus. Venus as an instrument of selection enables her to make the right choices and take her own decisions. It provides the higher reason that becomes wisdom. When she has studied the teachings of eternal wisdom, and has found all values to be absurd, she can get right to the heart of things. She experiences through her own centre of being that this is the only goal worth striving for, and is then able to let the others go.

The esoteric seed thought for Gemini expresses this clearly:

"I recognise my other self and in the waning of that self, I grow and glow."

Virgo ♍ ☽

The sign of Virgo combines the element earth with the mutable cross. The mutable diversity therefore has a certain structure; the earth quality provides a certain resistance to change. For a Virgo Moon, this means being concerned about matter and physical survival and working until everything is in order and every detail is consistent. These people also actually enjoy work, are outstanding at carrying out detailed tasks and feel guilty if there is something they cannot cope with. They are always working on improving or refining things. They are practical and efficient and are always thinking about how they can accomplish both their professional and domestic duties perfectly.

The Virgo Moon is a "Helping Moon", with all the virtues of thoughtfulness and the willingness to work. These people always notice if something is not right. They have an instinctively helping, immediately reacting Moon ego. If something drops on the floor, they pick it up without giving it a second thought. It must be put back in its place straight away. People with a Virgo Moon are usually nice to have around; they always make themselves useful and like to give people a helping hand. They are efficient in many areas and intervene where necessary. They feel responsible for everything and don't hesitate before they jump in and help. They are reliable and willing co-workers, who do their job carefully down to the last detail. They don't need to search for errors, but spot them immediately. People with a Virgo Moon know exactly what is good for them and what is not. They are also concerned about other people's health. The Virgo Moon is nearly always oriented towards the You, and focused on serving and helping other people. A person with a Virgo Moon is ideally suited to the caring and helping professions.

Material Level

On the material level Mercury rules over the feeling self, giving it a special analytical ability. The Virgo Moon is more oriented towards the practicalities of life, and not really towards thinking in itself (as in the case of Gemini, the other Mercury sign). It can therefore analyse both its own feelings and other people's. It has an instinct for the niceties of love, can detect nuances and has hypersensitive reactions to all external influences and vibrations. Disturbances can have a negative effect on its emotional disposition and even make it seize up. The principle of order that characterises it needs perfection and completion.

These people are very irritable in emotional matters. The slightest excess and imperfection disturbs the harmonious flow of their feelings. This gives rise to a magnifying effect; the Moon ego only sees the negative and suffers from the imperfection of life – its overreactions place obstacles in the way of love. Such people have an "allergic" reaction to everything that is not in order or that could possibly be dangerous. On this level, they are extremely critical and demand the utmost purity from themselves and others in all things. They point the finger at everything that is wrong. They get upset about the slightest mistake and criticise everyone around them. Virgo's pedantry is a well-known trait and is also present in the Virgo Moon.

Another emotional feature of the Virgo Moon is its fatal tendency to demean itself by being too servile. This submissiveness is only rewarded by ingratitude and rejection from the environment, leading to deep feelings of inferiority and disrespect, and great suffering. The Virgo Moon's feelings fluctuate between superiority and inferiority. Its censoriousness gives it a superior attitude and its servility brings it back down again. Then it usually attracts people who are stronger than itself, and allows them to abuse it by making it do menial tasks. It actually humbles itself, because devotion makes it willing to do everything for love. It then fights back in the wrong way by shouting, criticising, remonstrating and scolding. Instead of bringing the love and appreciation it really wants, this just brings further rejection.

Others worry endlessly over things which are nothing to do with them. This happens because they have trouble distancing themselves from the suffering of others. Some even fall victim to other people's illnesses. Empathy and compassion can be worthwhile qualities, but the Virgo Moon must be careful not to lose itself in the process. Otherwise, the positive qualities of serving, avoiding what is dangerous and maintaining order or health can degenerate into the denial of life. Then the transformation crisis starts, catapulting Virgo into the opposite sign of Pisces and into confusion, meaninglessness and chaos – where the Moon as esoteric ruler is finally awakened.

Transformation

The crisis spans the Existence Axis (Virgo/Pisces) from the physical ability to survive to the infinite space of love. This space initially has a boundary-breaking effect and is experienced as chaos. Here there is no protective order, no security. The world that the Virgo Moon used to serve and for which it worked and sacrificed itself is left behind. Everything that went before is finished and no longer matters. All security arrangements and preventive measures are useless here, disappearing into nothingness. It is a death and rebirth process, similar to that experienced by the Scorpio Moon, but in the case of the Virgo Moon it goes right to the root of its being – it is both an identity crisis and an existential crisis. However, the transformation leads to the experience of a higher existence, a love that is not of this world. It is that unbounded, unconditional love that emanates from the universe. In the conversion crisis, all formalistic and tangible emotions dissolve into nothingness and lose their value and meaning. The dissolving tendency of Pisces helps to cross boundaries, so that one realises that the material and formal things that were so important to the little Moon ego, that it clung to, are transient – and one lets them go. In the end, nothing is left but love. The conversion must be thorough; it is a profound purification process.

The Transformed Virgo Moon stands before open doors and in contact with the transcendental world, where it learns the universal laws of development, which it can now use for the benefit of its fellow men. Just when it thinks it has lost itself, it is caught by something else completely different. It becomes aware of a new experience, unlike anything experienced before, because it has been too obsessed with formal and material tasks. From the depths of the cosmos, from another dimension, he receives a flow of energy that stimulates him to serve and enables him to heal. Although at first this is frightening for the Virgo Moon, who feels surrounded by alien forces, he learns to have more and more confidence in his own inner voice and healing powers. These benevolent transcendental powers simultaneously awaken and strengthen the Moon as the esoteric ruler of this sign.

The Moon now radiates love as a real quality into Virgo, so that the analytical Mercury ability can now be used for making accurate diagnoses, healing and caring. Love and ensuring survival become the primary motivations. It is a journey from matter to spirit, where the highest is combined with the lowest. A person with a Virgo Moon is then able to be present when lives have to be saved and people need love. He can live the law of serving and healing completely; he has transcended the boundaries, has seen the breadth of universal consciousness and returns refined as a true servant.

The esoteric seed thought for Virgo expresses this process as follows:

"I am the mother and the child. I God, I matter am."

Sagittarius

A combination of the mutable principle and the fire temperament, Sagittarius is the third fire sign. Fire is an ego temperament associated with the development of the personality, and in Sagittarius with individualisation and the ability to think for oneself. Ego development begins in Aries, the ego is tested in Leo, and in Sagittarius it is individualised. So a Sagittarius Moon loves independence, strives for freedom and always has its own point of view. It is closely linked with mental processes as much as with feelings; mind and feelings take turns to predominate.

The Sagittarius Moon is strongly influenced by the mutable principle, as demonstrated by its search for breadth and its inability to remain in one place for long. It is emotionally inspired by distance and therefore needs to travel frequently and move about even more often. If he feels trapped in a relationship or situation, the yearning for experience and adventure will always drive him away. Only out in the big, wide world can he can learn about his spontaneous feeling self. He is open to all encounters and interested in everything living, organic and natural. He has a big heart, a lot of understanding for human weakness and is generous in his judgements, all of which influence his environment for the better.

People with a Sagittarius Moon are positive, always bringing confidence and new faith in life, despite bad experiences. They are passionate about learning new things, are avid readers and are always busy expanding their knowledge and improving themselves. They take a keen interest in human affairs and feel compelled to find logical answers to deep philosophical questions. They are in their element when philosophising about God and the world, and share their feelings and thoughts on the matter with others. They are able to talk about feelings and give them a philosophical interpretation. They fight for an idea and their enthusiasm makes others want to get involved. Like the Gemini Moon, the Sagittarius Moon also has a sense of humour which tends towards silliness.

They can sometimes hurt others with their honesty, often doing this quite matter of factly, not thinking that their frankness could cause offence. This sometimes brutal candour can also make them unpopular. Usually their empathy is not particularly developed, because the main objective of Sagittarius is to find the truth and nothing but the truth. This openness also has a positive side, because you nearly always knows where you stand with a Sagittarius Moon. They make no secret of openly admitting what they feel and think. A Sagittarius Moon cannot stand furtiveness, and tries to get things out in the open immediately. They do not make any bones about their opinions, and win many battles by speaking bluntly. But Sagittarius Moon's openness is more than some people can take.

Material Level

People with a Sagittarius Moon react quite selfishly and subjectively. They claim individuality and insist on it, cannot be told anything and do not listen to advice, no matter how well-meant. They identify with their feeling self and it is hard to know where their erratic behaviour will take them next. Their behaviour can neither be defined nor predicted; they are as spontaneous as they are individual. They often forget what they have promised other people and react completely in the moment, especially in sudden encounters. They are even proud of this, as they class the ability to make direct contact as a virtue. Reproaches from the cardinal or fixed areas are not taken seriously and scoffed at. This philosophy and the emotional arbitrariness that goes with it often bring problems in partnerships, not only because they give their opinion openly to their partner, but because they more frequently say things that just do not add up. And they stubbornly stick to this.

The Sagittarius Moon does not like to feel tied down or owe a debt of gratitude and prefers to organise everything itself. The ego dominates and such people have a limited understanding of their partner. If love restricts their individuality, they demand freedom and set conditions. If they feel too trapped by the daily grind, they suffer terribly under the pressures of life. Women with a Sagittarius Moon hate being stuck at home all the time; they often take their baby everywhere with them in a sling. Their ego demands a lot of freedom and independence.

They usually avoid marriage and prefer to remain single. Love must never become a duty – they would rather not bother at all. The Sagittarius Moon always has a kind of fear of commitment. It is afraid of losing the expansiveness brought by Jupiter, ruler of Sagittarius. Having its holistic awareness reduced is unthinkable. Limiting its horizon or being caged in is the worst thing that could happen.

Transformation

For people with a Sagittarius Moon, the opposite sign of Gemini is activated in the transformation crisis. This is the relativising, levelling principle that reduces personal pride. They find that they are not so special after all and that in love they must develop humility so that they can really learn how to feel. Their claim to uniqueness is overcome in loneliness when nobody wants to know them. At the end of the crisis, the esoteric ruler, the Earth, can develop and enable real comprehensive relationships on every level. Love is then experienced as an inclusive, universal phenomenon, in which there is neither high nor low, neither rich nor poor. Through his need for love, the Sagittarius Moon will realise that there is no point in enjoying life's pleasures by himself, and that he will enjoy life more in community with others. It is this question of meaning that is part of the conversion for Sagittarius. He finds that he should do things for those he loves and focus on a romantic goal. He will learn to think of other people too, and find out what kind of love they need to be happy. Then he will be capable of loving deeply. The devotion to the You should be completely true, real and genuine. The esoteric ruler Earth allows no half-measures; here it is only real, first hand experience that counts.

In the Transformed Sagittarius Moon, thoughts and feelings work together. Heart and head are in harmony. This Sagittarius Moon can be trusted. He gives the impression that he tries hard to understand everything in order to be able to judge fairly. He radiates generosity, because he treats everybody fairly and defends the underdog. The breadth that Sagittarius is looking for and his desire to reach the horizon mean that he sometimes overlooks important details. He can explain many things very clearly so that people can understand how they are related.

As usual, the Moon is concerned with the kind of love represented by the great inclusive principle. The Sagittarius Moon realises that love is the greatest power in the universe and that it is all-healing. He wants to spread this insight and live accordingly. They are people who, once they have discovered a truth, share it with everyone with a delight in the discovery that comes right from the heart via the feeling self. They then become great teachers and educators, and are able to portray the eternal wisdoms convincingly and communicate them intelligently. A Sagittarius Moon usually has educational and pedagogical abilities. He is a teacher with a philosophical background who wants to improve the human race. The attraction of distance is a force driving him forward towards new hopes on the horizon. He is therefore always prepared to defend innovations and attack with the necessary moral courage where old-fashioned or anti-social attitudes predominate. Emboldened by hope and faith, he is always ready to embrace new experiences.

The esoteric seed thought for Sagittarius expresses this aspiration as follows:

"I see the goal. I reach that goal and then I see another."

Pisces ♓ ☽

The sign of Pisces combines the mutable cross with the water temperament. Water is compatible with the mutable cross, so people with a Pisces Moon are emotionally flexible and adaptable. They long for infinite love, harmony and understanding, for a country that speaks their language. They have a rich imagination, and are often multi-talented and interested in the media and the arts. They are already capable of all-inclusive love and feel an intuitive connection with all people. The unlimited nature of their feelings allows them to participate in an even greater world, in a universal love that lies beyond good and evil.

Pisces Moons are mostly passive in love and with other people. They wait for others to approach them. Once contact has been made, they are highly adaptable and completely reflect their environment, taking in all the emotional nuances, but often giving the impression that they have no feelings of their own. Many react only to outside impulses, but show hardly any real emotion themselves. The impulses must be subtle and gentle though, as Pisces just ignores crass demands. It is hard to force them to do things, or they slip away like a fish in the water. People with a Pisces Moon have a unique insight into how things are related. They live in two worlds at once and understand human motivations as well as those of the transcendental world.

Material Level

On the material level, Pisces Moons are often the victims of those stronger than themselves. Because they cannot defend themselves, they are easily abused. On this level, the Pisces Moon has no will of its own; it is other-directed and manipulated by those around it. Many fall into the hands of strong-willed people whom they serve slavishly. The environment can do what it wants with such a "selfless" Moon, which is easy to extort and cannot say "no". As the inner motivation of the Pisces Moon is selflessness and infinite love, abandonment of the self is no great sacrifice for them.

Many know nothing at all about their own feeling self; they just want to feel devotion and a love in which they lose themselves. They are neither willing nor able to be themselves or to create solid foundations for themselves. Such people drift and become dependent either on a person or on drugs and alcohol. What a Pisces Moon really needs in order to feel emotionally secure is a deep spiritual connection with a higher power, a real religious experience, which is not easy to achieve on this level. Many suffer long periods of insecurity and feel lost inside.

Jupiter is the traditional ruler of Pisces, which is why they are basically looking for a comfortable life and want to avoid conflict. They make themselves materially dependent on people they love so that they do not lose the luxury of a quiet life. They are grateful for this and show gratitude by giving love in return. They are good listeners, are sensitive, helpful and feel a vocation to serve and help others. Some look for a partner who needs them or who is ill, who they can help and who is dependent on them in another way. However, constantly caring for others can leave them exhausted. For the Pisces Moon, it is important to recognise this co-dependence and to want to free himself from it. But that requires a deep inner conversion, an activation of the highest willpower in Pluto, the esoteric ruler, and this can only happen when the crisis reaches its climax.

Transformation

In the transformation crisis, a great divide appears, because the real world of Virgo does not correspond to the infinite scope of the cosmic sign of Pisces. The Pisces Moon experiences this divide on the Existence Axis, where the two poles are furthest apart. He now stands between them, feeling suspended between heaven and earth and unable to do anything about it. The universal consciousness of Pisces and small-minded reality are two very different things. Taking the little things of life that are so important for survival along into the great cosmic space almost never works. He finds it pointless and wants to escape. In this identity crisis, the Pisces Moon can become very desperate, depressed and even suicidal. It is like the "dark night of the soul" which can even lead to psychosomatic illness, sometimes in order to get other people to look after him. At least he doesn't feel so miserable and useless when he is ill, because he is receiving loving care and attention.

This dependency goes very deep. He hides this feeling of neediness from himself and others, compensating with surrogates, because he cannot cope with the world. This leads to existential crises in which the Pisces Moon is confronted by the esoteric ruler Pluto. He is thrown back onto his own resources, as Pluto wants to activate the higher self, the inner core. Pisces Moons also undergo processes of death and rebirth that are almost deeper than those of the Scorpio Moon. Pluto often takes away from them everything that they have clung to. They touch rock bottom and look death in the face.

If we see Pluto as the nucleus or the core substance, then the change must be radical; it is a thorough purification process that starts with letting go of everything that he used to serve. Once all external dependencies have become meaningless, he goes back to his centre. It is an experience of nothingness, an identity crisis leading to a profound change in motivation. Isolated, lonely, left to his own devices, the Pisces Moon sets out on the journey back to find his parental home, his inner core, his real home, his roots.

It is usually love that causes the Pisces Moon to experience this crisis. They are abandoned, replaced or pushed away, and do not get the attention they deserve. The parable of the prodigal son originates from this experience. They are often misunderstood and forced to be a scapegoat. This experience hurts and is impossible for the feeling self to understand. After all, they did everything for love, sacrificed themselves, deprived themselves of many pleasures to make the other happy; was it all for nothing? This self-pity is one of the last ravines that must still be negotiated at the highpoint of the transformation crisis.

The Transformed Pisces Moon can both extend his feeling of love to the furthest horizons and reconcile the great divide between spirit and matter in his own core. It is a synthesis between external and internal life, between above and below, between heaven and earth. Now it has been given structure by Virgo, the Pisces Moon can say "yes" to life and develop the ability to give help where it is needed. People with a transformed Pisces Moon are born helpers, the doctors or nurses who care for the sick with dedication and sensitivity, the therapists and psychologists who never tire of always hearing the same thing, the good Samaritans who only think of themselves when everyone else is provided for and satisfied. In the religious sense, they are the true priests and helpers, who possess the ability to get rid of and transform the evil in the world. They have a kind of redeeming function, because the sign of Pisces also has the ability to heal.

A transformed Pisces Moon can look more deeply and see how the spiritual and the mental are connected. He can often heal with his presence, openness and willingness to listen alone. He is selflessly there for everyone in need or going through an emotional crisis. He possesses a psychological flair and knows intuitively with few words what is wrong. The refined Pisces Moon is characterised by a spiritually pure sensitivity. In other words, the sign of Pisces has produced the Christ-like consciousness, the highest form of love. It is no coincidence that Christ was born at the start of the Age of Pisces and established the principle of love on our earth.

The esoteric seed thought for Pisces makes this development clear:

"I leave the Father's home and turning back, I save."

Fish Fossil: Depalis Macrurus
About 35 million years old (Bassin de Monasque, France)

7. Special Planetary Positions

Planets at The Ascendant

- The Influence of the Birth Process on the Ego -
- Sun • Moon • Saturn • Mercury • Venus -
- Mars • Jupiter • Uranus • Neptune • Pluto -

The Family Model

- Sun: Father, Saturn: Mother, Moon: Child -
- The Parents as Archetypal Role Models -
- Aspects between the Family Planets -
- Phases of Ego Development -

Exposed Planetary Positions

The Psychodynamics of Fear in the Horoscope
Article by Wolfhard Koenig

- What is Fear? -
- Planetary Configurations and the Development of Fear -
- 1st Case: the Normal Position -
- 2nd Case: the Weak Position -
- 3rd Case: the Strong Position -
- 1. Unaspected Planets • 2. Pulling Position -
- 3. Congestion Position • Example Horoscope -

Planets at the Ascendant

The Influence of the Birth Process on the Ego

Astrological Psychology has found that birth conditions are reflected not only in the zodiac sign at the ascendant, but also by any planets at both the ascendant (AC) and the descendant (DC). They mark the beginning of our lives. The manner in which we enter the world is our first formative influence and remains stored in our feeling self for the rest of our lives. The nature of our birth also has a strong effect on our ego. If we were warmly welcomed, we always feel accepted by our environment. However, if the opposite was the case, we tend to assume that "I am not wanted at all".

Knowing and analysing the exact circumstances of birth are very helpful for understanding the psychology of ego problems. That is why clients should be asked this in every consultation. You will notice that everyone has their story, which is why we cannot establish universally valid rules. But astrology allows us to make a graphic representation of the planets that the Age Point (17) was running through or was in opposition to when we were born. It is clear that the effect of Saturn at the AC is different to that of the Sun, for example.

It is commonly known that in the age progression life begins at the AC. The birth "thrust" of the cardinal cross pushes the baby out of the womb. Planets before or exactly on the AC, as well as those just before or after the DC, reflect the conditions of the birth. Planets between the 12th house low point and the AC indicate the conditions before birth, or prenatal influences. Below we describe the effect of each of the ten planets when positioned on the AC or DC and activated by the Age Point (AP) during the birth process.

Sun at the AC

The Sun at the AC or DC (or just before or after) has a strong influence on the formation of the ego. Birth was largely uncomplicated for the baby. The Sun made it accepted, the environment was proud and joyful at the baby's arrival. If we are cheered on our arrival, acceptance is guaranteed. The Sun ego therefore 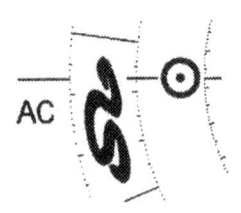 experiences approval of its identity right from the start, especially from the father. He was usually present at the birth and his joy validated the newborn baby as an independent being and affirmed its identity.

Such a person knows who he is and where others are. His ego is autonomous from the start and has a precocious charisma that delights those around him. He is sure of his own power and strength and wants to take control of his own life. Depending on the sign, he feels called upon to influence others and to attract their attention. He radiates energy and warmth, has a positive and energetic attitude to life and is determined to make something of himself.

The shadow side of this influence is egocentricity. He believes in himself so strongly that he does not give anyone else a chance. Depending on sign, ambition and competitiveness predominate. He has a great deal of self-esteem, often over-estimates himself and gets involved in rivalries with other people. If his place in the Sun is challenged, he becomes a dangerous enemy. He wants to be respected and admired for what he has achieved. Anyone who does not respect his competence and rights is spurned. Other people only have a place in his life if they are good for his own self-image.

Moon at the AC

If the Moon lies at the AC or DC (or just before or after), the ego is emotionally open so that environmental influences can act without a filter on the feeling self. It soaks up everything, good and bad, like a sponge. Every thought and feeling coming from the mother or the environment are passed on to the baby.

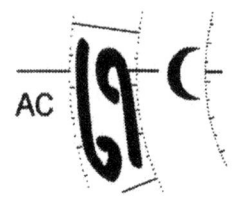

Such openness characterises this personality throughout life. They are sensitive, receptive and have a childlike openness that is attractive to others. Depending on sign, they find it hard to say no, they adapt and are malleable and influenced by circumstances. Many are dependent on the surrounding environment, react over-sensitively to every change in mood, and take in everything and relate it to themselves, even if it has nothing to do with them.

As already described in chapter 6, the Moon ego is naturally subjective and ruled by the moon's phases; it is a reflector, and is unstable and inconstant. That is why such people can sometimes be open and trusting, then suddenly become gripped by fear, and become closed and unapproachable. Some even display regressive, childish and insecure behaviour, especially when feeling stressed. Such people are basically dependent on the benevolence of their environment, on approval and praise, and have trouble finding their own identity. These people's I is focussed on the You.

It is not easy either for them to set boundaries *vis à vis* other people. Many must learn to adapt their openness or naivety to reality. Again and again they find that they are so receptive to the needs of other people that they cannot assert their own. Some become dependent on another person and become the pawn of those stronger than themselves, doing what they are told. They suffer emotionally from any kind of rejection or withdrawal of love and carefully avoid doing the same to other people.

Saturn at the AC

At the AC (or just before or after), Saturn as the limiting principle has a clearly restricting effect on development of the ego, burdening it with feelings of inferiority, guilt and atonement, and often with a terrible fear of life. The same is true if Saturn is close to the DC. If the Age Point passes right after the birth in a primary aspect (conjunction or opposition) to Saturn, there were nearly always complications in the birth that made the start of life difficult. With Saturn, the burdens are usually connected to the mother. It is very revealing to find out what really happened in each individual case.

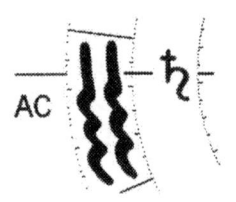

Here we would like to give you some examples from our counselling work. One mother often had trouble making ends meet; she was alone and received no support from her family. Sometimes she was very ill and near death. Other mothers suffered and transferred the pain to their children. People with this type of birth influence feel a lifetime of guilt towards their mother; they think that they are responsible for her problems.

By reliving the birth phase, these people experience a tightness that they must wriggle through, as though the cervix were still closed. During their lives, they find themselves in situations in which they find "no way out". In astrology, we talk about a "refusal to be born". The ego does not want to be born; it expects difficulties from the outset and protects itself against them. Often it is precisely this refusal that causes the problems. However, the ego is strengthened by having to overcome these difficult conditions during its life, leading to the creation of a "strong, tough ego" that can cope with difficult circumstances. Although Saturn's effect makes these people appear unapproachable and ruthless, their character possesses a certain strength and tenacity that evokes admiration from others. They are also capable of achieving anything they want later in life.

Mercury at the AC

If this planet of intellectual expression lies at the AC or DC, the person is closely associated with language. He is able to attract attention to himself using the spoken word, is brilliant at telling stories and knows how to captivate listeners. Depending on the sign in which Mercury lies, and also on the aspects it forms, it can assert itself with words and intellectual knowledge. Such a person talks a lot, either about himself or about everything that happened to him in his life. Everything revolves around him; he relates all that he has learnt, read or experienced to himself.

As Mercury is a thinking planet that likes to excel at deduction, the ego is revealed in all its glory. It can talk about itself, tell other people what it thinks, how it feels and what it wants. In a well-balanced person good social skills are indicated; with an excessively narcissistic person others are drowned in a deluge of words.

The birth was a varied experience. At times there were tears and those present either talked a lot or the baby announced its arrival by crying heartily. Eager discussions about all kinds of trivia, not just about the birth, can also incite the ego with Mercury to talk about itself, in order to attract other people's attention. These people often go for effect in their approach to others. When Mercury lies at the DC and the primary aspect was an opposition, some people also experience the opposite: the more they talk about themselves, the more they are ignored because they get on other people's nerves.

Venus at the AC

When Venus, symbol of the feminine, beauty and harmony, is at the AC, the ego is sensitised in advance to the fine things in life. Usually these people are physically attractive and fascinate others with their charm and good manners. They attract good things and are cherished and loved by their fellow men. They are thought to be incapable of doing anything bad; they radiate goodness and warmth and inspire trust and sympathy. The birth was a harmonious event. Their parents really wanted them and everything was prepared to give them a good life. Great efforts were made to keep negative or disturbing influences away from the child. Such harmonious conditioning of the ego naturally also spills out onto the environment. The ego is characterised by popularity and expectations of goodness throughout life.

But the conditioning that makes the ego so charming also has a shadow side. It is the exact opposite of Mars. Although beauty and charm make a good impression, this Venus position does not enable the ego to assert itself. It shrinks from situations in which it has to push itself forward, face conflict or be consistent in the pursuit of its own objectives. If it is in a cardinal sign, there can be some attempts at self-assertion, but they quickly disappear. The energy is directed to activities other than self-assertion. It wants to spread harmony and beauty and refuses to see the negative side of things, so that situations are not seen as they really are. Anything adverse or unpleasant is elegantly pushed to one side. This keeps the ego wrapped in cotton wool and prevents further attempts at assertion.

Both women and men with Venus at the AC (or just before or after) work hard to attain personal well-being. There is often a narcissistic attitude, they massage their own ego, overestimate themselves and their abilities and can become a burden on others. Some people can even find it hard to cope with life. They have been protected and spoilt for too long and have not had the opportunity to develop their own strengths. Later they have to learn how to cope with life even with this Venus position and to balance out their dependency on the You.

Mars at the AC

This masculine, powerful planet at the AC or DC has a particular influence on the ego, giving it a pronounced tendency to fight and defend. It puts all efforts into self-assertion and gaining approval. This Mars is constantly on the go, defending itself, showing off or trying to outdo other people. Before the AC, this is a typical stress planet, as noticed by Gauquelin (12) in his statistical research on elite athletes. Here Mars greatly stimulates the ego to assert itself, eliminate resistance, fight and triumph over others. Mars as the planet of drive and motor function provides a lot of energy, which the ego can use to assert itself. The person has to be the best, the first, the invincible in any field. Depending on the sign, this can be in the field of sport, at work or even in sexual matters.

There was often a forcible operation involved in the birth process. As Mars is also connected with cutting in astrology, the baby may have been delivered by Caesarian section or by forceps. We can imagine that such an operation endangered the baby's ego and that all its energies were focused on defending itself.

If a woman's horoscope has Mars in this position, she often has the feeling that her parents were expecting a boy. After the birth, when they saw it was a girl, they felt a sudden feeling of rejection for the little creature. The first influence on the ego was a feeling of general disappointment that it was not a boy. That affects the sexual self-image and is usually perceived as debasing and rejection. Sometimes this is also felt by people who have Mars or Venus at the IC or MC, i.e. at right-angles to the AC. This makes the girl wish she were a boy. A girl who is conditioned in this way tries hard by behaving like a boy, by over-achieving either in sport or at school to gain the father's approval. This primary influence makes it difficult for some of them to feel comfortable as a woman.

Jupiter at the AC

In classical astrology, Jupiter has always been seen as the bringer of luck. In astrological psychology, it is the sum of all sensory perceptions. Someone with an open mind reacts positively to everything that comes their way in life. Jupiter assimilates everything coming in and turns it to its own advantage. With Jupiter at the AC, all the senses are heightened and focused on the positive, so that the newborn baby assimilates a lot of good vibes. The fact is that people with Jupiter at the AC (or just before or after), and similarly at the DC, always had good birth conditions. They were wanted and warmly welcomed, which gave them a great sense of self-worth. There was rejoicing and happiness at the arrival of the baby. Perhaps bells even rang out, or celebratory gunshots were fired at the birth of the "Little Prince or Princess".

Such conditioning at the start of life is naturally very positive for the ego. Throughout life, they have the feeling: "Wherever I go, everyone is happy". This makes them believe that their whole life long they are welcomed with open arms. The ego feels flattered and approved of. Such a person gets used to the feedback, attention and respect that she is greeted with everywhere. This influence on the ego often makes other people trust her and expect her to help them. Some are discriminating and keep bad things at a distance, while others are credulous and let people use them. They only perceive what is pleasant and what makes them feel good; the negative is assiduously ignored. Sometimes this focus on the ego can also be interpreted as being spoilt, and can actually weaken the ego in difficult situations. People with Jupiter at the AC often have trouble with self-discipline and tend to avoid the harsh realities of life.

If the ego is affected by difficult circumstances and situations, the person can react badly. She is unable to stand negative experiences or to defend herself against them and reacts over-sensitively to criticism or rejection. Some are at the mercy of external forces and become a victim of circumstance - firstly because they are too optimistic, credulous or naïve, and secondly because they are incapable of fighting back and are always prepared to compromise to retain their comfortable situation. They have not learnt to cope with harsh realities. Someone with Jupiter in this position has problems tolerating redundancy, injustice and attack. She just cannot imagine that such bad things could happen to her. No matter how bad things get though, she nearly always manages to save her skin and often gets help from unexpected sources.

Uranus at the AC

At the AC, Uranus frequently causes a quick or even an emergency birth. There will be sudden events, like births on the stairs, in a taxi, in an aeroplane or with unexpected guests. Each person has their own story and it is astonishing what tales people with Uranus at the AC or DC (before or after) have to tell. Uranus is the planet of creative intelligence and it always wants to experience new things. It looks for revolutionary and extraordinary solutions to problems, does not take existing structures seriously but tries to do away with them. At the AC, it indicates an interest in modern technology, research, discoveries and fringe science. As such, at the I-point it brings a great need for personal originality, independence and freedom, and in any case a tendency to eccentricity. Some are suddenly seized by a violent craving for something out of the ordinary.

Uranus at the AC causes a lot of moving around, upsets and various life changes. The breaking through and transcending of barriers is one expression of the ego which other people find surprising and sometimes shocking. They find unexpected solutions in difficult situations; if nobody else can see a way out, they have the idea that saves the day. The ego becomes an improver of the status quo. It has an insight into cosmic connections and can even become a reformer, like Mikhail Gorbachov, for example.

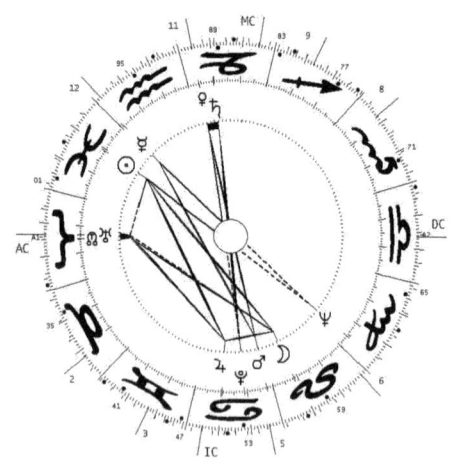

Mikhail Gorbachov
2.3.1931, 8:00 Privolnoja/Stavropol/USSR

Neptune at the AC

Neptune at the AC brings vast amounts of love and care to the birth. Some experience the opposite, indifference and coldness. They report that as newborn babies, they were too small, or delicate or sickly. They could not eat anything, or were premature and had to be put in an incubator. Such people long for spiritual protection throughout their lives. They dream of a world that does not exist here. This often causes them to lose their grip on reality and can lead to their reinterpreting life and giving it new meaning. These people are not interested in asserting themselves. Especially when young, their tendency to daydream and get distracted means that they miss out on many opportunities. Music is a good distraction and consolation when they are feeling down. Their creative fantasy knows no limits and in many cases leads to brilliant compositions or to illusionary representations. Neptune transforms some people's ego and makes it open to universal human kindness, which they express in a caring, healing or artistic profession.

Pluto at the AC

In the region before or after the AC or DC, Pluto activates all the elements of its archetype. Such people experienced their birth as the work of a higher power; they felt that they were helplessly at the mercy of a powerful force. That evokes very intense ego-forces and creates a strong willpower. People with Pluto near the AC protect themselves with all their might against intruders; they cannot tolerate any encroachments into their personal space and get rid of anything that looks threatening. Their defensive energy is increased when under attack. At such times it is advisable to leave them alone and not to excite them unnecessarily.

When there is excessive mental or physical stress or stimulation, they can cross boundaries that trigger fear of destruction of the ego. People born during bombing raids in the war or other life-threatening situations have Pluto near the AC. These people are always on the defensive; they want to survive at all costs. The ego core does not want to be disturbed.

In reality, as the planet of metamorphosis, Pluto only wants to change the persona, the false ego-image, the mask. Many people with Pluto at the AC or DC feel constantly exposed to these conversion forces and in the course of their lives go through several transformation crises of their life motivation. Some even alter their facial features, posture or body shape. (chameleon effect).

Further descriptions of the effect of the AP transiting planets in the natal horoscope can be found in *Life Clock*, pages 137-179 (17).

The Family Model

Sun: Father, Saturn: Mother, Moon: Child

We can broaden the theme of the three factors that shape the personality, Sun, Moon and Saturn, if we also use them as a model for the family. The connection becomes very clear when considering the three cross qualities. We already know them as the "three pillars of heaven", which gave rise to all of creation. They are the basic principles with which we in astrological psychology begin every reading, be it of the planets, the houses, the signs or the aspects. The cardinal cross provides an impulse and produces ideas; it corresponds to the Sun and therefore the father principle. The fixed cross receives the ideas and gives them the structure they need; it corresponds to Saturn and therefore the mother principle. The mutable cross corresponds to the principle of the child; it produces constant movement and change by growth and development.

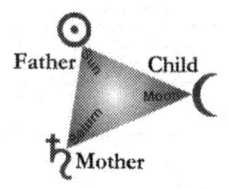

So in the cardinal and fixed crosses we see the paternal and maternal principles. The fixed cross not only provides the form, but also permanence, because it knows the laws of matter. There is an obvious connection with the term "matter": "mater" means "mother". The earth on which we live is our "great mother", she provides us with food, growth and security. To take this idea a stage further, we have classified the three planets Sun, Saturn and Moon according to cross quality and also with the three stages of ego awareness, to produce the following correspondences:

Father	Sun	Cardinal	**Self awareness**
Mother	Saturn	Fixed	**Reality awareness**
Child	Moon	Mutable	**Emotional awareness**

This family model enables us to get a clear idea of our own relationship with our parents in our horoscope. We know that a personality consists of three layers of being: physical, emotional and mental levels, or body, feelings and mind. As mentioned above, during the course of our development, these personality areas form an ego-centre. In the physical body it is Saturn that represents the physical self and is connected to the mother. In the emotional body it is the Moon that corresponds to the stage of childhood and reveals our emotional needs, and in the mental body it is the Sun that embodies the father in the horoscope, and which is instrumental in the later formation of self-awareness. From the positions of these three planets in the chart, we can learn about the functions of the ego as well as people's relationship with their parents. To use the family model in the chart, we first need to establish the positions of these planets and find out whether the parents were suitable role models for ego development or not.

The family model and the developmental tendencies can best be understood from the house positions. Their position shows a role assignment that determines behaviour (= house system). As described in chapter 5, these three family planets either lie in areas of the horoscope that correspond to them, or they do not. As a reminder, these are: Saturn is strong in the maternal, bottom part of the chart, the Sun in the paternal top area, and the Moon on the contact level.

The Parents as Archetypal Role Models

Saturn: Mother

The position of Saturn shows the role and influence of the mother, who is responsible for protecting the child in the first years of life. She sets boundaries in order to protect the child and makes it aware of life's dangers. How often does a mother say: "You shouldn't do that", "Stop it or you will fall" or "You will get dirty" etc. This constant "boundary setting" is something she shares with the quality of Saturn. From the position of Saturn in the horoscope, we can see which restraints, obstacles, checks, dangers and stresses the ego has to deal with and overcome. If Saturn is at the top of the chart, the mother was in charge.

Sun: Father

The Sun represents the father as a key figure for self-awareness. Development initially requires a role model of the father or a person who the child can respect or admire and trust. From the position of Sun in the horoscope we can see what kind of role model the father was. If Sun is in a strong position, then the child should be led and taught by the father. If Sun lies at the top of the chart, the father was usually dynamic, had a positive attitude towards life and could guarantee survival, and the child could follow in his footsteps. The child's ethical and intellectual powers can develop, be ingrained and become habits, until at the end of this learning phase he has developed the ability to think for himself and become a unique individual.

Moon: Child

The Moon ego plays a prominent part in the development of the feeling nature; the self is mainly experienced as a reflection of the inner and outer worlds. The reflective principle of the Moon and the feelings also awakens the imitative instinct, which is very pronounced in the first years of life, as is curiosity. The abilities to learn and socialise that develop later on are also dependent on them. From Moon's position in the horoscope, we can see how the child lived and felt, and how harmonious or problematic development of the personality was. If Moon lies in the top part of the chart, the parents projected their own wishes and goals onto the child.

Aspects between the Family Planets

Any aspects between the family planets are also important. They reveal various basic family structures and the general family situation. Among other things, the aspect connections show how the family members communicated with each other and what the bonds between them were like. We describe them systematically below.

Aspects between all three Family Planets

If Saturn, Sun and Moon are all interconnected by aspects, the family is usually close-knit and kept together by destiny or by similar interests. This interaction of forces does not necessarily indicate a "good" family, but there are plenty of families that are held together by the need to survive, by financial or internal problems, or because the members depend on each other. The family gives the outward impression of being a closed unit, in which the role of each member is predefined and predetermined.

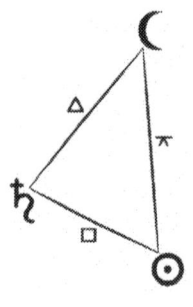

The comparison with the adult who has all three ego planets connected is interesting. Such a person has a closed personality, in which body, feelings and mind are all coordinated. Of course, it depends on which aspect figure and which aspect colours are involved. You can read more about this in *Aspect Pattern Astrology* (21) and in *Astrological Psychosynthesis*, part 2 "Personality and Integration" (19).

Conjunction of two Family Planets

If only two of the three family planets are connected, one of them feels excluded.

The **conjunction of Sun and Moon** shows a close relationship between father and child and they are very dependent on each other. The father is a role model for the child, whose self-awareness needs his approval. Sun and Moon understand and support each other, but Saturn, the mother, is not included. There is often a polarisation 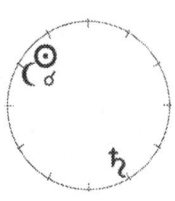 of relationships or people take sides within the family. If Saturn is detached [not connected (directly or indirectly) by aspects], this means that the child was usually unable to consciously make real contact with the mother. They live in different worlds, and the mother is either absent or otherwise somehow unreachable.

A **Saturn/Moon conjunction** indicates a strong maternal bond. This is often a symbiotic relationship that makes mother and child interdependent. Each knows what the other is feeling from a distance; if things are going badly for them, they suffer too. Separation from the mother is often delayed, and sometimes never happens at 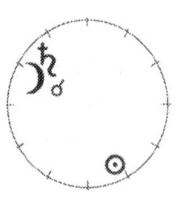 all. If the Sun is detached, the father's influence is negligible; he leaves the upbringing to the mother. Sun is rarely actually unaspected; if it is part of a disconnected aspect figure, some paternal influence can be exercised through the content of this figure.

The **Sun/Saturn conjunction** causes the attitude of the parents towards the child to be harmonious. The child finds it hard to distinguish between their influences. The parents stick together and do not let their identical opinions be swayed by doubt. This is why the parents often have a strong influence over the child. If the Moon is 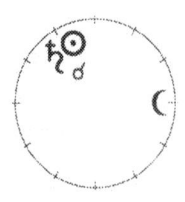 also alone [not connected (directly or indirectly) by aspects], the child is misunderstood. As the contact planet, Moon reacts sensitively to this solitary position; it suffers from isolation, so one can assume the childhood was unhappy. If, in addition, it has no aspects at all with any planets, we talk about an "Orphan Moon".

Red Aspects - Square, Opposition

If there are red aspects between the parental planets **Sun and Saturn**, the child experiences the parents as very different from each other. With an opposition, they often have differing opinions and argue about things that do not matter. With a square, there is always cause for conflict, and

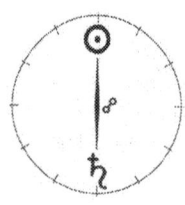

the parents often fight about making ends meet, about their position and spheres of competence. Sometimes they are even separated or divorced. Red energy aspects don't always indicate conflict though; they can also reveal a strong, passionate relationship, which can lead to joint creativity.

In the **Saturn/Moon** square or opposition, the child's Moon ego usually reacts contradictorily. On the one hand, there is a certain idea of how the mother should behave; on the other hand, her efforts are resisted. Many are let down by their mother, she does not put herself out for the child,

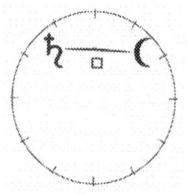

which gives him pessimistic tendencies. Some react over-sensitively to contempt, exposure and ridicule. Thomas Ring (11) characterises the square as follows: "One sacrifices oneself so that one can complain about it afterwards".

If **Sun and Moon** are connected by square or opposition, the relationship with the father is very intense but also conflictive. The child is very firmly under the father's influence and is constantly trying to please him. They certainly learn how to produce the desired performance, but do not enjoy it. All

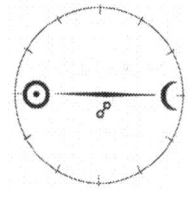

excessive pressure to achieve is perceived by the Moon as coercion. The self-awareness must be constantly checking what reduces inner security and weakens self-esteem.

Blue Aspects - Sextile, Trine

The blue substance aspects between the family planets promote harmonious coexistence. They indicate a calm and peaceful relationship, and sometimes also an idealistic philosophy that stifles and allows for little development. A trine or sextile between Saturn and Moon means a strong maternal

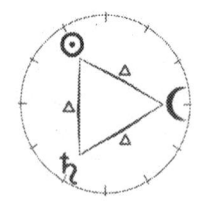

bond, which provides protection and security, but also possibly overprotection. The mother often finds it hard to let the child go and

vice versa. The same bond exists with the father if Sun and Moon are connected by a blue aspect.

Green Aspects - Semi-sextile, Quincunx

Green thinking aspects between the parental planets indicate both a learning process, and a rather loose bond between them. One of the parents was often not present, which is why there is a permanent feeling of unrequited longing for security and protection. This causes insecurity and doubt when the other is not immediately accessible.

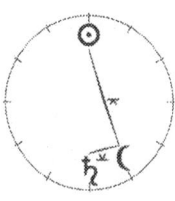

Some people with a quincunx between Moon and Saturn or Sun often have a life-long yearning for their father or mother, because they did not have real parents. A few people look for surrogate parents or a guru and so idealise the father or mother image to compensate for the pain of being abandoned.

Phases of Ego Development
According to the Family Model

To evaluate the family model in counselling using astrological psychology, one should also know something about the phases of ego development. This involves both counselling the parents and understanding the children, as well as the work in itself. The human ego develops in many different stages and forms. But there are some basic phases to be aware of, which are also clearly seen in psychological research. These phases are not clearly separated from each other, but run into each other and occur several times during a lifetime according to an individual rhythm that depends on the progression of the Age Point and its aspects to the three main planets.

1st Stage: Saturn - Body - Mother

In astrology, we can equate the stage of physical self-awareness with Saturn. Here, the infant's ego is still at one with the mother's. It is even said that the first two years of life are a continuation of the embryonic state. The infant's self is merged with that of the mother; it lives through and with the mother as a unit, and can barely distinguish itself from her In this symbiotic state there are no mental boundaries, as there are in the adult personality, so the individual psyche is not yet clearly discernible. This interconnectedness is only slowly dissolved during the development of the individual's self-awareness.

2nd Stage: Moon - Feelings - Child

This mental or emotional stage of ego development corresponds to the Moon. It is the most important for the child as the Moon represents the infant's ego. As mentioned above, it shows how we felt as a child and how we reacted to our environment. In the "anonymous phase of symbiosis" (c.f. Erich Neumann: *The Child* (33)), the awareness of unity is responsible for a healthy sense of existence and basic trust in the child. If circumstances separate the child from the mother too soon, it suffers throughout life from a lack of basic trust.

In this second phase, an ego relationship with the mother and the surrounding environment slowly develops. The experiences of these first contacts mark us deep within our still unformed and wide-open infant's psyche. If the first contacts were loving, gentle, tender and understanding, the child's own later social and romantic contacts with the You can develop correctly. But if the first contact was rough, abusive, loud and inconsiderate, this behaviour is repeated in later relationships. This emotional phase is therefore also important for personal social and human development, for learning the correct social behaviour. A lot can be learnt from the Moon position in the horoscope in this respect.

3rd Stage: Sun - Self-Awareness - Father

This brings us to the next stage in the development of the ego, which can be equated with self-awareness and therefore with the Sun. In this phase, we can talk about the child's intellectual self, which controls the world of the emotions and its own body, so that thoughts can be transferred directly into physical actions. The Sun as the autonomous principle always indicates the father in the horoscope, and the vital self-awareness. Our habits, moral attitude and temperament – in short our character or mentality – are formed by and are visible from the position of the Sun in the chart. Its sign, house position and aspects tell us how the person thinks and what his mindset is like.

The functions of intelligence always develop by learning, experience and memory. Intellectual capacity starts with the ability to assimilate, which increases from simple perception via concentrated observation to profound understanding. Memory enables the child to retain what has been perceived and to compare it with newer perceptions. Through practical experiences, he learns to regulate the tasks of daily life and to manage what he is asked to do gradually and logically instead of chaotically.

4th Stage: Formation of the Personality:
The Urge to Experience – Letting Go – Becoming Independent

Finally comes a great hunger for personal experience, in which the young adult wants to experience things for himself. This stormy and stressful period, which usually begins when the Age Point runs through (17) the fourth house and reaches its peak in the fifth house, i.e. between the ages of 18 and 27, is also the time for leaving the parental home.

This process of liberation or evolution of the self corresponds to the urge to experience things for oneself and for self-actualisation that takes the young person by storm and usually causes an internal and external crisis. This force comes directly from the innermost self and should under no circumstances be repressed or prevented by his educators, but should be channelled in the right way with understanding, constructive sympathy and broad-minded honesty. This is a kind of "creative self-actualisation", a primal human urge coming directly from the person's core. It is initially chaotic but contains more potential than he will ever experience again. This powerful concentration of living creative forces takes hold of people during adolescence. Anything can come of it, both the best and the worst, depending on how this force is managed.

5th Stage: The Evolutionary Urge of the Innermost Self

All human creativity, from the simplest manual action to the most complicated intellectual achievement and the finest work of art, come from the same inner source. The parents should treat this evolutionary urge of the innermost self with great care and intelligent responsibility, so that the adolescent can fully develop his/her individuality. This is the primary objective of education, in which the psychological interpretation of the horoscope can also be helpful. By using astrology in this way, we can make a contribution to a new phase of human history.

Exposed Planetary Positions

The Psychodynamics of Fear in the Horoscope
Article by Wolfhard König, Dipl.Psych., Dipl.Math., Psychoanalyst

What is Fear?

Fear is a very complex psychological phenomenon. Basically, realistic fear is an important warning and protective mechanism. Only the lapse into neurotic (excessive) fear is a problem. There is always a complex combination of motives, wishes, expectations and traumatic experiences involved.

So I will not give a simple astrological recipe for how problems of fear are represented in the horoscope. We must discredit both the mediaeval tendency to give simplistic solutions and the modern view, which can still be found in some textbooks, whereby only one planet, Saturn, is responsible for fear.

Planetary Configurations and the Development of Fear

Let us imagine the case of a man aged 38 who suffers from social phobia (we will discuss his horoscope later). He lives day in, day out secluded in his apartment, and only has contact with his immediate family (brother and parents) and his therapist. He started the first session with his therapist with the words: "I am a male virgin", meaning that he had never been intimate with a female. How much fear of contact, of intimacy and of being hurt in a close relationship must he feel to let this fear isolate him so much and for so long, and dominate his social life so completely?

We have ten planets in our horoscope: they represent the ten archetypal human motivations, or primal needs. Using energy as a metaphor, the ten planets represent ten sources of energy that drive us in our lives. For so much anxiety, or such strong energy, to be produced as in the above example, the energies of several planets must be working together.

Pronounced fears, phobias or anxiety neuroses are depicted in planetary configurations, groups of planets forming aspects with each other – in other words, aspect figures, which form a sort of motivation network. Such a configuration, with three or four (out of ten) planets linked, produces a correspondingly large amount of energy. These energies (or motivations) can "split off", and become no longer consciously controllable by, or even accessible to, the consciousness. When the unconscious can no longer meaningfully (constructively) use them in life, symptoms appear. This means not only fear disorders, but all kinds of symptoms, including psychosomatic disorders, depressions, addictions, etc.

Why such splits occur and which symptoms they tend to cause is the vital issue for psychology. The issue for astrology now is: Which configurations of planets in the horoscope show the tendency for fears, and what kind of fears do they show? A problem arises here that is typical for the field of fear: there is no other symptom that is so changeable and diverse. People can have fears about anything: about intimacy, separation, heights or all kinds of animals, anything unknown, even about the (unknown) future, and finally there is also a fear of fear itself.

In astrological terms this means that, in principle, every configuration of planets can give rise to the development of fears under certain conditions. So all ten primal motivations or primal needs can be connected to fears. And conversely, there is no one single planet or combination of planets that is necessarily involved in the development of fears!

Our next question is: Under which conditions can a configuration of planets indicate the development of fears? This happens when planets have a so-called "exposed position". These are variations of particular strong or weak positions in signs, houses and aspects, as already defined in Chapter 4. Such positions, surprisingly both weak and strong, can always be found in the chart of someone who experiences symptoms of fear. The reverse is also possible, i.e. such exposed positions can be beneficial for the psyche and can be used constructively in life so that no symptoms develop.

The chart itself can only show the potential, the possibility of a challenge to the personal powers that can lead to symptoms of fear. There are two approaches to interpretation when dealing with the issue of fear.

1. If a person suffers from fear, we can ask which exposed position in the chart has "split off" and can therefore not be controlled. This can then be discussed in counselling or therapy.
2. If we have a chart but no other knowledge of the person concerned, we can only make an analysis of the potential for fear, or explore the question of which positions are so exposed that they could lead to fear symptoms if they cannot be controlled.

Let us now look at three different astrological cases: the normal, weak and strong positions.

1st Case – The Normal Position

Take as an example a Sun at 8° Virgo at the Balance Point of the 2nd house with two blue aspects (to Moon and Saturn) and one red aspect (square to Jupiter). The Sun is well positioned in the sign and in the house and is well aspected. There will be few challenges or problems (2nd house BP), and the problems that concern the house theme, e.g. possessions, should be easily dealt with using the available abilities (good position in the sign, helpful aspects to Jupiter and Saturn). This kind of "normal position" usually neither causes particular flights of fancy or idealistic objectives nor particular failures or disappointments, so it can hardly be associated with the development of symptoms.

2nd Case – The Weak Position

Imagine the horoscope of a man with the Sun at 2° Pisces at the Low Point of the 6th house in a learning triangle with quincunx Mars and square Jupiter. When performance requirements come from the 6th house, possibly at school, but particularly later on in professional life, this person with the Pisces Sun will always find that he first withdraws and meditates and prefers only to undertake social duties that correspond to his sensitivity. The Low Point also calls for reflection and a clarification of personal motives, and the development of at best spiritual, but at least ethical, motives for the development of one's own Sun.

This is why he will often find that he needs "too long" to formulate his ideas, and has to watch others seize opportunities more quickly and resolutely than he does. This can lead to a feeling of weakness and inferiority, and eventually a fear of any kind of test, performance and professional challenge. This fear can sometimes lead to a test (or examination) phobia or an interruption of work. Only in the second half of life can the person concerned start to experience the sensitivity of the Pisces Sun and the ability to reflect at the Low Point as positive attributes and deliberately look for a career suited to them (which can be a difficult and lengthy process).

In general we can say that the fear of failure is usually associated with weak positions. There is actually a wide variety of possible weak positions, depending on whether a planet is weakly placed in a sign (at the beginning or the end), in a house (around the Low Point), or is unaspected, or which combination is present (e.g. normal in the sign, weak in the house, etc.). The nature of the fear depends very clearly on the planet concerned and on the house in which it lies. In the above example, the Sun had developed other performance anxieties in the 8th or 1st house. And Venus or Neptune instead of the Sun would have had a different effect, for the Sun is naturally sensitive to failure. But this is not the place to go into all these variations.

3rd Case – The Strong Position

You would probably not imagine that strong chart positions could also (or particularly) give rise to great fears; you might expect that they should be easy to put to good use in life. Bruno Huber once remarked: "The strong point can also be the weak point, and vice versa." There are two possibilities for this, in my opinion. By strong positions we mean: when there are groups of planets (large conjunctions, stellium); when planets lie right on an axis, particularly one of the main axes; when planets are strong in the sign (around 12°); when planets are linked through a number of aspects. Of course, not all these criteria need to be met.

Imagine a chart with a Sun-Mars-Pluto conjunction in Leo at the MC. This is undoubtedly a very strong configuration. In the constructive case, the person will set their goals high (Pluto), fight for a spiritual goal (Pluto-Mars) and in the process solve problems with leadership skills (Leo Sun at the MC). One would concede that this is the best imaginable case, which is unfortunately rather rare or only possible after lengthy maturing processes. In the worst case, it can lead to bitter rivalry and power struggles. The person must absolutely be the number one and has a tendency to delusions of grandeur. They want to be the saviour of the human race or the most generous politician of all times. This can lead to two problems:

Problem Case 1

There is a fear of losing control and of the aggressive forces breaking through. Particularly during puberty one gets an idea of what kind of energy, like a "bomb", one has inside. This can generate an acute anxiety-controlled counter-reaction, leading to forced ideas of peaceableness and great fears of aggression. Anna Freud (1936) discovered this "reversal into the opposite" as a defense mechanism and called it "fear of the strength of one's own drive", from the field of drive psychology.

Problem Case 2

Such a strong configuration can lead to delusions of grandeur and unachievable demands for perfection, particularly if planets like Pluto or Saturn are involved. This can give rise to a strong fear of falling short of one's own inner ideals. Either I do everything perfectly or

I am a failure. This can lead to performance blocks and to the above forces never being turned into real, good achievements.

Strong positions are therefore often associated with the fear of losing control or fear of breakthrough. And likewise with the fear of failing – not real demands but unachievable demands for perfection. Even with strong positions there are again so many variations depending on which planets are involved, at which house cusp and in which sign they are situated and how strong the aspects are. We cannot go into this in any more detail here, but would like to explore three special cases, which occur quite frequently in practice.

1. Unaspected Planets

If planets are unaspected and in a weak house position they usually have trouble coping with life and are supplanted by other planets (e.g. Sun by Jupiter, etc.) But if they are important planets, (like the ego planets) lying on a house cusp, there is stimulation from the environment to become active and achieve things. However, it is hard for the will and consciousness to reach a planet without aspects, leading to a feeling of inadequacy. This can create the impression that one is not in control of the situation and does not understand what one has to do. First aid and support coming from the environment bring relief. The planet concerned can then develop a little (e.g. in the case of Saturn, taking care of security). Otherwise, the fear of failure can easily return.

2. Pulling position

Here the problem is that the "inner position" of a planet is weak, but its "outer position" is very strong. By inner position we mean the position in the sign and the type of aspect. The planet is weak in the sign and receives little stimulation, having few or only weak aspects. Its outer position is strong as it lies on a house cusp. This is the root of the problem: the planet 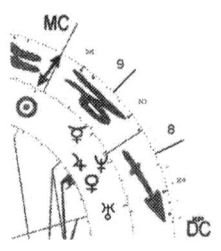 is naturally not very confident and receives little stimulation from the sign, but the house position indicates great expectations and demands from the environment. The individual tends to perceive this as a strong pull ("The environment keeps on pulling me, wants to take something from me, I am out of my depth").

The example shown is part of the chart of a young musician,

with the Sun just after the MC, at 2° Aquarius and with only a weak quincunx. This is a typical pulling position. As the father of this young man was a very famous musician, the son received premature praise and received concert bookings much too soon, without really having time to grow into this role. The result is a pronounced performance anxiety. His stage fright is sometimes so strong that he has to be gently forced on stage by his friends. He then goes on to perform well, but afterwards is completely exhausted.

3. Congestion Position

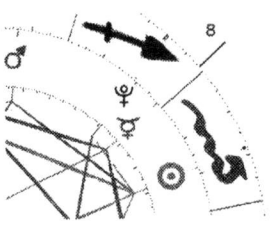

Here we have a very strong inner position of a planet, but a weak outer one. A typical example of this would be the Sun with three or four strong aspects at 12° Scorpio, but at the same time at the Low Point of the 7th house in an intercepted sign. While the Sun's assertiveness and ambition are strongly marked in the consciousness and will and Scorpio has "fighting energy", the environment stops all his efforts from being seen, respected and acknowledged.

Low Point positions and intercepted signs show that the person's abilities and wishes are not acknowledged or supported by their environment. Bruno Huber says about such a position: "It is like having a Porsche in the garage and not being able to find the key." The person concerned develops a strong fear of social situations. There is an inner mixture of two fears: "I will show the world, by force if necessary" (breakthrough anxiety) and "I will never be able to do it, I am a loser" (fear of failure). Both fears focus on encounter situations in the 7th house. In both these cases, the problems can only be dealt with and solutions found through long-term and intensive work on the development of awareness (possibly with the aid of therapy).

This may have clarified how diverse what I have described as an "exposed position" can be, depending on the planets involved (out of ten), the signs involved (out of twelve), the house concerned (out of twelve), the aspects present and depending on the combination of inner or outer strong and weak positions. The generation of fears resulting from overstressing the exposed position can be just as individual. For this reason, this article can only be a stimulus to think more about the subject and gather your own experiences.

Example Horoscope

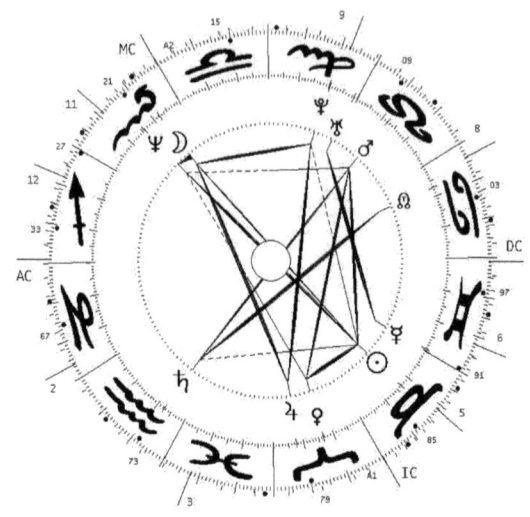

Client Natal Chart
7.5.1962, 23.00, Simbach am Inn/Germany

To conclude, let us take another look at the chart mentioned at the beginning of this article. As already indicated, Mr X suffers from pronounced social and relationship fears that have made him avoid any close contact, particularly intimate relationships, during the last 30 years. We could now try to understand from his biography, and from a deep psychological point of view, which experiences and traumata have affected him so deeply. We cannot explore this any further here. Instead, we try to gain a better understanding of his fears from his chart. Is there an exposed position that would explain these strong social phobias?

The conjunction of Moon and Neptune stands out immediately. Both planets lie well inside Scorpio in the 10th house, but around the Low Point. Then there is the opposition to Sun, which causes the mind to be influenced by romantic desires and fantasies. Furthermore, both are situated at the highest point in the chart and act something like a tension ruler. Seen in this way, this is a strong position in this chart.

The conjunction of Moon and Neptune naturally causes an excessive longing for love, an almost unrealisable system of ideals, a certain insatiability relating to devotion, closeness and understanding. This leads to an extreme fear of disappointment, that these vital needs will be rejected and could remain unfulfilled. In his life, the client has experienced how his father and brother had suffered in similar circumstances. The brother was suicidal after separating from his wife, and found it difficult to recover. The client is afraid of the same thing happening to him. His favourite saying is a classic quote: "He who has never been hurt by love should congratulate himself." The client has managed this as he has never fallen in love and has never suffered. But the price is high and feeling unloved is also a kind of suffering.

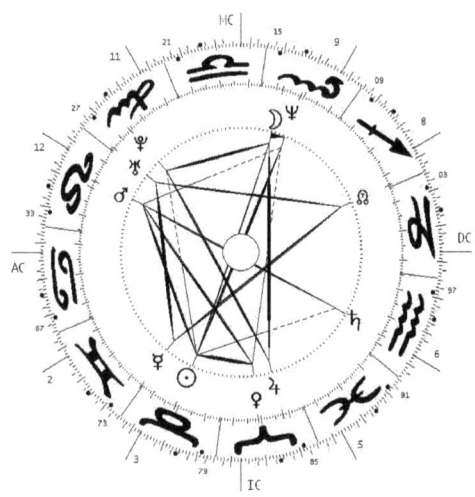

Client Moon Node Chart
7.5.1963, 23.00, Simbach am Inn/Germany

The depth of this problem is revealed when we take a look at the Moon Node chart: here too the Moon-Neptune conjunction is situated at the highest point, but this time in the 9th house. So this is an overall, karmic problem concerning the existential issue of how much love, closeness and understanding is actually possible between people and how we can avoid being deeply hurt by the experience.

As the client has still not found a satisfactory answer to this question, the defensive mechanism of relationship anxiety protects him from the suffering he fears so much. The conflict can be understood on a deeper level if we consider the natal positions of Pluto in the 9th house, the Sun-Mars square and Venus in intercepted Aries in the 3rd house.

An even deeper and more holistic perspective on the problem can be obtained from looking at the three charts together (next page). You will see the foundations and inner psychodynamics in the natal chart, the influence of the environment and possibilities for development in the house chart and the potential from many lives in the Moon Node chart. However, the overall reading requires a good knowledge of this method, which is described in *Moon Node Astrology* (18).

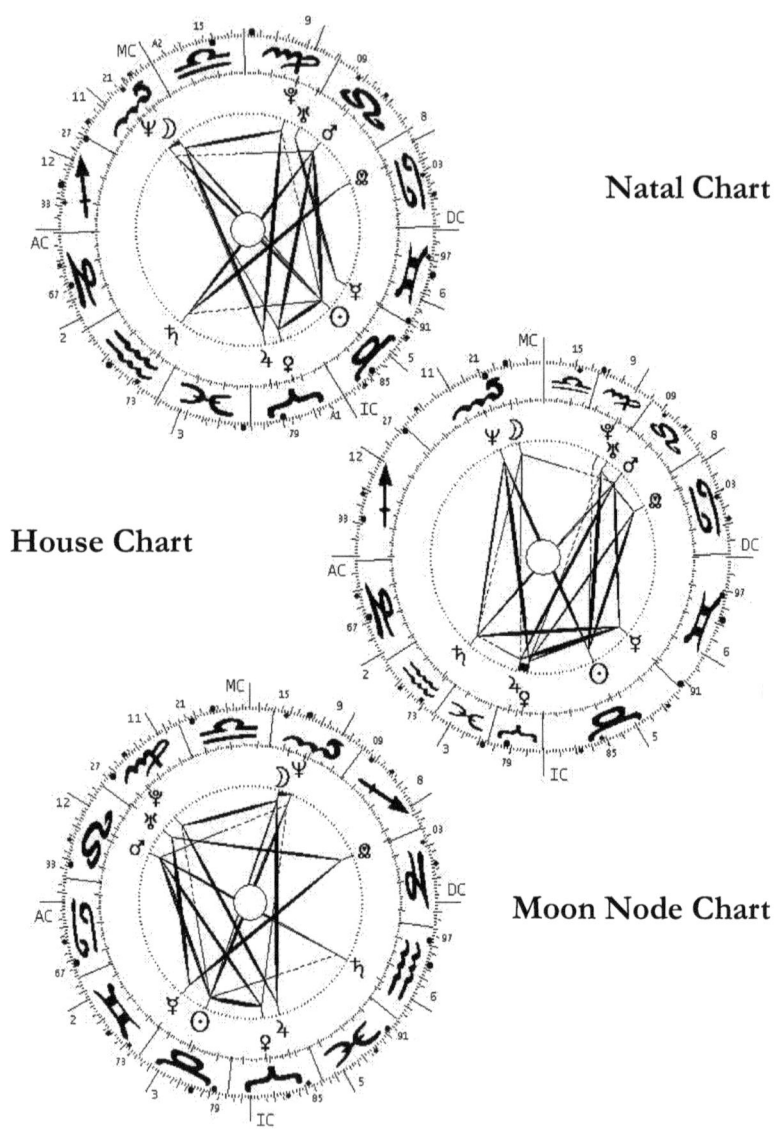

The Three Charts
Client 7.5.1963, 23:00, Simbach am Inn/ Germany

Data for Example Horoscopes (Koch House System)

Bach, Johann Sebastian	31.3.1685 GC (JC:21.3.85) 11.30 Eisenach/Germany	211
Client	7.5.1963, 23.00 Simbach am Inn/Germany	308,9, 310
Cousteau, Jacques	11.6.1910, 13.15 St. Andre-de-Cubzac/France	206
Einstein, Albert	14.3.1879 11.30 Ulm/Germany	130
Example Horoscope	10.5.1942, 11.30 Zürich/Switzerland	7
Gandhi, Mahatma	2.10.1869, 07.45 Probanda, India	227
Gorbachov, Mikhail	2.3.1931, 8.00 Privolnoja/Stavropol/USSR	292
Hartmann, Dr. Franz	22.11.1838, 14.30 Donauwörth/Germany	199
Huber, Bruno	29.11.1930, 12.55 Zürich/Switzerland	223
Huber, Louise	10.5.1924, 03.15 Bamberg/Germany	197
Jung, Carl Gustav	26.7.1875, 19.20 Kesswil/Switzerland	193
Kästner, Erich	23.2.1899, 03.30 Dresden/Germany	177
May, Karl	25.2.1842, 22.00 LT Hohenstein-Ernstthal/Germany	184
Psychiatric Nurse	13.5.1945, 21.30 St. Gallen/Switzerland	136
Savalas, Telly	20.1.1924, 05.00 EST Garden City/New York/USA	174
Tinguely, Jean	22.5.1925, 05.30, Fribourg/Switzerland	191
Tolstoy, Leo	28.8.1828 JC = 9.9.1828 GC/23.00 Jasnaja Poljana (Tula) USSR	181
Voltaire, Francois	1.12.1694, 17.30 Paris/France	188
Wagner, Richard	22.5.1813, 04.00 Leipzig/Germany	170

Bibliography

English language references are given in normal text, where known; *original references to materials in German are in italics.*

(1) Huber Bruno: *Astro-Glossarium, Band I, API-Verlag, CH-8134 Adliswil, 1995*

(2) *API-Kursunterlagen farbig, API-Verlag, Adliswil.* [API study materials. Equivalent information is contained in English in the API(UK) course manuals and publications. See "Contacts" on page 314.]

(3) *API-Computer "CORTEX", Adliswil*

(4) API-Software: AstroCora, MegaStar, Regulus UK/ Spain/ Argentina. Also, Regulus Special Light Huber Edition produces natal charts only. *Also Astrosys Berlin, Astrovisa Munich, Galileo Erlangen.* [See "Contacts" on page 314 for how to obtain the English-language software.]

(5) Arroyo Stephen: "Astrology, Psychology and the Four Elements", CRCS Books

(6) Assagioli Roberto: "Psychosynthesis Principles and Methods"

(7) *"Astrolog", Zeitschrift fur Astrologische Psychologie, 1981-99 Verlag API, CH-8134 Adliswil.* [Magazine of API Switzerland.]

(8) Bailey Alice A.: "Esoteric Astrology" and "A Treatise on White Magic", Lucis Trust, London

(9) Brunton Paul: "The Wisdom of the Overself", Rider, 1943

(10) Durckheim Karlfried Graf: *"Vom doppelten Ursprung des Menschen", Herder-Verlag, Freiburg, 1973*

(11) Ring Thomas: *"Astrologische Menschenkunde", Kombinationslehre, Bauer-Verlag, Freiburg, 1994*

(12) Gauquelin Michel: "Cosmic Clocks", Paladin 1973

(13) Huber Bruno and Louise: "Astrology and the Spiritual Path", Weiser 1990. This book contains part of *"Transformationen, Astrologie als geistiger Weg", API-Verlag, Adliswil, 1996.*

(14) Huber Bruno: "Astrological Psychosynthesis", Weiser 1996 – Part 3 "Love and Relationships in the Horoscope." Also, a booklet on "Clicks" is published by API(UK).

(15) Huber Bruno und Louise: *"Horoskop-Berechnung und Zeichnung", Verlag API 1973, 4. Auflage 1982.* Hoscope calculation is also covered by a course offered by API(UK).

(16) Huber Bruno and Louise: "The Astrological Houses", Weiser 1978, 1998

(17) Huber Bruno and Louise: "Life Clock", Weiser 1982,1986,1994

(18) Huber Bruno and Louise: "Moon Node Astrology" Weiser 1995, HopeWell 2005

(19) Huber Bruno: "Astrological Psychosynthesis", Weiser 1996 – Part 2 "Personality and Integration"

(20) Huber Louise: "Reflections & Meditations on the Signs of the Zodiac", AFA 1984

(21) Huber Bruno, Louise and Michael "Aspect Pattern Astrology", HopeWell 2005

(22) Huber Michael A.: *"Dynamische Auszahlungen" API-Verlag 1997,2. Auflage 1984.* ["Dynamic Calculations" are covered in the API(UK) Diploma Course.]

(23) Huber Bruno: "Astrological Psychosynthesis", Weiser 1996 – Part 1 "Intelligence in the Horoscope".

(24) Jung C.G.: "Memories, Dreams, Reflections" Fontana 1967 etc

(25) Ptolemy Claudius: "Tetrabiblos", Kessinger 1997

(26) Weiss, Jean Claude: *Horoskopanalyse Bd. I, "Planeten in Zeichen Und Hausern" Edition Astrodata, Zürich 1984*

(27) Hamaker-Zondac, Karen M.: *"Deutung der Planeten", "Verlag Hier und Jetzt" Hamburg 1994*

(28) Rudhyar, Dane: "The Astrological Houses: The Spectrum of Individual Experience ", CRCS Publications 1986

(29) Sasportas, Howard: "The Twelve Houses", Thorsons 1985

(30) Greene, Liz: "Saturn: A New Look at an Old Devil", Weiser 1976

(31) Neumann, Erich: "The Origins and History of Consciousness", Random House 1954

(32) Neumann, Erich: "The Great Mother: An Analysis of the Archetype", Princeton University 1991

(33) Neumann, Erich: "The Child", Shambhala 1990

(34) Piaget, Jean: "The Psychology of Intelligence", Routledge 2001

(35) Szondi Leopold: *Schicksalanalyse, Verlag Hans Huber, 1969*

(36) "The American Ephemeris: 21st Century", ACS Publications 1997

Contacts and Resources

The Astrological Psychology Institute (UK)

A MODERN APPROACH to SELF-AWARENESS and PERSONAL GROWTH

Astrology has become recognised as a valuable tool for the development of self awareness and human potential. Bruno and Louise Huber researched and developed this approach over many years, combining selective astrology with Roberto Assagioli's psychosynthesis. Our courses are based on their results and inspiration.

PERSONAL GROWTH Most of our Diploma students not only learn astrology, chart interpretation and astrological counselling skills, but find that the course helps develop their own self understanding and personal and spiritual growth.

COURSES We offer Foundation Modules to those new to astrology or to the Huber Method. Our Modular Diploma Course teaches the Hubers' psychological approach to chart interpretation for working with clients. Details are in our prospectus.

EVENTS Our programme of seminars, workshops and conferences includes annual workshops that are an integral part of the Diploma in Astrological Counselling.

CONJUNCTION Our magazine *Conjunction* contains articles, news and supplementary teaching materials.

API (UK) Enquiries and Membership
P.O. Box 29, Upton, Wirral CH49 3BG, England
Tel: 00 44 (0)151 605 0039; Email: api.enquiries@btopenworld.com
Website: www.api-uk.org

API(UK) Bookshop

Books and API(UK) publications related to the Huber Method.
Linda Tinsley, API(UK) Bookshop
70 Kensington Road, Southport PR9 0RY, UK
Tel: 00 44 (0)1704 544652, Email: lucindatinsley@tiscali.co.uk

API Chart Data Service

Provides colour-printed Huber-style charts and chart data.
Richard Llewellyn, API Chart Data Service
PO Box 29, Upton, Wirral CH49 3BG, UK
Tel: 00 44 (0)151 606 8551, Email: r.llewellyn@btinternet.com

Software for Huber-style Charts

AstroCora, MegaStar, Regulus, Regulus Light Special Huber Edition.
On CD: Elly Gibbs Tel: 00 44 (0)151-605-0039
 Email: software.api@btinternet.com
Download: Cathar Software Website: www.catharsoftware.com

Recent Publications on Astrological Psychology
A Modern Approach to Self Awareness and Personal Growth

Astrological Psychology was developed by Swiss astrologers/psychologists Bruno and Louise Huber and links with the psychosynthesis of Italian Psychiatrist Roberto Assagioli. Based on extensive research, it combines the best of traditional astrology with modern growth psychology, providing a powerful tool for self understanding and psychological and spiritual growth. These books complement the six already available in English on the Hubers' comprehensive approach.

A practical introduction to Astrological Psychology

by Joyce Hopewell & Richard Llewellyn
Illustrated

The Cosmic Egg Timer offers a new and exciting way of using astrology, and is intended for all who are interested in finding out more about astrological psychology - and themselves!

Using your own birth chart alongside this book you will gain insights into the kind of person you are, what makes you tick, and which areas of life offer you the greatest potential.

The first overview of the Huber Method available in any language.

ISBN 0-9547680-0-0

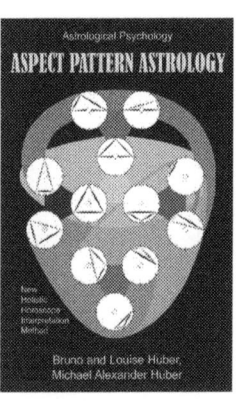

Understanding motivation through aspect patterns

by Bruno, Louise & Michael Huber
Translated by Heather Ross

Aspect Pattern Astrology provides, for the first time in English, details of a key feature of this holistic method of interpreting the horoscope.

The overall pattern of the aspects reveals the structure and basic motivations of an individual's consciousness. Whether novice or experienced astrologer, aspect patterns can provide immediate significant revelations about yourself and other people.

A basic reference work on astrological psychology.

ISBN 0-9547680-1-9

Published by HopeWell, PO Box 118, Knutsford WA16 8TG UK

www.ingramcontent.com/pod-product-compliance
Ingram Content Group UK Ltd.
Pitfield, Milton Keynes, MK11 3LW, UK
UKHW041415180426
11947UKWH00007B/153